WE ARE ROVERS

WE ARE ROVERS

An Oral History of Shamrock Rovers FC

EOGHAN RICE

NONSUCH

First published 2005

Nonsuch Publishing Limited
The Mill, Brimscombe Port,
Stroud, Gloucestershire, GL5 2QG
www.nonsuch-publishing.com

A catalogue record for this book is available from the National Library.

ISBN 1 84588 510 4

Typesetting and origination by Nonsuch Publishing Limited
Printed in Great Britain

CONTENTS

Acknowledgements

I AM GREATLY INDEBTED TO a number of people without whom this book would not have been written. John Dorney was of tremendous help during the interview process, while his refusal to worry about offending me during editing made that task an easier one. John Byrne was a huge source of encouragement throughout the project, as was Robert Goggins.

My family – Rodney, Margo, Cian and Caitriona – was a constant source of support. It was also they who first introduced me to Rovers and for that I will remain indebted. My friends convincingly feigned interest for twelve months while I bored them to tears about the exploits of Paddy Coad, Bob Fullam and the foundation of the League of Ireland. Sorry about that.

Richie Philpott conducted the interview with Alan O'Neill, while Les Lowe was always willing to share the details of his contacts book. Thanks to Ste, Keith, Ralph, Joe and the rest of the Ultras for allowing me to hijack their forum, and thanks to my closest circle of Hoops for making the journey so interesting – Adam, John, Fergus, Mac, Peadar, Scouse, Hugh, Rowan, TJ, Paj, Paul and the rest. It's always a pleasure, gents.

Thanks to Eoin Purcell and the staff at Nonsuch Publishing, who showed great patience and interest throughout the course of our dealings.

There are a number of publications to which I owe a great deal. Firstly, The Hoops by Robert Goggins and Paul Doolan was an invaluable encyclopaedia of knowledge. Football Association of Ireland – 75 Years by Peter Byrne was also a useful resource, as was Sean Ryan's Ireland's Greatest Goalscorers and the Guinness Record of World Soccer by Guy Oliver.

Thanks also goes to the following people, in no particular order: Ger Siggins, Paul Lynch, Tony Heffernan, all the staff at the Sunday Tribune, George Carthy, Michael Connell, Mark Lynch, Gerry Matthews, Seán Pádraig Mac Giolla Eáin, Steven Wall, Rayista, Rennie, Niall Keenan, Eamon Keenan, John Lyons, Sinead Switzer, John Barrington, Anthony Graham, the Berminghams and Gino Brazil. Special thanks to James, Jonathan, John, Eamon, Thomas and Dave of the 400 Club, and also to everyone who is a member of that group.

Finally, a massive thank you to everyone who agreed to meet me for interview or who emailed me their contributions. The past twelve months have seen me cycle across the entire city of Dublin meeting people who all took time out of their lives to share their thoughts and recollections. Writing this book offered me the opportunity to meet players whose names I have idolised for years, but it also gave me the chance to share time with a group of supporters whose passion, dedication and belief in all things Rovers was awe inspiring. Truly, you never cease to amaze me.

FULL LIST OF INTERVIEWEES:

Supporters:
Frank Allen; Ned Armstrong; David Byrne; Pat Brady; John Byrne; Marie Craddock; Brendan Costelloe; Jimmy Conroy; James Cooke; Fergus Desmond; John Dorney; Thomas Freyne; Macdara Ferris; Robbie Foy; Pauline Foy; Robert Goggins; Michael Kearns; Martin Keating; Alan Kinsella; Nell Little; Justin Mason; Fergus McCormack; Kitty Melon; Martin Moore; Pat Moore; Rowan McFeely; Peter Murphy; Ronan O'Donoghue; Maureen O'Hara; Sonny O'Reilly; Hugh O'Connor; Pat O'Dwyer; Jim Palmer; Richie Philpott; Frank Whelan; Jack Wilson.

Players:
Mick Byrne; Pat Byrne; Liam Buckley; Dick Dunne; Theo Dunne; Peter Eccles; Terry Eviston; Robbie Gaffney; Tommy Kinsella; Mick Leech; Mick Meagan; Kieran Maher; Gerry Mackey; Ossie Nash; Ronnie Nolan; Liam O'Brien; Alan O'Neill; Terry Palmer; Larry Palmer; Mick Smyth; Liam Tuohy.

There were countless other people whom I would have liked to have interviewed, but a halt had to be called at some stage. I'll cover myself by thanking anyone who has every followed Rovers and anyone who has ever pulled on that famous green and white jersey.

I also wish to think James Connors, Peter Synnott and Michael Walshe for their contributions. Whilst we have our differences, the Football Association of Ireland offered to help with the book, while Labour Party leader Pat Rabbitte and An Taoiseach Bertie Ahern both personally offered their support for the project. Louis Kilcoyne also offered himself for interview and for that I thank him.

By way of dedication, the book goes to Lynsey and to my families, both biological and green and white.

Eoghan Rice
Dublin June 2005

INTRODUCTION

'We are Rovers, super Rovers,
No one likes us, we don't care'

IT IS A CONVERSATION THAT WILL be all too familiar to any League of Ireland supporter. It begins with somebody asking what football team you support; it ends with them, having heard your reply, saying, 'but who do you really support?'

Irish football isn't cool. Its stadiums are run-down; its clubs bankrupt; its supporters – the few who remain – viewed by the rest of society as oddities, an almost subversive group of misfits not to be trusted. While the rest of society cheers on the English Premiership – the Emperor's clothing of the twenty-first century – the supporters of the domestic game are marginalized and ridiculed.

I was originally going to write a book about the domestic league and its curious relationship with the Irish public, but an event in late 2003 made me change direction. After an outbreak of crowd violence at a game between Rovers and Bohemians, the national media began a witch-hunt. The witch-hunt was primarily aimed against Rovers, but it wasn't difficult to read between the lines: 'League of Ireland: rubbish grounds, rubbish teams, thugs as supporters'. It was 'who do you really follow' journalism.

I attended my first Shamrock Rovers game in September 1990 when St Patrick's Athletic provided the opposition for the club's first league game at the RDS. Glenmalure Park, the club's home since 1926, was gone; an act which many sports journalists hoped would kill off this troublesome league forever. In the fifteen years since my debut, the League of Ireland in general, and Rovers in particular, has become something of a cult. It has provided me with some of the happiest moments in my life, together with some of the saddest. Friends have been made, friends have been lost.

It occurred to me that one of the reasons why the League of Ireland is so marginalized in Irish society is because people tend to view it as a side-show to the larger football story. England, Spain, Italy – these countries have real football clubs that real people care about.

9

Who could actually care about a local, part-time club? Who do you really support?

Maybe, I thought, if people could hear League of Ireland supporters talk about their experiences and emotions, they might understand that it isn't a side-show, it is part of the global football narrative, just without the millionaire stars and twenty-four different camera angles. Just because the standard of football in Ireland is not as high as in other European countries does not make it any less relevant. To confine your football interest to only the top two or three leagues in the world is to dismiss 99.9 per cent of the world's football as meaningless. If you support the game, you support the game, not merely the top 0.1 per cent of it. Someone who truly worships at the church of football would surely go to any lengths to see a game, which would surely encompass those games being played on their doorstep.

I began interviewing supporters and former players in late 2003 and the concept of what this book was to be changed several times. On its most basic level, football is simply a marvellous game – a sport whose complicated simplicity is so perfect it has been absorbed into every culture on Earth. Yet, to examine football on a purely sporting level is to miss the point – it is arguably the most powerful global cultural phenomenon of the new century.

I say I made my Rovers debut in September 1990, but I recall nothing about the actual game. What fascinated me – even as a nine-year-old – were the supporters. They sang, they waved flags, they unmercifully taunted the opposition in a way that ran counter to every rule of polite society. They weren't dangerous, they weren't thugs, they just genuinely cared about what was happening on the pitch. For ninety minutes they became different people – they entered a trance.

This book is not a history of Shamrock Rovers. It doesn't contain statistics or match results. What it does do is chart the history of the club – and the entire league – through the eyes of those who saw it. From the league's inception, Rovers has always been the biggest club and their story reflects the wider story of the league. I hope it's of interest to Rovers fans, I hope it's of interest to all League of Ireland fans, but I also hope that people unconnected to the domestic game may read this book and realise that the domestic league is a great product crying out for your support. It's not a sideshow; it's the main event. We really do support these clubs, and we do so in a way that can't be compared to watching foreign teams on television.

To support a club through the television is to simply follow its team. By absorbing yourself fully into a club, it becomes precisely that: a club. It is something that runs much deeper than last weekend's result; it is something that crawls inside of you and becomes an intrinsic part of who you are. After all, We Are Rovers.

Eoghan Rice
May 2005.

Note on the method:

We Are Rovers is largely an oral history of Shamrock Rovers. However, the oral aspect is more prominent in certain chapters than in others. It is a sad fact of our existence that the further you go back in time the fewer people there are remaining to tell the tale. Therefore, the early years of the club are covered through a straight narrative, with the first oral section introduced during the section covering the 1930s.

The chapters dealing with specific time-frames tend to be oral-based, with chapters 1, 2, 3 and 11 more narrative-based. Where possible, I have tried to allow the story be told through eyewitness accounts. This is surely the way any story should be told.

CHAPTER 1

THE CONVERTED

Iт sтаrтед оuт аs sıвⅬıng rivalry. Every Sunday Kitty Melon would stand at the door of her Dundrum home and watch as her father and brother made the half-hour walk to Milltown to watch Shamrock Rovers FC Kitty, a child growing up in 1930s Dublin, would protest at the injustice of being denied a day out but her protestations were destined to fall on deaf ears. Every Sunday, as her brother waved goodbye, Kitty's determination to be included in her father's Sunday afternoon visits to Milltown grew strong and stronger.

'I always wanted to go with them but my mother said that a football match was no place for a girl because she thought there'd be too much bad language', recalls Kitty. 'I begged her and begged her to let me go and eventually she told me that I could go to a game once I'd made my first communion. I prayed and I prayed and eventually, when I was six years old, I made my communion and she let me go to a game'.

Kitty's reward for making her first communion would grow into a lifetime's obsession. Travelling to every game, home and away, from the mid-1930s, Kitty became one of the most recognisable and most loved supporters of the Irish domestic game. Since the turn of the century, seven decades after making her first pilgrimage to Rovers, Kitty Melon has resided in a home for the elderly in south Dublin. Confinement has not diluted her love of the green and white - a weekly supply of match programmes and newspaper clippings enable her to follow her beloved Hoops.

The nurses who attend to Kitty's needs are probably as informed as the average Rovers fan as to the goings on at the club: 'That club is all she talks about', says the matron with a sigh.

Kitty is sitting in a chair looking out onto the garden. She is perplexed by a major problem: Tony Grant has just left Rovers. 'It's all about money now', she says disdainfully regarding the striker's move across the city to Bohemians.

Physically frail but mentally strong, Kitty makes a tough interview because she is as eager to ask questions regarding the future of the club as I am to extract information regarding its past. In one breath she talks about the genius of 1940s centre forward Jimmy Dunne and her frustration at the constant delays to building the new stadium in Tallaght. By the time

I was born, Kitty Melon had been following Rovers for half a century, yet her enthusiasm remains the same.

The Ireland of the 1930s and '40s was very much male dominated. In De Valera's Ireland, the role of women was reduced to cooking and reproducing, a state policy enshrined in the constitution. While crowds of over 10,000 flocked to Milltown to see the Hoops, only a handful of women would have been inside the ground. This, of course, is highly ironic given that it was a woman – Mary Jane Cunningham – who was effectively running Rovers.

The male dominated atmosphere of football did not dissuade Kitty and she was soon a regular fixture at Milltown. Throughout the '80s and early '90s Kitty's fame spread across the country due to her travelling companion: Cindy the dog. Kitty and Cindy the Jack Russell travelled Ireland supporting the Hoops, never missing a game. Dressed in a green and white jumper, Cindy became a legend of Rovers.

'Cindy loved the matches', says Kitty. 'I'd say we were going to a match and her ears would shoot up. She loved travelling too, she loved going on the buses with all the Rovers fans. I even used to sneak her onto planes for European games by putting her in zip bags. She loved putting on the jersey and going to the match. When we got to the ground I could say, 'go on in there and find me a seat' and she'd run in and jump on an empty seat. She was almost human, that dog'.

Kitty and Cindy became two of the most recognisable faces in Irish football. The pair were so well known that when Cindy passed away in 1992 her death was announced on national radio and in the Evening Herald newspaper.

'She died on a Sunday and even when she was dying I said to her, 'you have to get well because we're going to a match' and her ears shot up, with her dying and everything. We made a little coffin for her and we buried her in her Rovers jersey'.

As the interview draws to a close, I offer Kitty my Rovers Ultras scarf as a sign of my admiration for a woman who has followed Rovers for over seventy years. 'I'll treasure it', she says, wrapping it up neatly and placing it on her lap, clenched tightly into her ailing fists. It seemed like the only logical present to give. As I walk out of the nursing home, I turn to give a final wave. Kitty sits in her chair by the window starring at the scarf, transfixed by a

"She was almost human, that dog': Kitty Melon and Cindy the dog'.

12

lifetime of memories. Kitty and Cindy Mellon: the original Shamrock Rovers' Ultras.

★★★★

The football fan is the modern sociologists dream. Countless books and articles have been written attempting to explain the power the sport of football has over the planet. What makes millions of people across the globe so obsessed with the actions of twenty-two men kicking a round ball around a park? What makes people like Kitty Melon devote her entire life to a semi-professional football club in south Dublin?

The birth of football and its spread across the planet during the latter stages of the 19th century and the early part of the 20th century touched a nerve with humanity. Over the course of a couple of decades, what started out as a simple game developed into the most powerful global phenomenon of the century. The game of football has more followers than any church, more power than any state and more loyalty than any nation. While non-believers may argue that it is 'just a game', the evidence shows quite clearly that it is not.

With the exception of praying and procreation, football is humanity's most popular past time and over the past century the sport has shaped our world in an unprecedented manner. From South America to Africa and Asia, football has helped integrate people, easing racial tensions and creating a common focus and bond. It has also acted as a negative force, leading to sporadic violence and, in at least one case, full-scale war. As society becomes increasingly consumerist, more and more people are suffering from alienation, particularly working class males, who have always been the most enthusiastic football supporters. In uncertain times, football clubs have offered focus, order and meaning to the lives of millions of people.

The final half of the last century also saw a remarkable decline in the power of religion in European society. The three monotheist religions – Christianity, Islam and Judaism – have always been the prevalent religions of Europe, yet all three were imported from the Middle

Rovers fans with flags v Cork.

East. Even minor European religions, such as Buddhism and Hinduism, were imported from the Far East. With football, Europeans finally found a religion of their own.

Of course, as with most things, we do football a little differently in Ireland. Gaelic games have traditionally ruled the roost here, with football playing second fiddle[1]. With the exception of North American and Australasian countries, Ireland is one of the few countries in the world in which football is not considered the premier sport.

Being a supporter of Irish football can be an odd experience. Consider, for example, a derby fixture between Rovers and Bohemians. To the supporters of both clubs, this is the highlight of the season. The countdown to the fixture begins weeks prior to the actual event; the day of the game is merely a collage of nerves and panic. Yet, as much as the game means to the 4,000 or so people who will witness it, the majority of the population of the city do not even know that it is taking place.

The important aspect to remember is that being a football fan is not about numbers or about glamour. You can be as passionate about a team that no one else follows as you can be about Real Madrid or Manchester United. Being surrounded by 70,000 fellow addicts is not a prerequisite for devotion.

Over the past number of years, two of the most popular football books have been 'A Season With Verona' by Tim Parks and 'Barca: A Peoples Passion' by Jimmy Burns. These books conjure up the emotion and feeling behind the supporters of Verona and Barcelona. Yet the reason why these books sold so many copies around Europe is that they are about the same thing: being a football fan. It does not matter whether it is the biggest club in Europe or the smallest team in Dublin; the emotions experienced by football fans are the same.

When Parks writes about the Verona supporter's frustration with the board of directors, the problems with poor policing, the boredom of being stuck on long bus journey's, the addiction to Internet message boards, he could as well be writing about Shamrock Rovers as Verona. Supporters encounter the same experiences. Behind the glamour of the continent's big clubs, the supporters still have to endure the monotony of travelling the length of the country, of arranging accommodation for themselves, of standing in ice cold conditions while your team is being humbled. Whether you're Manchester United or Kilkenny City, these are the same obstacles you face. As the saying goes, even the highest of kings still sits on his arse.

The countries and the clubs may be different (and in this particular case the politics behind both clubs are wildly different), but Verona and Barca fans are both part of the one community: the international community of the football fan. As Verona slide towards relegation and obscurity, Parks brilliantly describes the scene on the terraces of one of the final league encounters of the season. It is a scene which cuts through the false glamour of football and offers the reality of what it is to be a football supporter:

'"My world is falling apart," the boy beside me starts to curse rhythmically. He has his face in his hands. "Let it be over now. Let it be over. I don't want to hear anybody talking about hope. I don't want to hear anyone saying that it's not mathematical yet, that they still believe we can make it…It's too painful. It's too painful. All we do is go to games and suffer and suffer and suffer and suffer to no end. There's no hope, that's the truth. We've got to get used to there being no hope. Let it end." The boy keeps shaking his head. He's crying. He's seriously upset.'

In Burns' book, he interviews a group of Barcelona supporters known as the Cules. When discussing their feelings for F.C. Barcelona, one of the Cules remarks:

'I don't know if you can call us tribal. I don't like the word. I prefer to see myself as part of a collective fiesta in which I can celebrate the great opportunity of being surrounded by others who feel the way I do. The club belongs to us; we are linked to it as if it were a vital element of our existence'.

You do not have to be a supporter of Verona or Barcelona to identify with either of these extracts. You simply have to be a supporter of any football club. Supporting Shamrock Rovers is no different to supporting Barcelona. The club is smaller, the fans fewer, the players less glamorous, but the emotion is exactly the same. Rovers belongs to us; we are linked to it as if it were a vital element of our existence.

★★★★

It is four weeks before the kick-off of the 2004 season and the Hooped faithful are crammed into a small bus destined for Monaghan. Rovers are lining out in Century Homes Park for a pre-season friendly. For The Converted, this is the first chance to see the team play since November. It has been an unusually long pre-season break and the stress of not having seen Rovers play for three months in beginning to show. On board the Rovers bus the fans exchange tips on how to pass a weekend with no football. Pre-season is a different life; a life that the football fan does not want to know.

In terms of glamour, Monaghan United ranks up there with a used public toilet. After a brief spell in the Premier Division in the 1990s, the club has been rooted to the lower half of the First Division for nearly a decade. This is a graveyard of football. Only a complete lunatic would be willing to bare a five-hour return trip to watch a pre-season friendly in Monaghan, which is precisely why Rovers have had no problem filling a coach.

Boarding the bus on Dublin's Tara Street, the usual suspects welcome each other back after a gruelling winter break. 'Jaysus, it feels like years since the last game'; 'I've had the shakes for the last two months'. Handshakes go around as the family is reunited. A dysfunctional family perhaps, an unconventional one certainly, but a family none the less.

As the usual seats are assumed, it's business as usual for the Hoops. On the back seat of the bus sits John Byrne, together with his nephew Dave Byrne and Fergus McCormack. As the Sunday papers are sifted through, occasional observations on the world are made public. It's a scene which is replicated on football supporters' buses around the world: the supporters talk about anything and everything except football. While football may have brought the group together – although some, such as John and Dave, are linked in deeper ways – the social dynamic of the group has evolved far beyond sport. The men on board the bus are friends: they know each other's lives, interests and problems.

John Byrne, journalist and Rovers fanatic, attended his first game in 1962 when, as a two year old, he was among the 32,000 people to witness Paddy Ambrose and Tommy Hamilton demolish Shelbourne 4-1 in the FAI Cup Final in Dalymount Park. John's appearance at Rovers was no accident - the club is a family heirloom.

'Ours is a Rovers family', he says. 'My brother, my nephew and two of my sons all go now, before that my dad went. My granduncle actually died for Rovers. In the late 1920s he was at a game in Milltown and the place was so packed that he couldn't get under the cover. It was lashing rain; he got pneumonia and died. So someone in the family actually died for the Hoops'.

Attending his first game while still in nappies, Rovers became a huge part of John's childhood. He grew up with the club. It's a devotion which he has thought long and hard about, but one which even he does not fully understand.

'It's a religion to the hardcore supporters', he says. 'There is no two ways about it, being hardcore gives your life a new meaning. You're obsessed with it. There are people who need to be hardcore. It's not even about what the club are doing, it's about finding something that they need to be a part of. There are many reasons why people need it, I'd imagine that the bottom line is that there is something lacking in their lives. That's not being judgmental, it's just stating a fact. Blokes are obsessed by cars, by naked women, by drink, by football, by comic books, by whatever it may be; women aren't like that'.

The parallels between religion and football are often made, but is calling football a religion placing too much importance on the sport? Are we losing the run of ourselves by elevating a sport to the level of spiritual belief?

'There is a religious aspect to it', says John. 'I remember one of my friends was being interviewed for a job and they asked him whether there were any religious reasons why he couldn't work on Sundays. He told them that he couldn't work on Sunday's for religious reasons because he went to Rovers. 'Milltown is my church', he told them. We all understood that perfectly, but he didn't get the job. They just thought he was a nutcase.'

Dave Byrne sits beside his uncle, flicking through the day's newspapers. He has no qualms about going to Monaghan - last season Dave went to every single Rovers game, home and away. 'It becomes a challenge after a while', he says. 'If you get so far you become determined not to miss any'. Dave's youth was spent on the terraces of Milltown, watching the likes of Liam Buckley, Alan Campbell and Pat Byrne drive Rovers through the glorious 1980s, when the club won four league titles in a row.

'I'll never forget the first time I was in Milltown', he say. 'I was eight years old and it was a pre-season friendly against Liverpool. They were the European Champions at the time but we drew the game. When you paid in the turnstiles at Milltown you came to a set of steps at the back of the terrace. When you went up them you were overlooking the entire stadium. The floodlights were on and the crowd was huge and I remember my uncle turning to my dad and saying "would you look at the smile on his face". I was totally dumbstruck. "That's it", he said, "he's a Hoop".'

Like any young child attending football, the players soon became idols to Dave. While his friends were admiring players like Ian Rush and Mark Hughes over in England, Dave was busy imitating the moves of Mick Byrne and Neville Steedman: 'It was only when I got older that I realised that these are normal lads with normal jobs. I remember once I saw John Coady working as a postman and I couldn't believe it. A Rovers player being a postman!'

Rovers grew from a childhood hobby into a true obsession. The surge of the Milltown crowd, the glamour of the green and white hoops, the sense of family surrounding the weekly outing to Rovers – it all conspired to make Dave a Rovers addict. With twenty years 'active service' under his belt, Dave has been around long enough to see the good and bad times. However, he says, the test of being a true fan is not about length of time, it is about depth of feeling.

'Whether you're going to Rovers a year or sixty years it doesn't matter', he says. 'If you love it you love it, there's no difference. I love going to Rovers and if that was taken away from me life would be impossible. I don't know what life would be like without Rovers.'

Fergus McCormack remembers how he felt when he first stood on the terraces of Milltown in the late 1970s. He was a young child, excited and terrified in equal measures at what surrounded him.

'I remember standing there in the Shed and being half terrified and half in awe of the Rovers fans', he recalls. 'I was quite young so I loved the feeling of standing there beside all these big men, but I was also shitting myself. You felt as if you were really part of something, but also scared that someone was going to tap you on the shoulder and say, "alright sonny, what are you doing here?"'

Like John and Dave, Fergus has grown up with Rovers. From the age of eight, he has stood on the terraces with the same people. It is these people, he maintains, that he has forged the closest bonds with in life.

16

'They say that most people meet their friends through work, school or college and that you are very lucky if you make friends outside of that', he says. 'Well, I've been very lucky because some of my best mates I met through Rovers. What it is that holds us together is very hard to put your finger on, but there is something there that unites fans. It's a common bond'.

We arrive in Monaghan. There is no rivalry here, simply because there is no one else here. Monaghan is a rural area of Ireland where football is very much the poor sporting relation. Two sides of the pitch lead onto fields where sheep sit by the sideline. It is a surreal scene. One small stand – which was built out of funds raised by the club's small, but loyal, group of supporters – fits the few locals who have turned up to witness the fixture. Arriving early, the Rovers bus turns into the ground before the match-day officials are in position. Without anyone to take our money, we walk in for free.

Monaghan United do offer one facility that any football fan will appreciate: a bar. And a big one at that. Within seconds of the bus arriving, a large queue has formed. Aside from fulfilling the dietary requirements of Rovers fans, the bar does serve a more valuable purpose: it is the life-blood of Monaghan United Football Club. If Irish society is dogged by apathy and bandwagon-jumping when it comes to sporting matters, alcoholism is the one Irish trait that football clubs have been able to exploit. Bars are vital sources of revenue for Irish football clubs and, in the case of clubs such as Monaghan United, possibly the only major source of income.

That is not to say that clubs do not attempt to open up new revenue streams. On the wall to the right of the bar are photographs from one of Monaghan's more ingenious marketing ploys. Every year at the Miss Monaghan Ball a local woman is named 'Miss Monaghan United'. It mightn't be the most glamorous of titles but the Ball provides the club with valuable cash.

Underneath the Miss Monaghan United 2003 picture, a Rovers fan is selling bootleg copies of The Football Factory, a new film depicting football violence in London. Others are busily signing people up to various supporters clubs, while another group plot the up-coming season's Ultras displays. Monaghan is suddenly a hive of activity.

The game itself is a non-event. The supporters do not recognise most of the Rovers team, which is primarily made up of members of the underage squads. At half time the fans retreat back into the bar. Most don't return for the second half. Rovers lose 1-0. The supporters in the bar feel vindicated.

By the time the bus pulls out of Century Homes Park, the supporters have been in the bar for over three hours. It's getting messy. We pile back onto the bus and stop at the first off-licence. The Rovers' fans come out armed with alcohol in preparation for the journey home.

The Sunday papers have been tossed aside; the fans have now found their voices. Starting at the back, each supporter takes turns in starting a chant. The once-quiet bus is now consumed by song. Sitting in the middle of the emerging madness are Robbie Foy and Martin Moore, veterans of Rovers bus journeys since the 1970s. If a drunken singsong is as out of control as today's away trips get, things were a little different in the '70s. The supporters clubs were actually disbanded in 1972 because the club's owner Louis Kilcoyne claimed that they were little more than 'cheap trips for hooligans'.

'My whole family were steeped in Rovers', says Robbie. 'Our house was only around the corner from Milltown so Sunday afternoons were fairly interesting. As a kid, you were more or less taken out of the area because windows would be put in, buses were going to be wrecked'.

The 1970s was a violent decade throughout society and that reflected itself in Irish football, where battles between rival fans were a weekly occurrence. A Rovers bus to anywhere outside of Dublin would inevitably be met by local football fans eager to 'have a pop' at the lads from the capital. Rovers fans responded in kind and were known as the most vicious supporters in the country.

On the pitch, the club took a downward turn, although the glory days of the 1960s – which saw Rovers win six cups in a row – still ensured that the club was supported well throughout Dublin, even amongst those with little knowledge of football.

'My cousin was a huge Rovers fan, as was my father', says Martin. 'We were from Synge Street, which was very much a Rovers area of Dublin. I wasn't into football as a kid but the only name I ever heard was Shamrock Rovers. People would ask me, "do you follow football?" "No", "What team do you support?" "Shamrock Rovers". I couldn't have told you who Liverpool or Manchester United were'.

RICHIE PHILPOTT
'I started going to Rovers in 1970. My family was very much a GAA family but I had a friend in school whose dad was from Milltown and so they used to go to matches together. I started going with him and I suppose it was an act of rebellion going to Rovers games.'

THOMAS FREYNE
'My first game was a 0-0 draw against UCD, which, needless to say, was a pretty poor game. Luckily, the next week we played Bohs and beat them 3-1 with Stephen Grant and Aaron Lynch getting two late goals. I just remember the Rovers fans were going ballistic, jumping on the pitch and everything. That game got me hooked, I suppose.'

MACDARA FERRIS
'I was around nine when I first went to Milltown. My father brought me just to get me out of my mothers' way on a Sunday afternoon really. My dad put me in the children's entrance and he went into the adult entrance but when we got into the ground we were separated by a large fence. So my dad had to climb underneath the fence to get on the same side of the

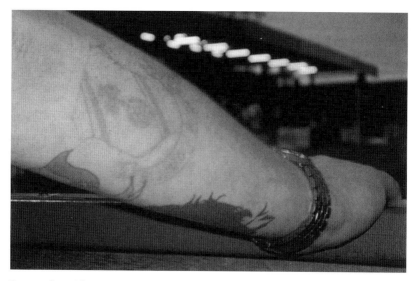

Rovers fan with tattoo.

ground as his kid. We stood on the terrace on the Milltown Road end. I was young and it looked massive to me. I was really impressed by the floodlights, I used to love when it got dark at games and the big lights came on. '

Peter Murphy

'I started taking an interest in football after the World Cup in 1990 and so my dad decided to bring me to a game. Rovers had just moved into the RDS, so we went to their first game there. There were 22,000 people there but dad was warning me that it wasn't always like that and that if we went to the next game only the hardcore fans would be there. Two weeks later a crowd of 11,000 turned up to watch Rovers take on Derry. Vinny Arkins scored early on and Derry got a late equaliser. I remember being completely devastated coming out of that game and suddenly realising that I was hooked. I was thinking, "that's only my second match and I feel like this". I knew I was hooked.'

Robert Goggins

'I'd consider myself to be a late starter; I didn't go to my first game until January 1980. I had friends who went to Rovers and they were always onto me to go, so one Sunday afternoon I decided to go and watch Rovers play Galway. I went up to the ground and paid my money in and as I entered the ground it was as if something magical had grabbed me. It wasn't a particularly big crowd, probably only around 3,000, but there was great atmosphere. I hadn't been prepared for that. To me, that day was like being on Stars in their Eyes – people go to that show as themselves and they walk through a door and come out as a different person. That was me at Milltown, I went as myself and when I walked through the turnstile I came out as a different person.

Hugh O'Connor

'I was around 14 and I saw the highlights of a game on TV. I remember that when Rovers scored the fans went berserk, and I just thought to myself "that looks like a bit of craic".

Fans looking at game v Carrick.

There was a lad in school who I knew went to the games so I bullied him into bringing me along. My first game was against Sligo in the RDS. We actually lost the game but we had a bit of fun and I never looked back. When you're around 14 or 15 going to games offers you a bit of independence. I had my first pint at a Rovers game, had my first trip out of Dublin on my own. I had a lot of firsts at Rovers, with the exception of the most obvious one. It's a great sense of freedom to run amuck in a controlled environment.'

PAT BRADY
'When you follow a team there's a romantic attachment to a lot of its symbols. On a winter's day, when the lights are on and you see the green and white shirts coming out onto the pitch it certainly has an emotional connection with you.'

JOHN DORNEY
'The first time I went to a game on my own was when Rovers beat Dundalk 3-0 in the RDS, with Jody Byrne scoring an hilarious own goal. I'll never forget the Rovers fans that day – the way they taunted Jody and showed their absolute contempt for the opposition and their fans. At school and at home behaviour like this was restrained but here, in public, you could do what you wanted. Standing in Dalymount and screaming "we fucking hate Bohs" felt incredibly liberating for a teenager.

MACDARA FERRIS
'My support lapsed for a while and then one day I decided to bring a few lads from college to see Rovers v Bohs. I didn't even know where Dalymount was but a few of the lads were from the country and I've always found culchies are better for knowing Dublin Bus routes than locals, so they knew where it was. We stood on the terrace and the atmosphere was electric. They had lots of ticker tape and they gathered it in together in the middle of

Eoghan Rice & Rowan McFeely in Marseille.

20

the terrace and lit a bonfire and started singing Johnny Cash's Ring of Fire. That was me hooked, I went to every game from then on.'

MICHAEL KEARNS
'I was brought up on Rovers. As a kid I'd be brought to Milltown and told, "here's your crisps, here's your coke, now shut up and watch the match because this is your father's whole weekend".'

★★★★

The crowd surged forward as security men struggled to control order. The assembled crowd were getting angry; a man begins to remonstrate vocally with those charged with maintaining order. 'This is mental', one of the security personnel, his hands on his head, mutters to no one in particular.

It was a scene replicated outside of football grounds across the planet every week. Only this time it was different. The crowd was not comprised of angry young men, but of elderly couples. The security was not made up of Gardai, but of students working part-time jobs. This was no football ground, this was Easons bookshop.

Behind the madness, an 84-year-old woman sits at a table, her walking stick leaning against her side. Seemingly oblivious to the scene of chaos in front of her, the lady calmly signs a never-ending line of books. If this is no ordinary day in Dublin's famous bookshop, that is because this is no ordinary 84-year-old woman. This is Maureen O'Hara – Hollywood legend, film icon and Rovers fanatic.

It's a Saturday afternoon and O'Hara is in Dublin to promote her autobiography, Tis Herself. The flame-haired actress from Ranelagh who became the queen of the silver screen is only in Ireland for a limited amount of time. Which means that I have a limited time to act. Working for a Sunday newspaper means that Saturday deadlines are quite rigid. Excusing myself 'for ten minutes', I make a hurried journey to O'Connell Street in a bid to meet the retired star. I'm gone ten minutes by the time I reach Easons. Deadlines are passing. The scene of madness which greets me inside the shop ensures that any hope of meeting O'Hara today quickly disappear. After ten minutes battling with old women for a place at the top of the queue, I retreat back to fast approaching deadlines.

Although Rovers can boast the likes of Colin Farrell and Paul McGinley amongst its list of celebrity supporters, Maureen O'Hara is without doubt the most famous Hoop on planet Earth. Born Maureen Fitzsimons in 1920, two decades after the club's formation but two years before their entrance into the League of Ireland, the future star was virtually raised on the terraces watching Rovers.

Her father, Charles Fitzsimons, was one of the first directors of the club, working closely with the Cunningham family to turn Rovers into a force in Irish football. Fitzsimons played Gaelic football for County Meath but fell out with the association over their ban on players attending soccer matches. Fitzsimons left the GAA in protest and threw himself behind Shamrock Rovers. Young Maureen was inside the inner circle of the club, assuming her seat on match days in the directors box. A self-confessed tomboy in her youth, Maureen never missed a game.

Upon her rise up the Hollywood ladder, Maureen changed her name from Fitzsimmons to O'Hara. Therefore, the link between father and daughter – and, therefore, between daughter and club – is not well known. Having learned of O'Hara's devotion to the green and white, I was determined to speak to her. Having failed in my quest in Easons, I fell back on any journalist's Plan-B: the PR person. Within minutes, the interview is arranged.

'I grew up on Churchtown Road', she says from her home in West Cork a few days later. 'My father played GAA but he got caught at a soccer game and so he gave it up and got involved with Shamrock Rovers, who played just up the road from us. I was mad about Rovers; I never missed a game. When I was young all I wanted to do was play for Rovers, I couldn't understand why they didn't have a ladies team'.

Maureen grew up in the 1920s and early '30s, during the era of players like Bob Fullam and Paddy Moore. Rovers were sweeping the city by storm, attracting huge crowds wherever they played. However, with an acting career to pursue, Hollywood beckoned and by the late 1930s Fitzsimons left her native city.

In Hollywood, Maureen enjoyed almost instant success, first with Jamaica Inn and then with The Hunchback of Notre Dame, both of which were released in 1939. The Dublin actress was instantly propelled to the top of the Hollywood ladder and in 1941 starred in the Oscar-winning How Green Was My Valley. However, success came at a price. The outbreak of World War II meant that Maureen was not allowed to leave the US. For someone so fiercely attached to her home country, it was virtually like being a prisoner: 'I wanted to go home to Dublin but there was no chance - we were forbidden from going home because of the war. We finally got permission in 1946 and I jumped at the chance.'

The chance to return home also offered the now established movie star the chance to pop into her old friends in Milltown. While the opportunities to visit Rovers dwindled over the years, Maureen can still recall those days when as a teenager she would accompany her father to Milltown to watch the Hoops. 'I idolised players like "Sacky" Glen and Paddy Moore', she recalls. 'Paddy was some player! Sacky Glen was a marvellous player too. He was great at getting balls into the box, where Paddy Moore would just throw his head at them and score! Paddy was the best. It was very, very exciting to watch.'

O'Hara's career soon exploded and soon she was making three or four movies a year. Trips to Ireland were infrequent and short as the young actress went from strength to strength. By the early 1970s, Maureen had married and all but retired from the big screen to concentrate on raising a family.

The Hoops always remained close to her heart, however, and even now she can chat freely for twenty minutes about the great players and the feeling of being a small girl in a crowd of 20,000 men. One of the greatest shocks of her life, she says, was the news that Glenmalure Park in Milltown, the ground where she watched 'Sacky' Glen and Paddy Moore carve up opposition defences, had been knocked down to make way for a housing estate.

'Glenmalure Park was like a second home to me', she says. 'Every weekend the crowds used to flood past our house on the way to Milltown for the big game. I couldn't believe it when they knocked it down. I still haven't gone back to Milltown, I don't know if I could bear to look at it'.

★★★★

Internet message boards have revolutionised the existence of football fans. Just like millions do around the world, Rovers fans spend hours each day online united by their common love. The Rovers message board is where I go for my laughter and my tears; where the most profound issues facing the globe are discussed alongside the most ridiculous.

As I began to research this book, I placed a plea on the Internet for fans to send me accounts of their experiences at Rovers. Amongst the contributions was one written by Rovers fan Alan Kinsella. Above all others, it put into words how important a football club can be to an individual in a time of trouble:

'On the 23rd of December 1995 I was diagnosed with a cerebral abscess. Two months, two brain surgeries and my father's death later, I emerged. Two months of twice daily being asked, "What is your name?" "Do you know where you are?" "What year is it?"

'I was confined for long spells in occupational therapy putting wooden shapes through the correct holes; writing my name; doing simple addition. Recuperating at home, I found that I had forgotten or at least failed to remember things. Nothing major but mundane things. Was it significant? Would I have forgotten them anyway?

In such situations it is common to look for a form of mental affirmation, a reassurance that nothing's damaged. In a few months I would be starting a FAS course, but in the meantime I felt the urge to do something to prove my mental ability to myself. Something to prove I was still sane. I had always wanted to appear on Know Your Sport, but had done nothing about it. Needing a mental challenge of sorts, I applied.

At the time Know your Sport was one of the top programmes on RTE, attracting up to half a million viewers. Appearances by locals on the show were regularly mentioned in the local press and the 1989 Christmas frenzy for the Know Your Sport Quiz Book makes recent festive hysteria over Playstations and Pokemon seem mild.

In the show's early years, viewers were asked to send in questions for Jimmy McGee, nicknamed The Memory Man. Floods of tough questions like "What colour are Ray Tracey's eyes?" and "Who was the Irish fencing champion in 1948?" arrived in RTE. "What size boots did Paddy Coad wear", Joe Kelly from Waterford would ask. Jimmy would never settle for simply giving the answer, he'd have to get a lot more bizarre trivia in and so he'd ponder the question for a moment as if he was gathering his thoughts, and off he'd go in his distinctive breathy voice: "A very good question Joe. I see that you're from Waterford yourself, things going well down there at the moment. In fact I bumped into Jimmy McGeough the other day, lovely man. I don't know if you know this Joe, but Paddy was the first ever sub to score for Ireland, in a 3-2 victory against Norway in 1951. Did you know Paddy yourself? A lovely man and a lovely footballer too. By the way the answer to the question is size seven boots. I'll tell you how I know this one...." Cue some ridiculous set of coincidences and name-dropping.

The craze for trying to catch out The Memory Man with obscure questions peaked with a tour of various venues around the country. The posters ran: "Jimmy McGee - The Memory Man - Ask him a question". Pubs and clubs around the country were full with people asking Jimmy obscure questions about archery in North Korea which they didn't even know the answers to themselves. It was great fun, especially when Jimmy would go off on a tangent about some great North Korean boxer that nobody had ever heard of. As the evening progressed more drink was taken and the questions became more obscure and sometimes even vulgar.

A few weeks after I had applied to RTE, I was called in for an interview. At the interview I was given twenty sports questions to answer and I got fifteen correct. I'd made the cut. One thing remained: a contestant had to choose a specialist subject. In order to prove myself to myself, it had to be Shamrock Rovers.

As a young lad Rovers were the glamour team and the first club off everyone's lips when asked their favourite Irish team. So it was without having gone to a match that I became a fan. My Rovers debut day arrived when my father - a Drums fan - and a pal of his took me along to see the Hoops play UCD. I only realised afterwards that one of the UCD players had a soft spot for my Dads pals' daughter and that I was being taken on a spying mission rather than to watch a game.

A few weeks later, I was on Georges Street with my mother when we entered a Tony Quinn – an entrepreneur at the time - bric-a-brac bargain shop that had been in business for maybe a year. There, in a pokey corner downstairs, I found some posters of the Shamrock Rovers team for 15p each. I reached into my pocket, counted the pennies and had enough to buy one.

The poster took pride of place on my wall. The players, with fashionable haircuts and

Quinnsworth sponsored hooped jerseys, stared down on me. As it turned out, those players were just a short bus journey away, and so I soon began to venture to Milltown on the 46A. Going to a soccer game unaccompanied by an adult was a rite of passage. At the game, I'd meet a lad from school whose claim to fame was that he had spat on Graeme Souness. We were in with the crowd. It was a status symbol on Monday to say that you were at a game.

Then, the year I did my leaving cert, Milltown was sold. I wasn't involved in any of the protests, but kept an eye on the goings on and like any sports fan was sickened by the whole deal.

Having been accepted onto Know Your Sport, I nearly killed myself reading anything I could get my hands on - books on the Hoops, League of Ireland Annuals, books on the Olympics, The Sporting Life. I'd get up in the morning to be met by my Mother asking:

"What time did you get in from the pub last night? Who did Rovers beat in the 1978 Cup Winners cup first round?".

"Eh… 11.30. Eh…Apoel Nicosia."

"That's a lie!",

"It was so Nicosia"

"It was 12.05, not 11.30. I hope you won't be telling RTE any lies."

When the big day came, I went into the studio and was shown to the dressing room. After depositing my stuff it was in for the rehearsal, where the contestants got into action, feeling their buzzers and answering questions. My questions suited me like a dream; I was as good as into the final and the grand prize of a trip to the Olympics awaited.

Filled with confidence, I returned to the dressing room, cleaned myself up and went into the studio. Mother, aunties, brothers, sisters and friends were there to greet me. The nerves had started. I sat down and thought about the circumstances that had me sitting there: I was here to prove myself to myself.

I was in the Green seat and the computer chose the colour that would go first. After much tension it stopped on Green. Pictures of six hurlers hit the screen. My mind went blank. I would have blurted them all out an hour ago, but now… 'Eh, umm … No.1 is Mike Galligan, eh...' Out of the corner of my eye I saw my pal throw his head in his hands in frustration. 'No 3 is Pat O'Neill .. eh…ummm… No. 6 is Adrian Fenlon ..ummm is No.4 Tommy Dunne?…'

I could do no more. I got one correct, was shaking with nerves and the sweat was pumping out of me. By the time the specialist topic round came up I was last but within

One fan standing beside flags in Cork.

'Supporters watching the game from the roof of Glenmalure Park celebrate a Rovers goal'.

striking distance of third place. In an attempt to compose myself, I thought back to the last Rovers match I had gone to before I got ill, an October Friday night in Cork. I was actually living in Cork at the time and so I got the bus to Bishopstown and then marched out to what was Cork's ground at the time.

Unlike Dublin's urban sprawl, Cork just stops. A few yards past Bishopstown it's farmland and we were hit by one of those awful country smells, the type you always seem to get on a nice summers day with the windows down when stuck in traffic in the vicinity of Enfield. The type even country people can identify. Eventually we got there to find the handful of Rovers fans down the far end. There was one lad who roared non-stop for the whole first half.

"Jaysus Paddy, your making some racket there"

"Ah sure didn't she leave me off the leash"

"Pity she didn't leave the fuckin' muzzle on"

The second half came and we had Rovers attacking the goal in front of us. Cork had Phil "Biscuits" Harrington in goal and when he came to position himself in the goal he got showered in raspberry creams. Great fun it was too. Then, towards the end of the game, Eoin Mullen scored with a brilliant shot from outside the box to claim a 1-0 win for Rovers. Suddenly, I found myself in the hot seat. Could Rovers save my sanity?

"Up until 1987, at which ground did Shamrock Rovers play?"

"Glenmalure Park, Milltown."

"Who is Shamrock Rovers all time top league goal scorer?"

"Paddy Ambrose"

"Who were Shamrock Rovers first ever opponents in European competition?"

"Manchester United"

"What was the aggregate score of the tie?"

"9-2 to United."

The round eventually finished. I missed one question, answering Mick Leech instead of Paddy Coad, got a few on the buzzer round, got to meet Ciaran Carey and finished third in the heat. For my trouble, I got my sanity back and the prized possession of a Know Your Sport umbrella. Suspiciously, the umbrella got left in the pub that evening. Rovers, however, continue to test my sanity.'

CHAPTER 2

FOUNDATION – 1949

JOHN MCALERY WAS THE FIRST ever Irishman to argue with his wife about wanting to watch a game of football. The Belfast merchant was married in 1878 and soon after departed with his bride to Edinburgh for a honeymoon. McAlery's short break was romantic, but perhaps not in the way his blushing bride had hoped: McAlery fell in love with football.

The game had only recently made its way to Scotland and had not yet crossed the Irish Sea. Upon his return to Ireland, however, this new sport was all the young merchant could think about. On 28 September 1878, McAlery placed an advertisement in a local newspaper looking for people interested in forming a football club. Within days, Cliftonville Football Club was born.

In order to promote the new sport in Ireland, McAlery invited two Scottish football clubs - Queen's Park and Caledonians – to play an exhibition game in Belfast. The match, which took place on 24 October 1878 at a cricket ground in Ballymafeigh, was the first football match to ever take place on Irish soil, Queen's Park running out 3-1 winners. The young merchant – his unsuspecting wife in tow – had unleashed a sport that would forever change the sporting makeup of the Irish nation.

Association football had been gaining popularity in Britain for almost twenty years by the time McAlery transported it across the water. The history of every football club on the planet begins in 1862, the year in which football enthusiasts in Nottingham, England, held a meeting which resulted in the formation of Notts County FC, the world's first football club. The game was being played across the country but had no fixed rules. The founders of Notts County made contact with enthusiasts from other English towns and on 26 October 1863, the Football Association was formed at a meeting in the Freemasons Tavern in London's Great Queen Street. At a further four meetings held between that date and 8 December 1863, the rules of the game were developed, paving the way for the establishment of football clubs the length and breath of Britain.

Supporters of the English national football team still sing about the now-distant British Empire, yet in the nineteenth century Britannia really did rule the waves. From India to

Australia, from large tracts of Africa to the Middle East, British imperialism was alive and well. Through the medium of imperialism, football would become a more powerful global superpower than the British ever were. When British sailors set off across the world they brought footballs; when British merchants went in search of new treasures they brought footballs; when young army personnel were sent to quash local dissent they brought footballs. As an offshoot of the British monarchy's insatiable lust for land, football was brought to every corner of the globe. It is fitting that the empire on which the sun never set gave the world the sport on which the sun never sets. At any given moment there are literally millions of games of football in progress around the globe – from the streets of Montevideo, Nairobi and Bangkok to the great football monuments of Rio's Maracanã, Madrid's Bernabau and Manchester's Old Trafford.

Before the game travelled out of Britain, it penetrated the Scottish and Welsh borders in the late 1860s. Tellingly, the first football clubs to be established in European countries were founded in large port towns, implying that British traders brought the game with them. The maritime nature of football can be seen from all the earliest clubs founded in Europe – Le Havre Athletic Club (1872), KB Copenhagen (1876), Royal Antwerp (1880), Hamburg Sport-Verein (1887), Sparta Rotterdam (1888), Panionios Athens (1890), AIK Stockholm (1891). By the 1880s a new British Empire was conquering the world. Argentina – whose rich reservoir of football talent would astound the world over the following century – was the first country outside of Britain to play football, when members of the sizeable British community founded Buenos Aires Football Club in 1865. In 1896 Bolivian football was established with the foundation of Oruro Royal Club, whilst in Brazil Charles Miller established Sao Paulo Athletic Club in 1901.

Ireland's earliest football clubs were all set up in so-called garrison towns – towns in which members of the British army were stationed – which later gave rise to the sport being christened 'the garrison game' by those who opposed its emergence. The tense political situation, coupled with the Gaelic revival, made the introduction of football controversial. For this reason, it is no surprise that the earliest clubs on the island were formed in the predominantly Protestant north of the country. Following the establishment of Cliftonville FC in 1879, clubs began popping up like mushrooms. In 1881 McAlery's Cliftonville battled it out with Limavady, Moyola Park, Distillery, Knock, Oldpark and Avoniel in the 1881 Irish Cup, the first competitive football competition held on Irish soil, which was ultimately won by Moyola Park.

The first football club founded in what is now the Republic of Ireland was Dublin Association Football Club, which was founded in 1883. It was closely followed by Dublin University FC, with the two sides competing in the first ever Dublin derby on 7 November 1883.

Of course, to say that football was invented in 1862 in England is a gross simplification. Football has been played across the globe for thousands of years in one form or another, all the British did was export a common set of rules and the notion of organised clubs. Humans have been kicking stones in some sort of organised fashion since before anyone thought to invent fire. The Ancient Chinese had a game called Tsu Chu – Tsu referring to the action of kicking, Chu meaning a stuffed ball of animal skin. Played roughly 3,000 years ago, Tsu Chu, together with the Japanese game of Kemari, bore a remarkable resemblance to modern day football, involving as it did two bamboo posts which the players had to kick to Chu through. The Romans played Harpastum, whilst the Greeks played Episkyros, both of which had much in common with what we now call football. There are many other examples of games related to football which we now know to have been played in ancient times around the world – La Soule in Brittany; Giuoco del Calico Fiorentino in Italy; Pilimatun in Chile; Tchoekah in Patagonia. The Eskimos played a game called Aqsaqtuk,

28

whilst German explorer Max Schmidt was amazed to discover the Pareci Indians of Brazil playing a sport with a rubber ball which they named Zicunati. The fact Schmidt was one of the first non-Pareci to come into contact with the tribe is a wonderful example of the natural origins of the game. Football did not emerge out of a meeting held in London in 1863, it emerged out of mankind's natural desire to kick round objects.

In Britain, the establishment of the sport coincided with the Industrial Revolution, where millions of people flocked to the cities from the countryside. Living in squalid conditions, football was promoted as an escape from the mundane nature of a city-life to which so many were unaccustomed. This is still relevant today where football is primarily a working class, urban sport. When football was exported abroad, it was embraced by the working classes of other countries. Whereas cricket and rugby – the main two other popular British sports – became largely associated with the ruling classes, football, with its unique simplicity, was firmly claimed by the merchant and working classes. From its inception, football was the people's sport.

The period between 1875 and 1900 was perhaps the most revolutionary ever known in world sport. Those twenty-five years saw the creation of clubs across the world that would go on to play invaluable roles in the social fabric of cities for the next century. Clubs such as Manchester United (1878), Arsenal (1886), Juventus (1897), Barcelona (1899) and many more who have since become global entities, were all products of the football revolution of the late nineteenth century.

The oldest senior club still in operation in the Republic is Athlone Town, which was founded in 1887 in the large garrison town. In 1890 Bohemian Football Club was established by members of the Royal Irish Hibernians, who ran an orphanage for children of British soldiers killed in combat. Shelbourne FC, also a Dublin club, was founded five years later in 1895. By the mid-1890s there were 59 clubs in Leinster alone. Bohemians initially played in the Phoenix Park, although they soon moved to Dalymount Park in Phibsboro, the ground where the club is still located. Shelbourne, however, were conceived in Ringsend, a small fishing village outside of Dublin city centre. It was out of this same village that another football club was to emerge; a club who would dominate Irish football for a century. It was in Ringsend that Shamrock Rovers Football Club was born.

★★★★

Ringsend is real Dublin. It's not big; it's got no spectacular sights, no quaint features and few – if any – attractions. But it's real Dublin. Tucked away fifteen minutes walk from the city centre, it's the sort of Dublin old drunken men in pubs still sing about – a tight-knit community only recently infiltrated by hordes of young professionals seeking accommodation near the capital's bustling nightlife. Whilst Dublin has recently become known throughout the world as a vibrant and wealthy city, it was not always this way. At the beginning of the twentieth century Dublin was a city of tenement flats, where wealth was the exception to the rule. Life was harsh and short in a city that was starved of economic investment and plagued by disease and poverty.

Ringsend was uninhabited until the seventeenth century, when it became Dublin's main port. Over the next two centuries, the village became home to the city's fishermen and dockers, although a near-fatal blow was dealt to the area in 1814 when the village of Howth replaced it as Dublin's main port. Although the natural resource of the sea enabled the people of Ringsend to keep their heads above water financially, the emergence of Howth placed the area into economic decline. By the late 1800s, Ringsend was as poor and destitute as many of Dublin's other surrounding villages.

Above and below: Shamrock Avenue, Ringsend.

The area has, however, always had a sporting tradition and, together with the nearby area of Irishtown, was a famed venue for hurling in the eighteenth and nineteenth centuries. It was only logical, therefore, that it would be the people of Ringsend who formed two of the country's earliest football clubs: Shelbourne and Shamrock Rovers. The former was founded in 1890, but the foundation date of the latter remains hotly disputed.

Rovers do not have an official historian but if they did it would be Robert Goggins. The editor of the match-day programme and co-author of clubs' official history book – The Hoops – Goggins has spent over a decade researching the history of Rovers and he maintains that Rovers were founded in 1901. Others, however, argue that 1899 was the year the club was founded.

'I met with sons of people who were there at the time of the founding of the club and they all say that they were told that Shamrock Rovers was formed in 1901', says Goggins. 'I would love to say that Rovers was found in 1899 but I can't because I have no evidence. I went to the national library and painstakingly went through papers as far back as 1899 and the first mention I found of Rovers was in 1901'.

Throughout the '70s and '80s, the date 1899 was written on the gates of Glenmalure Park, the home which Rovers occupied from 1926 until their controversial departure in 1987. However, since the 1990s, 1901 has been adopted by the various regimes which have run the club. Officially, the centenary of the club was celebrated in 2001, although the more hardcore believers in 1899 claim to have held private celebrations two years earlier.

The divisive issue is the undisputed fact that Rovers played only friendly games for their first two years of existence. This, together with the fact that Rovers registered with the Leinster Football Association in 1901, are the only two certainties about the origins of the club. Essentially, the dispute is over whether the two years of friendlies were played before or after registration with the LFA in 1901. Goggins points to an article in the club programme of 28 December 1941, when the Hoops took on Cork United in Milltown. In the programme, an article penned under the title 'an old supporter' claims that the club was founded in 1901. Although the 'old supporter' could not have realised at the time, his article is now the centrepiece of the debate over the origins of the club over sixty years later.

Jimmy Conroy has been a Rovers' obsessive since he was a child in the 1960s. His love affair with the club has led him to conduct his own research into its origins and Conroy is defiant in his belief that 1899 was when the club was founded. Ironically, it was Conroy who first uncovered the article from 1941.

'If you are going to use that article as a source of proof, then I think it points to 1899', he says. 'The club registered with the LFA in 1901 but why would they spend two years playing friendly matches if they joined the association in 1901? The simple answer is that they were formed in 1899 and played two seasons of friendlies before joining up'.

Sadly, no official documentation from the era exists and so the debate will probably never be settled. Rovers will remain a club without a birthday.

Shelbourne FC had been active in Ringsend for over five years when a group of locals decided that they could do with some competition. Why this decision was taken remains unclear, although it is probable that nationalism played a role. Prior to Rovers' birth, Irish clubs tended to have links with the British military and it is probable that the people who founded Shamrock Rovers felt it was time for a non-aligned club to make it's presence felt.

At a meeting at 4 Irishtown Road, home of Lar Byrne, it was decided to set up a new football club. A series of meetings were held over a number of weeks during which time the club was established. One problem remained: what to call the new club. Several names were suggested and the founding members could not decide on one. Eventually, they met in a house on Shamrock Avenue and opted to name the club after the venue: Shamrock Rovers FC was born.

'Shamrock Rovers, Leinster Junior Champions 1914/15'.

Shelbourne and Rovers were immediate rivals. Shels, founded by a local man named James Rowan, played their football on the northside of the river Dodder, which runs through Ringsend, whilst Rovers played on the southside. Almost instantly, fixtures between the two clubs attracted thousands of spectators, with families divided down the middle between Ringsend's two great clubs. Little of the early heritage sites of Rovers remain. Rovers' first clubhouse – The Bandroom on Thorncastle Street – is now a shining block of apartments, whilst a similar fate was suffered by 'The Clinkers', the land where the clubs' first home ground stood. Even 4 Irishtown Road appears to be now missing. Modern Ireland has no place for sentiment – if they'll build a motorway through the Tara Valley, what chance did Lar Byrne's house ever have?

However, two areas of land are still identifiable from the club's history. At the beginning of Irishtown Road lies a small series of side streets. The first, St. Patrick's Villas, was home to many of the original players. Although Rovers and Shels both shared Ringsend as a home, Rovers fans will often point out that they were formed by the 'real' Ringsenders, whereas Shels were formed by locals from outside the village. St. Patrick's Villas appears to back up this argument, sitting as it does in the heart of Ringsend. Such was the influence of the Villas that the club was briefly named after it – being called St. Patrick's for a number of years after 1906. Next to St. Patrick's is The Square, which was formerly known as Shamrock Avenue.

Across the road in the local library Brendan Costelloe paces up and down alongside the great collection of books. His eyes light up at the mention of Shamrock Rovers. Brendan hails from Limerick but his sporting allegiances were settled as a child when Shamrock Rovers came to town to play. He has never forgotten being mesmerised by the green and white hoops, the travelling supporters and the brand of football that made Rovers such a spectacle in the 1960s. He ran on the pitch and asked Paddy Ambrose, the hugely popular Rovers centre forward, for an autograph. Ambrose – a player who was renowned for three things: his skill on the playing field, his mild manners off it and his obsession with pigeons – conversed with the youngster and reminded him as Gaeilge to keep up his Irish studies. Costelloe has been a hoop ever since. At least Ringsend still has some sentiment left for Shamrock Rovers.

****

Aside from winning trophies, Rover's greatest forte has always been tragic irony. Having lost their ground in 1987, Rovers have spent nearly two decades without a home. Homelessness is now what the club is best known for. It is, therefore, only fitting that it was this very problem which blighted the club's early years. In 1906, after merely a handful of seasons in operation, the club informed the Leinster Junior League that they were unable to provide a home ground and promptly dropped out of all competitions.

The history of Shamrock Rovers may well have ended before it had begun if it were not for the determination of the locals to revive it. At a meeting in 1914 Rovers was resurrected, playing their matches in Ringsend Park. However, the rejuvenation of the club was only a temporary measure and when in 1916 Ringsend Park became unavailable once more, the club disbanded and played only friendly matches for the following five years. In 1921 Shamrock Rovers was born for the third and – so far – final time.

Football in Ireland developed differently than it did in many other countries. Although hurling had been a popular Irish pastime for centuries, Gaelic football only became popular at much the same time as association football. The two sports were seen as rivals by their backers, even though many ordinary people enjoyed playing both. Under the nationalist revolution sweeping Europe, the rivalry soon took on a unique political significance, with many viewing the new sport as an English game to be resisted.

On 1 November 1884 the Gaelic Athletic Association for the Preservation and Cultivation of National Pastimes was formed, largely through a series of articles published in two nationalist newspapers, United Ireland and Irishman. The association's conflict with the British government was immediate: in 1885 'non-Gaelic' players were banned from partaking in the association's activities; three years later all members of the Royal Irish Constabulary were banned from playing Gaelic games. Following the Easter Rising of 1916, GAA President James Nowlan was amongst hundreds of players interned and in 1920 when the British Army sought revenge for the deaths of their comrades they entered Croke Park and shot dead twelve spectators and a player. With its feet firmly rooted in the nationalist camp, the GAA was openly hostile towards all semblance of English culture, including the sport that was taking the globe by storm. Although southern Ireland secured independence from Britain in 1922, the continued British 'occupation' of Northern Ireland meant that relations between Gaelic and football remained tense. Right up until 1971, the GAA outlawed its members from playing or watching football. Ned Armstrong and Jim Palmer, who both began following Rovers in the 1930s, vividly remember the hostility towards football from certain quarters:

NED ARMSTRONG
'The GAA actually had a ban on people playing both soccer and Gaelic, which was ridiculous I thought. And it didn't really stop people either, because people would just play soccer under a different name. In fact, it was only the big players that would get caught, the average person could play both sports without too much difficulty. But you could get banned from the GAA for even attending a soccer match. They used to send fellas to soccer games to spy

on people. They viewed it as an English game, and in Ireland we shouldn't playing English games with them occupying the north of the country.'

JIM PALMER
'I went to school in Westland Row. All the boys were mad into Rovers but the Christian Brothers used to punish us for even speaking about them. They'd give us a few slaps if they heard us talking about the games. We weren't allowed to talk about association football at all. It was stupid. They called it "the English game". They were really rotten about it. If we wanted to go down to Ringsend Park we weren't allowed to tell them we were going to play football, we'd have to make something up. I never minded being made an example of by the Brothers because I didn't care if they knew I followed Rovers. If only they knew I played cricket too!'

The hostile attitude towards football which is still held by many in the GAA is ironic given the fact that football in Ireland was always fiercely nationalistic. Southern Irish clubs viewed the Belfast-based Irish Football Association (IFA) as being little more than a puppet organisation run from London and the association did not have an easy relationship with its southern members. Relations between north and south deteriorated to such an extent that in 1892 representatives from Bohemians, Montpelier, St. Helen's School, Dublin University and Leinster Nomads founded the Leinster Football Association (LFA).

The annual Irish Cup rapidly descended into a north Vs south affair, with clubs from Ulster maintaining the upper hand. This changed, however, in 1906 when Shelbourne took the trophy with a 2-0 defeat of Belfast Celtic. So delighted were Dubliners at getting one over their northern rivals that bonfires were lit all along Sandymount Strand and throughout Ringsend to celebrate the momentous achievement. The victory marked a shift in the balance of power from north to south and the LFA soon adopted a policy of outright separatism from their northern masters.

In this respect, football was used as a nationalist vehicle for Ireland to build its own structures and distance itself from Britain and the unionist elements in the north. In the north itself, Belfast Celtic became a highly politicised club, so much so that it would eventually have to disband for safety reasons. Bohemians, Shelbourne and St. James' Gate – the south's three top clubs – withdrew from the all-Ireland league but agreed to stay in the Irish Cup. However, with the War of Independence raging in the south and unionists in the north importing arms in preparation for a civil war should Britain retreat from the island, security surrounding north-south fixtures was tight. In 1921 Shels and Glentoran played out a scoreless draw in the Irish Cup final and when the IFA refused to schedule the replay for Dublin southern clubs withdrew from the competition altogether.

In June of that year – six months after the signing of the Treaty which partitioned the island of Ireland – the Football Association of the Irish Free State was formed. Three months later, eight Dublin clubs – St. James Gate, Bohemians, Shelbourne, Olympia, Jacobs, Frankfort, Dublin United and YMCA Dublin – kicked off the first season of the League of Ireland. Although the IFA made several attempts at reconciliation, the southern clubs refused to disband their new organisation. Southern clubs had sought to express their nationalism and had effectively severed all contact with their northern rivals.

★★★★

Frankfort and YMCA Dublin disbanded after just one year in senior football and, as the league expanded from eight to twelve teams for the following season, were replaced by

Shelbourne United, Athlone Town, Pioneers, Midland Athletic, Rathmines and Shamrock Rovers. Fittingly, it was to be Rovers who would finish the season on the top of the table, taking the league title home at their very first attempt. Not only had the club arrived in the big time and taken the prize home, they did so in some style, going twenty-one games unbeaten and scoring 77 goals, a record that still stands. The star of that side was Bob Fullam, who was born in Ringsend in 1897.

Fullam began his League of Ireland career with Shelbourne, whom he signed for in 1918, before crossing the Ringsend divide to join Rovers in 1921. The club was still in the Leinster Senior League at the time, but Fullam and his legendary left foot were soon to propel Rovers to the top of the senior league.

Although still only a Leinster Senior League outfit, Rovers reached the first ever Free State Cup final that season, narrowly losing out 1-0 to St. James's Gate. Amongst the Rovers players to line out that day were William 'Sacky' Glen, who went on to win eight cup winner's medals with Rovers, a record which was only equalled in 1977 by Johnny Fullam, also of Rovers.

It was, however, a cup final that was to be marred by violence and controversy. Incensed with the result, Rovers supporters invaded the pitch and scuffles broke out between supporters and the victorious St. James Gate players. The Rovers fans were soon joined by their own players, who, spurred on by a personal dispute between two rival players, invaded the opposition changing room and engaged in a mass brawl with the opposition. The scene was soon one of mayhem and was only halted when the brother of one of the St. James Gate players took a gun from his belt and fired into the roof of the changing room.

Fullam — a docker by trade who was never afraid of a physical confrontation — was central to the disturbing scenes that day and, along with John Joe Flood and Dinny Doyle, was suspended for the early part of the following season as a result.

Bob Fullam left Rovers for one season to try his hand with Leeds United, but he was soon to return to Ringsend and Rovers. His return, in 1924, saw the completion of a famous forward line still known as the 'Four Fs': Bob Fullam, John Joe Flood, John 'Kruger' Fagan and Billy 'Juicy' Farrell. Together, the 'Four F's' proved an unstoppable force and Rovers won the league title for a second time, again going the entire season unbeaten.

'The Four Fs', alongside players such as Dinny Doyle and 'Sacky' Glen, proved to be the base around Rovers' success was built. Indeed, Fullam, Flood, Fagan and Doyle all played in the first ever Irish international, a 3-0 defeat away to Italy. Fullam gained two international caps, both against Italy. The second outing was on 23 April 1927 when the Italians game to Lansdowne Road for the first Irish international played in Dublin. Fullam's ability to strike a powerful free kick was well known in domestic circles and it did not take long for the Italians to experience a Fullam special. The visiting full-back, Zarillo, attempted to clear a Fullam free kick with his head and was knocked unconscious. According to local legend, the Italians soon begged the Irish team not to allow the Ringsend man take any more free kicks.

By 1925 Rovers had won the league title twice out of three attempts, Bohemians edging them out on one occasion. Rovers were playing their home games in Milltown, although it was a different stadium to the one that would become so famously associated with the club. Big games were attracting crowds of over 15,000 and the club knew that a permanent home had to be found. Shelbourne Park and Dalymount Park were top class venues and Rovers, rapidly emerging as the country's top side, needed a venue to compete. A site was quickly identified off the Milltown Road. Although the land was owned by the Jesuits, Rovers were granted permission to construct a new stadium to meet their ambition to be the country's largest football club.

Although the Milltown stadium would grow to be loved by generations of Dubs, some

Rovers supporters were initially sceptical of laying down permanent roots in a village so far from Ringsend. Jim Palmer, whose father followed the club from the time it entered the league at the beginning of the 1920s, recalls that some fans thought Milltown was too far away. Although Dublin was expanding, the areas we now refer to as suburbs were at the time separate villages outside of the city.

'I remember my father giving out about moving to Milltown', says Palmer. 'He thought it was too far out. It was out in the country, he used to complain!'

Shamrock Rovers played their first game in the new Milltown stadium on 11 September 1926. The new stadium was christened Glenmalure Park, after the area of County Wicklow which the Cunningham family, who ran the club, originally hailed from. However, whilst the official name of the ground was Glenmalure Park, to generations of Dubliners it would simply be known as Milltown. The two terms – Glenmalure and Milltown – are interchangeable as both are used when talking about the ground which opened on that historic day in 1926, when Dundalk FC provided the opposition.

The stadium that was opened that day was a very primitive prototype of what would emerge. The main stand, which was, literally, constructed by the supporters of the club, did not open for several years and so the early ground merely consisted of a pavilion, some basic standing room and makeshift seating.

The stadium was officially opened on 18 September 1926, when Belfast Celtic travelled down for an exhibition match. Indeed, so strong was the friendship between Shamrock Rovers and Belfast Celtic that the Dublin club decided to model their look on their northern allies. Up until 1926, Rovers wore green and white striped jerseys. However, at the start of the 1926/27 season it was decided to copy the green and white hooped jerseys worn by Celtic. The Hoops were born. Although the green and white hoops would become the trademark of the club, the first outing in the new strip did not go well, losing 3-0 to the Bray Unknowns in the first round of the Free State Cup. So displeased were senior members of the club with the result that they considered dumping the hoops after just one game, a decision which would have forever altered the mystique surrounding the club. Indeed, 'Sacky' Glen, one of the clubs' earliest stars, once remarked, 'all we have to do to win is show them [the opposition] the green and white jerseys'.

However, although the club made an early exit from the cup, the season was to end in triumph, with the league title returning to Rovers. The club had now been in the League of Ireland for five seasons and had already amassed four major trophies – three league titles and one Free State Cup. With a home base firmly established and with the green and white hoops now the chosen strip, Rovers were on their way.

★★★★

Between 1922 and 1949 Rovers established themselves as Ireland's most successful football club, winning a remarkable forty-four major trophies – six league titles, eleven FAI Cup's, seven League of Ireland Shields, six Leinster Senior Cups, two Dublin City Cups, four Inter-City Cups and eight President's Cups.

During this time, the club became firmly ingrained in Dublin life. Growing from a local Ringsend club, Rovers quickly gained support from all areas of the city, with regular crowds of 20,000 flocking to Milltown to see the Hoops. The green and white hoops became a part of Dublin folklore.

'Joe Cunningham,
Chairman of Shamrock
Rovers from 1925 until
1972'.

'The new stand at Glenmalure Park, Milltown is officially opened,
1 September 1928'.

GERRY MACKEY
'We used to walk from Sandymount to Milltown, up along the Dodder. By the time you reached Eglington Road it was just a sea of faces, everyone going to the game. It was unbelievable.'

MICK MEAGAN
'I was born in Dundrum. Everyone in that area – Dundrum, Donnybrook, Ranelagh, Harold's Cross, Windy Arbour, Churchtown – we were all Rovers. The games were at half three but you'd always leave the house at two o'clock. I'd sometimes sell programmes outside the ground. You'd be given a load of programmes and if you sold a certain amount you'd be given two and six pence. It was the best way to get into the game.'

OSSIE NASH
'When I was playing for Rovers I'd leave the house at half two on match days. It was usually a ten minute walk but on match days it would take much longer because of the crowds. I'd always try and hide myself on the walk down, hoping no one would recognise me.'

NED ARMSTRONG
'I lived in Rathmines and we used to hear the cheers from Milltown from our house, which was three miles away. When I got a bicycle I would cycle up. The number of bikes outside the ground was unbelievable. There'd be thousands of bikes parked all the way down to Donnybrook. There'd be special buses put on from town to bring people to Milltown and you had the trams too.'

PAULINE FOY
'Everyone who lived in any of the areas around Milltown followed Rovers – it was all people talked about in work. Most people cycled to games. The bicycles would be parked three or four deep all the way up to Ranelagh. You couldn't even walk down the path because of the amount of bicycles. That's my abiding memory of that era: lots and lots of bicycles.'

JIM PALMER
'I used to get the 46A bus from outside the Screen cinema. There'd be fleets of buses waiting to bring people to Milltown. The amazing thing about Milltown was the amount of bicycles, especially during the war. You'd get a ticket off a man, he'd write a number on a bit of paper and lick it and stick it to the saddle. There only had to be a bit of mist and the numbers would be gone. I never knew a bike to go astray though, even though Dublin was notorious for bike theft back then. I'd sometimes leave mine in Dartry, which is a good bit away. There used to be lots of vendors outside the ground selling fruit and drinks. It was a bit like Moore Street. They'd do a roaring trade.'

JACK WILSON
'You'd have to be at the ground at 2:30 for a 3:30 kick-off in order to get a good area to stand. Especially since we were only kids. I was living in Crumlin at the time so I'd get the 18 bus from Larkfield to Ranelagh and I'd walk to Milltown from there.'

NED ARMSTRONG
'Games were usually on Sundays, although Bohemians would play on Saturdays. They were a Protestant team so they wouldn't play on Sundays. There was no segregation at games and there were always plenty of comments between rival fans. There'd be great fun. The Shels

games were great for the comments. They were mostly taken as a bit of fun but there was the odd scuffle. Sometimes someone would take a comment badly and the crowd would form a circle around them while they fought. Other times the crowd would close in and they wouldn't have room to fight.'

SONNY O'REILLY

'The atmosphere was different back then. There was no segregation and there was never really any trouble. There'd be great slagging during the games. Milltown was so packed one day that I climbed up on this little barn because I couldn't see anything. Next minute, everyone starts climbing up and the barn caved in! I climbed up on the pavilion in Tolka Park once too and it started caving in. Everything seemed to cave in on me.'

JIM PALMER

'I remember the surrounding wall collapsed once. It was only waist-high but the smaller children would sit against it on the side of the pitch. One day it fell on top of them. Lads ran down from the far end of the ground with stakes to try and prise it up to get the children out. It was very lucky no one was killed. '

GERRY MACKEY

'You could barely get your hands in your pockets you'd be so crammed in.'

NED ARMSTRONG

'A small crowd would be 10,000. You'd get up to 30,000 people in Milltown. The PA system – when it worked – would be asking people to take care. The perimeter wall fell down a few times because the crowd was so big. There'd always be a big crush leaving the ground. It was frightening at times. During the game, if there was a corner or a goal the crowd would push down and you could get crushed. People would often faint. There was an element of danger to it.'

PAULINE FOY

'There were a lot of sweet shops around the ground and with so many thousands of people going to games there would be a bit of pilfering. Some of the shops would close for an hour or two after games because of the pilfering. Most shops shut on Sunday anyway, but the ones around Milltown would generally open because of the matches. They were just family run sweet shops, there were no cafes or restaurants back then.'

SONNY O'REILLY

'I remember being at a Rovers v Shels game in Tolka on a Wednesday afternoon and there were 15,000 people at it. That's 15,000 people who should have been in work! After the games you'd go back into town and wait outside the Irish Press offices for them to put up the results of the other games. There'd be a huge crowd waiting outside the Press for the results. It was a real love-hate thing with Rovers. If they lost, people would be waiting for you in work or in the pub just to slag you. You either loved Rovers or hated them.'

'THE LOCAL LADS WERE OUR HEROES'

MICK MEAGAN

'I went to school directly opposite Glenmalure Park. We'd hang around the ground and the players would come out and give us old socks. They'd be covered in holes but we'd treasure them. You'd wear their socks to school the next day. You'd heard of the English players but the local lads were our heroes.'

JIM PALMER

'My father was great friends with Bob Fullam and "Sacky" Glen. I'd often be in the pub with them. It was a huge thing to be introduced to someone like 'Sacky' Glen or Bob Fullam – they were superstars.'

SONNY O'REILLY

'Larry Palmer was one of the greatest I ever saw. In one game against Dundalk, he was at the edge of the box and the ball got lobbed over him. Everyone was shouting "goal" but Larry got back and saved it. It was the most amazing save I've ever seen.'

LARRY PALMER

'I made a save against Dundalk in the Inter City Cup that became famous. It was down the Tramway end of Dalymount and I managed to stop the ball as it was going over my head. I still get reminded about that save all the time.'

JIM PALMER

'Larry Palmer was in goal when I started going. Palmer was an unusual name back then so people used to think he was my uncle. Of course, with all the adoration I was getting I didn't deny it! I used to go and see Rovers train on Tuesday and Thursday. All the convent girls used to stand outside and ask for autographs, that used to make some of the lads very jealous. There'd always be a big crowd at training sessions.'

NED ARMSTRONG

'When you're young you're easily impressed, but to my mind the best Rovers team was the side of the '40s. Matt Clarke, Shay Healy, Pat Doherty, Bob Bryson, Peter Farrell, Jimmy Dunne, Tommy Eglington – all great players. Football was a different game back then. They had the "W" formation, and the ball was a big, heavy leather thing. On a wet day the ball wouldn't bounce. It was so heavy that only the strongest players could get it into the box from a corner-kick.'

'Action from the 1936 Cup Final between Rovers and Cork. Rovers were to win the game 2-1'.

'Paddy Coad scoring against Bohemians, mid-1940s'.

From left to right: Tommy Eglington, Mickey Delaney and Bobby Rogers training in Milltown, 1945'.

SONNY O'REILLY

'You could talk about great Rovers players all day, but the three I'd put a golden circle around are Paddy Moore, Paddy Coad and Jimmy Dunne. Moore was an absolute genius. People would go to games just to see Paddy. He used to wobble in a way that sent everyone the wrong way. There's not many people left who remember Paddy.'

KITTY MELON

'Paddy Moore was brilliant – my God, he was a legend. He could have played on any team in England. He was quite a short fellow but his heading was so good that they used to say he had springs in his boots. It was very sad the way he ended, drink got the better of him.'

NED ARMSTRONG

'Paddy Moore was good in every way, he was of international standard. His downfall was the drink. We didn't talk about it, but everyone knew. People would try and keep him away from the drink on the days before a match.'

JACK WILSON

'My earliest memories are from 1945. Rovers won the cup that year, beat Bohs 1-0 in the final. We lost the cup final in 1948 to Drumcondra. I remember crying after that game because Rovers had lost the cup.'

NED ARMSTRONG

'The War Years helped Irish football because you had a lot of players coming from England and Northern Ireland to play here in order to avoid national service. They came down and as soon as the war was over they were gone. Davy Cochraine was one of those players. I got a lot of entertainment from watching him. He was a tricky player, but he was built so close to the ground that he'd never fall over. The crowds boomed too.'

JACK WILSON

'In '46 there were players at Rovers who came from England. We had Jimmy McAlinden and Davy Cochraine, who we got from Leeds United. Jimmy was from Belfast and had actually won a cup medal with Portsmouth in '39. He was a Northern Ireland international and Cochraine was a regular player in the Leeds side but he came back to Ireland so as he wouldn't have to do national service. We brought over a Scottish international player in around 1948 by the name of Jack Dodds. He was miles overweight but it was a huge thing to bring over a Scottish international into the club.'

★★★★

In 1925 Rovers introduced a young talent into the League of Ireland by the name of Jimmy Dunne. Aged just 21, Dunne was soon snapped up by English League side New Brighton. However, Dunne's introduction to the game was unique. His break into football came during the Irish Civil War, when he was interned by the Free State government for his republican beliefs. It was whilst playing a football game in prison that he was spotted.

Having signed for New Brighton, Dunne soon transferred to Sheffield United, where he spent almost a decade. It was at Sheffield United that Dunne made his name, becoming one of the club's all time record goalscorers. Three seasons at Arsenal – where he won the English Division One title – preceded a short time at Southampton, before Dunne returned to Dublin and to Rovers. Dunne took up the reigns of player/coach at Rovers in time for the 1937/38 season, leading the club to the title at his first attempt. Occupying the outside right berth on the pitch, Dunne proved the inspiration and the genius behind the Rovers side. However, disagreements with the clubs' owners led to Dunne's departure in 1942, when he joined city rivals Bohemians. The Ringsend native spent four seasons at Bohs before putting his differences with the Cunninghams behind him and joining up with Rovers for the third time in his career.

Sadly, Dunne's third stint with the club was to prove tragically short. In November 1949, Jimmy Dunne died suddenly at his home on the Tritonville Road, Sandymount. His death at the age of just 45 stunned everyone involved in Irish football and his funeral was to see a huge out-pouring of grief on the streets of Dublin.

For those who witnessed him play, Dunne is always mentioned alongside Paddy Moore and Paddy Coad as the greatest ever Rovers player. Jimmy Dunne had essentially replaced Moore at Rovers and, after Dunne's sudden passing, it was to be Coad who would take over the reigns at the club. Coad's great gamble – replacing the entire Rovers team with a group of teenage players – would bring glory back to Rovers and would mould arguably the greatest League of Ireland side ever seen.

CHAPTER 3

'POOR AULD PADDY'

ON 3 MAY 1929, THE unsuspecting onlookers who had gathered in Milltown to watch Shamrock Rovers take on Brideville were introduced to a player the like of whom they had never seen before. Eighteen-years-old and standing at a mere five foot four inches, Paddy Moore was an unlikely hero for the assembled crowd. Yet as the ninety minutes drew to a close – with Moore scoring the only two goals of the game – it was clear that the young forward was special.

Moore's dramatic burst into Irish football was matched only by his tragically premature exit. His entire career was to span just six full seasons, yet almost eighty years on he is still regarded as probably the greatest centre-forward – if not the greatest player – the island of Ireland has ever produced. A star by 18, a legend by 26, by 41 he lay dying in a hospital bed, beset by alcoholism. When Paddy Moore's light was extinguished so tragically, the city of Dublin came to a halt. From all corners of the city, thousands came to pay their respects to a man whose sporting genius has not been seen since.

The story of Paddy Moore is often regarded as the most tragic story in Irish sport. Like George Best three decades later, Moore was ravaged by an addiction to alcohol. Unlike George Best, however, there was to be no second chance for Moore. 'Poor auld Paddy' is the phrase you will most likely hear if you mention his name to those fortunate enough to have witnessed him play.

The tragic story of Paddy Moore begins in 1910 in the north Dublin area of Ballybough. Born in the shadow of Croke Park, Moore was obsessed by round balls from the age he could walk. At football and Gaelic the young Moore excelled, displaying a control and a balance far beyond his years. It was not long, however, before he made a choice between the two codes and dedicated himself solely to football.

Moore soon found himself making regular jaunts across the city to line out for Clonliffe Celtic, a schoolboy club who play their games in the Phoenix Park. A true sign of Moore's dedication to his side occurred in January 1928 when Clonliffe were due to play local rivals Strandville. Moore had taken ill with pneumonia and had been in bed for several days. That morning, Moore's mother was shocked to find that he had left the house and for several hours searched the neighbourhood for her son. Returning back to the house, she discovered two boys carrying a near-unconscious Moore back into the house. He had just scored twice in his side's 3-1 victory.

It was obvious to all who witnessed the young Ballybough lad that his talents were far superior to the schoolboy leagues and Moore soon opted for senior football with Richmond Rovers of the Leinster Senior League. Why Moore resisted a move straight into the Free State league remains unknown, but after one season with Richmond that is exactly what he did. Beating off stiff competition for his signature, Shamrock Rovers signed 18-year-old Paddy Moore, beginning a relationship that, although tragically short, would soon enter the realm of legend.

Pat Moore never saw his father play football. By the time he was born, in 1944, his father was seven years into his retirement from the game. They'd play together on street corners and in parks; games that were inevitably interrupted by strangers wanting to say hello to his father. He heard countless stories of his father's exploits, but thought nothing of them. To him, Paddy Moore wasn't a famous footballer; he wasn't an idol or a legend – he was a father.

'As a kid I never realised how famous my dad was', he says. 'People would always be going on about my dad but I didn't have a clue. I was only seven when he died, but I do have happy memories of him. He was always laughing and smiling. He loved kids and he'd always be playing football with us on the road. I didn't realise who he was though'.

While others would talk of his prowess on the pitch, Moore himself was a modest man and was not one to boast. It was a fact best illustrated through the story of how he met his wife, Una. It was during World War II and Dublin's North Wall had fallen victim to a German bombing. Paddy, at this stage retired from the game, was working as a labourer fixing some of the damaged area when he glanced upon a local girl.

'He started chatting my mother up', explains Pat. 'My mum is very shy and she was already going out with someone else. Her sister turned around and said, "Don't you know who that is? That's Paddy Moore the famous footballer". She hadn't a clue who he was, but she liked

'Shamrock Rovers 1935/36. Paddy Moore sits to the right of the colourful Mrs. Mary Jane Cunningham'.

him and she went out with him. When the other lad found out, himself and his friends went to confront my mother's new boyfriend, basically to beat him up, but when they saw it was Paddy Moore they just said, "we're very sorry, we didn't know it was you"'.

Having made his debut for Rovers in May 1929, Moore quickly rose to prominence. Two weeks into his Rovers career, the weekly newspaper Sport commented: 'Seldom has a forward made such a dramatic entry into senior football as Moore. In four games he has registered eight of the fourteen goals scored by the Cup holders'. Despite making his debut as the 1928/29 season came to a climax, Moore was soon the star of Milltown and that summer Cardiff City came calling.

Just turned nineteen, Moore packed his bags to sample the highest level of English football. However, homesickness kicked in and Moore never settled in Wales. Not only was he young, Moore had played just a handful of top flight games in Ireland, and had essentially gone directly from the Leinster Senior League to the English Division One. The move proved to sudden and Moore would spent the majority of his only season at Cardiff playing reserve team football.

Moore returned to Dublin for the 1930/31 season and instantly took up from where he left off, scoring twice in his first game back in the green and white of Rovers. Although initially deployed as an inside-right, an injury to David 'Babbie' Byrne gave Moore his chance to claim the centre-forward spot. In two successive games – against Jacobs and Bohemians – Moore struck hat-tricks and his form continued into the Cup Final, where he scored Rovers' goal in a 1-1 draw with Dundalk. It was this form that saw Moore earn international recognition and, eight days after the Cup Final, Moore took to the pitch in Barcelona's Montjuich Stadium where Ireland faced Spain.

It was just the sixth international game Ireland had ever played, and Spain – boasting Pepe Samitier, arguably the finest player of his generation – were huge favourites. However, it was to be Moore and not Samitier who stole the show, the debutant scoring the cheekiest of goals to put Ireland in the lead. Running onto a pass from team captain John Joe Flood, Moore lifted the ball over the head of Spanish 'keeper Zamora. So incensed at his

Newspaper clippings.

humiliation was Zamora – the second star of the Spanish team, considered Europe's finest goalkeeper – that he removed his jersey, threw it into the net and, in the words of Ireland player Charlie Dowdall, 'danced around like a demented ape'. Although the game was to finish 1-1, Moore returned to Ireland with a rocketing reputation.

Thirteen days later, Moore completed a remarkable period in his career by scoring the only goal of the game to defeat Dundalk in the Cup Final replay. At the age of just twenty-one, Paddy Moore had captured his first senior football medal. Events to follow would ensure that he would earn just three more during his prematurely short career.

As a boy, Moore had developed into something of a fitness fanatic. When not on the football pitch, he was swimming at Dollymount Strand, running in the Phoenix Park or climbing the Dublin Mountains. His stocky physique hid his impeccable level of fitness. In line with his strict regime, alcohol was an indulgence he seldom touched. However, having achieved super-star status in his native city, a dark side of Paddy Moore soon emerged. A single man with a desire to socialise, he could not enter a pub without every customer wanting to buy him a drink. What was once an indulgence soon became an addiction – the downward spiral into which Paddy Moore was plunged by alcohol soon had him in its grip.

It is not possible to pin-point one day or one event that pushed Moore over the edge. Alcohol doesn't work like that. Its addiction is a slow one; one that creeps up unnoticed until its devastating power is all too clear. During his formative years at Rovers, Moore had been taken-in by Bob Fullam, the undisputed king of Milltown. Fullam was a hard-drinker but he could see in Moore a quality he had never seen in any player before and would not allow him consume alcohol with the other players. Whether Moore's descent into alcoholism coincided with Fullam's retirement from the game is not clear, although it was certainly the early years of the 1930s that Moore's battle with alcohol began.

Regardless of his condition off the pitch, Moore's on-field antics were unaffected and he was the driving force behind Rovers' all-conquering side of 1931/32. The club won every honour that season with the exception of the Leinster Senior Cup, out of which they were eliminated during Moore's two-month injury lay-off. Despite a lengthy absence from the game, Moore scored a remarkable 48 goals in all competitions during the course of the season, including his second international goal which came during a 2-0 Irish win over Holland.

The legend of Moore was now at its peak in Dublin; his fame surpassing even that of legends such as Bob Fullam and 'Sacky' Glen. Since 1922, attendance for Cup Finals had constantly hovered around the 20,000 mark. However, with Paddy Moore now the star attraction, a record 32,000 people crammed into Dalymount Park to witness Rovers take on Dolphin in the 1932 Cup Final. Moore responded in style, scoring the only goal of the game to give Rovers their fourth successive cup final success.

At this stage, Moore's reputation was outgrowing Ireland and, sensing that it would not be long before the Dubliner moved abroad, Scottish outfit Aberdeen swooped. Dons manager Paddy Travers signed Moore and Paddy Daly from Rovers, together with Joe O'Reilly of St. James' Gate, in a bid to revamp the club. Of the three Irishmen who helped revive Aberdeen, Moore was the biggest success and was credited with single-handedly revolutionising the way Scots looked at the game of football. The Pittodrie crowd adored Moore, who responded with a flurry of goals.

Sadly, Aberdeen's club records were destroyed in a fire some years ago and so little statistical information is available for Moore's time in Scotland. However, one event is recalled in an edition of the Evening Press in 1961:

'In a Scottish First Division game, he [Moore] struck inspired form and went off on a one-man goal-scoring spree. Six times he hammered the ball past the opposing goalkeeper and his total would have been much greater but for the fact that he gave up trying. Even in the last quarter of the game, when he was presented with a "sitter" five yards out from goal, he beckoned to the unfortunate goalkeeper and then lifted the ball with his foot and tipped it into the goalkeeper's hands, much to the delight of a huge crowd. Paddy explained his action later: "That poor man was in enough trouble as it was. I didn't want him to lose his job".'

The Aberdeen years also presented Moore with his most famous achievements in an Ireland jersey. In total, Moore played five international matches while at Aberdeen – against Belgium, Holland, Germany and Hungary for the Free State side, together with a game against England representing Northern Ireland. Although he scored twice in Ireland's 5-2 defeat to Holland and turned in another solid performance in the 4-2 defeat to Hungary, it was to be the Belgian game that Moore will always be remembered for.

On 25 February 1934, Belgium and Ireland lined up at Dalymount Park in front of 30,000 spectators. David Byrne and Peadar Gaskins were Rovers' representatives on the day, with Moore sailing from Scotland to make the game. After thirteen minutes Capelle put the visitors in the lead, with Van Eynde doubling the score after 23 minutes. The Evening Press describes what followed:

'A pass from Joe O'Reilly reached Moore. Pappaert on one side and Welkenhuysen on the other, converged on him to seal off the gap that led to goal. Paddy feinted to go left, then right and suddenly, with inches to spare on both sides, he shot cheekily between the two Belgians and lashed in a vicious shot that beat the Belgian goalkeeper Van de Weyer'.

The sides went into half-time with the visitors 2-1 up, when Moore famously told his team-mates not to worry because for every goal Belgium scored he would score one for Ireland. His work was cut-out, however, shortly after play resumed when Van Eynde put Belgium 3-1 up. Again, the Evening Press describes the action:

'Now Paddy Moore decided it was time for swift action. Fastening on a ball near the centre of the field, he danced his way past Welkenhuysen and went streaking through the Belgian defence and slammed in a glorious goal'. 2-3.

'Jimmy Kelly of Derry City sent over a high centre and Pappaert and Smellinck jumped to head it clear. Much to everyone's surprise, Moore, just behind them, made no move. He waited and the ball dropped, after skimming over the heads of the Belgian backs, he shoved out a foot and tapped the ball neatly into the net'. 3-3.

When Van Eynde completed his hat-trick after 78 minutes to put the Belgians 4-3 in the lead, time seemed to be running out for Ireland. Just as he had promised at half-time, however, Moore wasn't finished yet:

'With perfect accuracy, Joe [Kendrick] lobbed it back into the Belgian goalmouth. And this time Paddy Moore did not wait when the Belgian backs jumped for it. He was a split-second ahead of them and to a sudden, shattering roar from the packed stands and terraces, his flashing header sent the ball high into the net'. 4-4.

The whistle blew for full-time, sending Paddy Moore into the record books as the first player in the world to score four goals in a World Cup qualifying match. The legend of Paddy Moore was now written in stone.

Behind the public image of Moore, however, his mask of stability was slipping. The centre-forward had descended into such a state of alcohol dependency that he was regularly failing to turn-up for games at Pittodrie and a member of the Aberdeen coaching staff had to accompany the wayward star on trips to Dublin to ensure he'd arrive at his destination in a state of sobriety.

As a result of his failing condition, together with a knee injury he had sustained, Moore was transferred back to Shamrock Rovers for the beginning of the 1935/36 season. In the three seasons in which Moore resided in Scotland, Rovers had won one Cup Final and finished in second, third and sixth position in the league. With the star attraction returning to Milltown, hopes were high that the club could challenge for the title which Moore's goals spurred them to in 1932.

However, Moore was feeling the effect of his injury and, despite some strong performances, could only help the club to a sixth place finish. Rovers did, however, manage to secure the cup with a 2-1 win over Cork, with Moore getting the first of the day. Moore had lived up to his reputation as a cup final player, getting a goal in each of the three finals he played with Rovers for.

The following season – 1936/37 – proved a major let-down, Rovers finishing the season in ninth place, which was their worst ever finish, and ending their participation in the cup with a 2-0 defeat to Waterford in the quarter-final. Moore's most outstanding contribution all season came in an Ireland jersey, when Germany travelled to Dalymount Park in October 1936.

Germany was under Nazi control and the event was marked by the visiting team, together with seven hundred of their supporters, taking the Nazi salute on the pitch before and after the game. Indeed, the German players had arrived in Ireland on a plane bearing the Nazi swastika and were treated to unprecedented levels of diplomatic nurturing during their visit, receiving a special state dinner in the Mansion House and complementary tickets to the Abbey Theatre.

The game itself saw Ireland record what was described at the time as their greatest ever result, crushing their opponents 5-2. Although Moore did not score any of the goals, the Rovers man set up each of them and was hailed in the press as the star of the show. Indeed, so impressed were the Germans by Moore that they offered him a coaching position, an invitation he declined.

Yet, unbeknownst to the Germans, and indeed the home supporters, Moore was actually hopelessly inebriated during the game. With hours to go before kick-off, Moore had been discovered slumped over a hotel bar. Some years later, Billy Lord, the Rovers trainer, recalled the events of 17 October 1936:

'I did what I could, but I was a very worried man when the Irish team took to the field', said Lord. 'Of the thousands of people in the ground, I alone knew how unfit the little fellow really was. The Germans were superbly fit and well trained and I didn't think Paddy would last fifteen minutes. But he had a dream game from start to finish and ran rings around the German defence. He was so good that towards the end of the game, the German coach, the famous Dr. Nertz, turned to me and said, "you know, our football association have sent me to London several times to watch Alex James at Highbury, but they should have sent me to Dublin to study Moore". I smiled but inside I was more surprised than he was'.

Moore played one more fixture for Ireland, a 3-2 home defeat to Hungary in December 1936, but by the end of the 1936/37 season it was clear that a combination of alcohol abuse and a knee injury were robbing Moore of his undoubted genius. Jimmy Dunne, who had played briefly for Rovers in 1925 before transferring to Sheffield United, where he would become a legend, wanted to come home to Dublin and Rovers offered him a position has player-coach. Moore's days at Milltown were over.

He transferred to Shelbourne but wouldn't even last the season. One of Moore's first games in a Shelbourne shirt was against Rovers. The game was billed as a contest between Moore and Dunne, with both players scoring in a thrilling 5-5 draw played in front of 15,000 people. However, while both players scored, it is a sad commentary on the decline of Paddy Moore that at 27 he was replaced at Rovers by a player almost six years his elder.

Moore's injury had finished him. Billy Lord, his long-time friend, recalls the day he broke the news to Moore that he would have to retire from the game: 'I worked on it [the knee] but it was no use. Sadly, I had to tell him, "it's no go Paddy. Your knee won't be right again. You've finished with football". It almost broke my heart to tell him. But he took it like a real star. He said: "Well, I suppose it had to end sometime. Anyway, it was good while it lasted"'.

Without football in his life, Moore's condition worsened. He was working as a labourer but was not earning much money. Not having saved much of his football earnings, Moore eventually traded in all his medals and Irish caps in order to get alcohol. It was, however, a story that almost had a happy ending. Having met and married a girl, Moore began a family and soon after moved to Birmingham to re-start his life. Without the fame that cursed his life in Dublin, he began to improve and, had he remained in England, may have lived longer. In 1949, however, his father died and Moore decided to return to Dublin to live. It was a fatal decision. Within two years, Paddy Moore was dead. He was just 41 years of age.

Pat Moore remembers the day his father died. Paddy's health had declined rapidly and on the morning of 23 Monday July 1951 a doctor was called to 147 Clonliffe Avenue, the house where he was staying with his mother. The doctor recommended that the former footballer be brought to hospital immediately, but Moore resisted. The following day, he deteriorated further and was rushed by ambulance to St. Kevin's Hospital where he died of heart failure within an hour of admission. Pat, his only son, was just seven years old and was playing football on the street when his father took his final breath.

'There was a rag and bone man coming down the street on a cart', he says. 'Rag and bone men were people you'd give rags to and they'd give you a balloon or something in return. I ran into the house to get some rags and there was a man from the army there. In those days they used to stick a white card with a black edge on the house door when someone died. I remember seeing the card and my mum crying and the army man giving a salute'.

Obviously, it was a tragic day for Pat, although he says that he was too young to fully understand his father's downfall. The struggle to survive kept all thoughts of his father out of his mind for years. Moore's earnings may have been small but without them the family were plunged into financial ruin and Una Moore was forced to uproot three children - Pat, Nuala

Pat Moore.

51

and Anne - and move back to England, where she remarried. The lack of financial aid from Rovers has remained a sore point for the Moore family.

'Aberdeen gave my mother £100 but Rovers gave her nothing', says Pat. 'They took all the glory but didn't give us anything. We were forced to emigrate just to survive. The least Rovers could have done was give us a testimonial'. It has only really been over the last twenty years that Pat has begun to acknowledge his father's legacy. Having lived in England for much of his life, it was only when Pat returned to Dublin that he would hear the stories of his father: 'People would always be coming up to me saying, "are you really Paddy Moore's son?"'

Pat researched his father's career and through a newspaper plea in 1984 managed to recover some of his lost possessions. Individuals who had acquired Paddy Moore's medals sent them to their rightful owner and even the Irish cap from the game against Belgium was returned. To commemorate Paddy Moore's legacy, Billy Behan, the former Manchester United scout and long-term friend of Moore's, organised for the cup winners' medal from 1931 to be mounted on a plaque. The company who performed the operation refused payment. The plaque is now Pat's prized possession. Above the 1931 medal lies a simple inscription: 'Paddy Moore: At his peak, he was the best footballer in Europe'.

Above: The trophy.

Left: Close-up of the trophy.

CHAPTER 4

Coad's Colts (1950–1959)

The Rovers side of the 1940s had achieved moderate success, winning four cups but failing to ever challenge convincingly for the league title. Paddy Coad – who was already established as one of the best players in the country – decided to shake the club up, opting for a radical youth policy. He scoured the schoolboy leagues and signed up the brightest talents. Over the course of his first three years in charge, Coad would sign virtually the entire schoolboy international side to Rovers. It was a risky move – the step up from schoolboy to League of Ireland football could easily have proven too much for the players. However, the side that Paddy Coad would form was to change the way Irish people viewed the sport of football and would go down in the history books as the greatest League of Ireland side of all time.

'By '53 we were up and running'

Coad had been plying his trade at Rovers since 1942, whilst Paddy Ambrose had joined the club in 1949. However, these were the only two players of the Jimmy Dunne era to stay at the club through the 1950s revolution. Ambrose was a powerful forward with devastating aerial abilities and scored 109 league goals for Rovers, a club record which still stands. Renowned as the quiet man of Rovers, Ambrose's first love was pigeon racing and the centre-forward would often miss pre-season training if it interfered with the pigeon season.

One of the first players to join Coad and Ambrose at Milltown was Liam Tuohy, who would go on to become a household name in Ireland through both his skilful play and, later on, his managerial success. Over the course of two years, Coad travelled across Dublin in search of new talent.

Liam Tuohy
'Paddy was going for youth, he was signing a lot of lads out of Under-18 football. I signed for the club in late 1951 and the following year we got players like Shay Keogh, Ronnie

Action shot from game v Bohs.

Team shot of the League of Ireland side v German Hesse league.

Nolan, Gerry Mackey and a few others. Youth was the key to the team that went on to be known as the "Coad's Colts". We were a great side.'

RONNIE NOLAN
'Before Coad took over, Rovers had a lot of players who came up through the ranks but had never played in the schoolboy leagues. They were doing well but they weren't winning trophies so Coad decided to delve into the schoolboy leagues. He signed every schoolboy international he could get his hands on.'

GERRY MACKEY
'Coad was signing up a lot of young players. People like Shay Keogh and Ronnie Nolan all came in shortly after myself. The only player of that side who had already been there was Paddy Ambrose, the rest were all brought in over a two year period. It was during that 1951/52 period that Coad assembled his side. By '53 we were more or less up and running. They called us the "Coad's Colts". It was a marvellous side.

JIM PALMER
'Coad brought in a lot of young players. My father used to say, "they're only juniors, we'll never win anything with juniors". They were only in their early 20s but they proved my father wrong. It was a very exciting era.'

'IT WAS LIKE SAYING THE ROSARY'

By 1953 Rovers had a core of twelve players whom the press soon christened the 'Coad's Colts'. Confusion often reigns over which players are deemed to have been a part of the side. Eamon 'Sheila' Darcy replaced Christy O'Callaghan in goals in 1957, and so both men were at one stage members of the Colts. Others players, such as Clem Dillon, Leo O'Reilly, Liam Monroe and Dick Dunne, father of current Republic of Ireland international Richard Dunne, featured in the side from time to time, although they are not traditionally recorded as being in the Colts. The Coad's Colts are generally acknowledged to have been:
   Christy O'Callaghan (goalkeeper), Mickey Burke (right full), Shay Keogh (centre half), Gerry Mackey (left full), Ronnie Nolan (right half), Liam Hennessy (left half), Jimmy 'Maxie' McCann (outside right), Noel Payton (inside right), Paddy Coad (inside left), Liam Tuohy (outside left), Paddy Ambrose (centre forward), with Tommy Hamilton acting as the replacement player.
   The Colts soon built an aura around themselves. With the exception of Coad, who was roughly ten years older than the rest of the side, the players were all in their late teens or early twenties when they were signed up to the Milltown club. The fast, passing style of football they played revolutionised the game in Ireland and no matter where they travelled in Ireland crowds of up to 20,000 would flock to see them. The twelve Rovers players became some of Ireland's earliest celebrities.

JACK WILSON
'Coad went about assembling his side. He put together a fantastic side: O'Callaghan, Burke, Mackey, Nolan, Keogh, Hennessy, Payton, McCann, Coad, Tuohy, Hamilton, Ambrose. Everyone of my era can recite that team; it was like saying the rosary.'

TOMMY KINSELLA
'The team Coad put together was the best ever League of Ireland side. I used to travel

Players looking at tactics board.

everywhere to watch them, even when I was ten years old. I'd get the bus fare off my mother and then get the man on the gate to lift me over the turnstile.'

RONNIE NOLAN

'We had twelve players in the squad, very few others players at the club made it into the first team. I often meet fellas who come up to me and say, "you know, I was at Rovers for three years and I never got a match". We had the same team every week, there was no such thing as resting players. Hamilton was the extra player, if there was an injury we'd have to jig around the team. They were great days for football. These days a League of Ireland player could be standing beside you and you wouldn't know him, but back then we couldn't go anywhere without people asking for autographs. People had nothing else back then. There was no television, the only entertainment was the radio and the cinema. The Theatre Royal would put on a one hour stage show followed by a film, that was a big high in the social end of things. So the game at the weekend was a big thing.'

DICK DUNNE

'It was a very tough team to get into. The side picked itself for years. I was signed to Rovers in 1958 and Mickey Burke got injured so I had a decent run in the first team that year – 1958/59 – and we won the league. But it was such a great side that you only got in if someone got injured. You couldn't just take Ronnie Nolan's or Liam Hennessy's place.'

Gerry Mackey tackling Duncan Edwards.

GERRY MACKEY

'We had nine full international players on that side. One of the highlights for me was the time the League of Ireland played the English League in Dalymount. They had a star-studded team, basically the full English international side. I was captain of the Irish side, Billy Wright was captain of the English side. There were eight Rovers players playing and the English had people like Tommy Byrne and Duncan Edwards, both of whom would be killed in the Munich crash. We drew the game 3-3 but we finished that game with nine players because Noel Payton and Ollie Conroy had to go off injured and there were no substitutes in those days. In the last minute Roger Byrne came from nowhere to clear a shot off the line to deny us victory. I can never remember feeling physically sick after any other game. We were totally and utterly exhausted playing against these full-time players.'

LIAM TUOHY

'We really became household names. We were a very attractive side to watch, everywhere we went we would fill the ground. I think we changed the face of Irish football because we passed the ball. Irish football before that was about either kicking it long or getting the ball and running with it, but Paddy Coad got us passing it around.'

RONNIE NOLAN

'It was a very professional set-up, that's why I think that team changed Irish football. Paddy Coad completely changed Irish training methods. He was doing coaching courses. Previous to that, training consisted of a few sprints and a lap of the pitch. Paddy had us practising with the ball. Eventually everyone started doing that.'

DICK DUNNE

'Coad was a great player but also a wonderful coach. He was way ahead of his time. If you look at teams in England, they train today the way Coad was training us back in the '50s.'

JIM PALMER

'Before Coad, players weren't very fit. They'd be wrecked very early into the game. Training was just running around the pitch a few times, but Coad changed that. He was great. I saw him getting sent off once. He told the referee to fuck off, which was very strange for Paddy because he was such a mild-mannered man.'

THEO DUNNE

'My first game for Shelbourne was against Rovers. Shels and Rovers had a great rivalry back then, you were either Shels or you were Rovers. My father was Shels but I'd always been a Rovers man. I was playing against Liam Hennessy in my first game. He was some player, he had a tremendous left foot. I missed a sitter in that game. I was put through but I blasted the ball into the side netting. The Shels fans knew I followed Rovers so they thought I did it on purpose!'

TOMMY KINSELLA

'At that time every kid in Dublin wanted to play for Shamrock Rovers, no other team in the world. I was playing with St. Joseph's in 1957 and Rovers were looking at bringing in some young players. Paddy Coad came to watch me but he turned me down. I cried and I said to him, "Mr. Coad, I'll prove you wrong". I eventually signed for Rovers in 1966 and I met Paddy in Milltown and I asked him whether he remembered me. "I do", he said, "and I remember what you told me. We don't always get it right."'

'ROVERS WERE THE ENVY OF EVERYONE'

RONNIE NOLAN

'Everything about the club was professional. Before the trains came into being, we used to travel to away games in limousines. They were rented from the local funeral home, they'd have three rows of seats in them. If we were going to Cork, we'd get the limos down and stay overnight in Cahir. The roads were so bad that it would take you five hours to get to Cork. Nowadays it takes five hours because of the traffic, so it's the same thing! The Cunninghams insisted that we all wear the club blazer and tie on away trips too. I remember one of the Cork lads saying that they used to be envious because we'd step out of limousines dressed in official club blazers and they'd be walking into the ground carrying their boots in brown paper bags! We had to wear the blazer, tie, a white shirt and grey flannels, they were very particular about that. We didn't carry our boots, they were brought into the ground with the jerseys.'

GERRY MACKEY

'Glasgow Celtic and Shamrock Rovers had a relationship with each other. Glasgow Celtic would ship their jerseys over to Belfast and the Cunninghams would drive up to Belfast and bring them down to Rovers, so we were actually wearing Glasgow Celtic jerseys. It used to be very amusing because the style of jersey would change over the years and Rovers were always the only ones in Ireland to have the latest fashion. A rule was passed in Scotland that all clubs had to have numbers on their jerseys but Celtic objected because they would have had to have a box for the number on their jerseys and they said it would ruin the hoops. They reached a compromise that numbers would be displayed on their nicks [shorts]. When the jerseys reached us, no one could understand why Rovers had numbers on their nicks because no one else did! I remember another game where it was lashing rain, we were all soaked, but the crowd started to buzz and the players became aware of this because it had nothing to do with the game. It turned out that the nicks were so wet that they had become see-through! There was a wide variety of jock straps on display! Billy Lord [the Rover's trainer] was having kittens over it; he made us change at half time because we were a disgrace.'

DICK DUNNE

'Rovers were the envy of everyone. We travelled to away games in these huge Austin Princess cars. The other teams would be going on a coach and would stop off for fish and chips but at Rovers we stayed in top hotels and were always given steak before every game. They travelled like any top club should.'

RONNIE NOLAN

'I remember on one occasion taking the limos down to a cup game in Sligo. There was a huge crowd that day, people were standing on the roof of the stand it was so packed. Mickey Burke, totally out of character, punched Johnny Armstrong, the famous Sligo player, and the crowd went crazy. There was war! They invaded the pitch and we had to be taken off. We were in the dressing room and the crowd were lashing rocks at us. We needed a Garda escort to the limos and the crowd were trying to overturn them. The driver revved up the car and scattered around 200 people.'

★★★★

As famous as the Coad's Colts became, they never enjoyed a complete monopoly of League of Ireland success. Domestic football was remarkably strong during the 1950s, a fact that is borne out by the labelling of the decade as 'the golden era' of Irish football. The Rovers side was strong, but so too were the sides assembled by Cork Athletic, St. Patrick's Athletic, Shelbourne and Drumcondra, whilst Limerick were never far off from challenging.

In 1953/54 Rovers won the league title for the first time since 1939 when they pipped Cork side Evergreen to the title by just two points. Liam Tuohy scored the decisive goal when the two sides met in a top of the table clash on the final day of the season in front of 15,000 people. Clashes between the top sides regularly drew five-figured crowds, with 22,789 people witnessing Rovers demolish St. Pat's 5-0 in 1955. Pat's were on the way to winning two league titles in a row but Paddy Ambrose single-handedly destroyed the Chapelizod based club, scoring four times.

The strength of the Rovers side of the mid-50s can be seen by one event which took place in 1955. Paddy Coad was given a benefit game in return for his fantastic service to the club over the years and Chelsea were invited to Dublin. The London club were celebrating their fiftieth years in football and had done so in style, winning their first ever English league title. However, the English champions were humbled by Rovers, who went 3-0 up inside twenty-three minutes. Leo O'Reilly, a reserve team player who only featured in the game due to an injury to Paddy Ambrose, struck twice, with Liam Tuohy also getting on the score-sheet. Chelsea pulled two back in the second half, but the Dubliners still ran out 3-2 winners, an extraordinary result and one which shows the brilliance of that side.

Rovers regained the league title from St. Pat's in 1957, only to surrender it to Drumcondra the following year. However, Rovers again won the league in 1959, making it four league successes during the 1950s. Not only was that decade the golden era of Irish football, it was the golden era of Shamrock Rovers. The successful Rovers sides of the 1920s and '30s were rapidly becoming a distant memory by the time Paddy Coad assumed the reigns at Milltown, but by the end of the 1950s Shamrock Rovers were yet again the most glamorous name in Irish football. Although other clubs had experienced equal success during the '50s, they never attracted the same mysticism about themselves as did Rovers. It was the era of Paddy Coad that forever immortalised the name of Shamrock Rovers.

'WE WERE HAPPY WITH WHAT WE HAD HERE'

With players in England subjected to a maximum wage, the lure of the English game was not as strong as it is today. Many League of Ireland players would have been equally at home competing in the English top flight but opted to remain in Ireland. Nowadays, the players that made up the Coad's Colts could command huge salaries in England, yet it was not until the beginning of the 1960s, with the abolition of the maximum wage, that moving to England became an attractive offer for Irish players.

Some players – such as Liam Whelan, Peter Farrell and Tommy Eglington – did move to cross-channel football, yet, as can be seen from the national side at the time, many of their contemporaries were content to stay in their native country.

GERRY MACKEY

'There weren't many of us at that time who were anxious to go to English football. I had a few opportunities, I was asked to Everton and to Blackburn Rovers but I wasn't interested. My father died when I was 11 and I was determined to look after my mother. My brother had to leave school to support us and there was no way that I was going to leave the country. I never regretted not going away. People like Ronnie Nolan, Shay Keogh, "Maxie" McCann, they were all perfectly happy with what they had here. Tuohy eventually did go to Newcastle for a few years but he was just as happy to come home. Mind you, two of my idols, Peter Farrell and Tommy Egglington, did go away and had very successful careers with Everton.

When I started at Rovers I was on around £2.10 shillings but that rose up to £5. Of course, we were paid £1 extra for each point we got, so when we won - which we usually did – we got an extra £2, which did make it worthwhile. I was lucky to have a good job too, so if you had £7 coming in on top of your wage you were earning good money. The maximum wage in English football was £20, so people like Stanley Matthews and Billy Wright were only earning £20. In 1959 my job was transferred to England and I played part-time over there but I was on the maximum wage. So I had £20 from football on top of my salary – it was great!'

RONNIE NOLAN

'At one stage I was supposed to be going to Preston North End but the maximum wage over there was around £20 and between Rovers and my job I was earning more than that over here, so there was no point in going to England to earn less money. The only incentive to go would have been to get a big signing on fee.'

'I USED TO MITCH OFF SCHOOL JUST TO LOOK AT HIM'

Paddy Coad began his League of Ireland career with Waterford, but was soon signed by Glenavon, who had intended on selling him onto an English outfit. However, the outbreak of World War II halted Coad's proposed move to England and he returned to the south-east. During the 1941/42 season, Waterford and Cork United finished joint top of the table and the title was to be settled by a play-off. However, the Waterford players refused to play the game after a dispute with the club directors over win bonuses. The result was that Cork were handed the title and Waterford were dismissed from the League of Ireland. With Coad a free agent, Rovers stepped in and signed the 22-year-old.

'Paddy Coad: Seventeen magnificent years of service to the Hoops'.

Coad played for Rovers from 1942 until 1959, when he returned to his native city of Waterford. The inside forward was capped eleven times by the Republic of Ireland and made 26 appearances for the League of Ireland inter-League side. He scored 104 league goals in his career at Shamrock Rovers, a feat second only to the record of Paddy Ambrose.

GERRY MACKEY
'The fact that Coad was still playing was a huge advantage for us. I was only 17 when I signed for Rovers but at that stage Paddy was in his early '30s. The fact that he was out on the field telling us what to do, as opposed to being on the bench, was the key. He guided us; we did the running for him. He was an incredible player, one of the best Irish players ever. I would put him on a par with John Giles. He was never interested in going to England but if he had there is no doubt that he would have been an outstanding player.'

NED ARMSTRONG
'Paddy Coad was excellent. He was a masterly player. He was the type of player that would get the ball and make a space for himself. That's the sign of a good player – if he can do a turn or a twist or something and he has space.'

ROBERT GOGGINS
'The Shamrock Rovers Supporters Club made Paddy the first entrant into the Hall of Fame back in 1987. We didn't actually tell Paddy that he was going to get the award, we just invited him to Dublin for the night. He was so taken aback when we gave it to him. Even with the star-studded Four in a Row team in attendance, people were queuing up to speak to Paddy. '

PAT O'DWYER
'Coad certainly would have made it in England. They always say that he was the best Irish player to never leave Ireland and I think that's true. A very intelligent footballer. Ronnie Nolan is another player I would put up there. Ronnie was a superb player.'

RONNIE NOLAN
'Coad was probably the greatest ever League of Ireland player. He was ahead of his time. His control, distribution, passing, it was phenomenal. In the days when they didn't have too many international games, only two or three a year, Coad had 11 caps. We used to play Everton on a regular basis, one year in Milltown and one year in Goodison. I remember Tommy Egglington and Peter Farrell saying that the Everton players used to love playing Shamrock Rovers because they loved watching Coad. Why he wasn't playing in England they could never understand. He changed Irish football.'

JACK WILSON
'Coad was the best player, without a doubt. No one comes close to Coad. What he could do with a big leather ball no one else could do. He was by far the greatest player I've ever seen. He worked in one of the Cunningham's bookie shops and I used to mitch off school just to go down and look at him. I wasn't allowed into the bookies because of my age, I'd just stand outside and look at him. I completely idolised Paddy Coad.'

★★★★

Coad had inherited the mantle left by Paddy Moore and Jimmy Dunne. These three players are considered amongst the greatest ever produced by Ireland. Coad is universally hailed as the greatest Irish player to have never left the League of Ireland. Both Moore and Dunne were to die tragically young – one through alcohol abuse, the other through a sudden heart attack. Paddy Coad did not succumb to the curse, and, after leaving Rovers in 1959, lived out his days in his native Waterford. On 8 March 1992 the League of Ireland lost one of its truest stars when Paddy Coad died aged 72.

'HE'D GET THE BALL, KICK IT PAST THE FULL BACK AND JUST RUN'

Alongside the great Paddy Coad was an emerging talent, a player who would become a legend of Irish football over the next two decades. The name Liam Tuohy was synonymous with Shamrock Rovers throughout the 1950s and '60s.

PAT O'DWYER
'They all say that Paddy Coad made Liam Tuohy, but Tuohy had what very few wingers back then had: pace. He had great pace and that was his whole game. He'd get the ball, kick it past the full back and just run. There was no fancy footwork like your Damien Duff's! Bunny Fullam, who was a right full with Drums, was asked whether he'd ever apologise to Liam Tuohy for all the kicks he gave him. Bunny says, "I'd be a hypocrite if I did because I'll kick him again next week".'

JACK WILSON
'Tuohy found it very difficult to get into Coad's team. He used to get the odd-game from time-to-time but Tommy O'Connor was played ahead of him. We were drawn against Sligo Rovers in the cup and we were short a few players so Tuohy got picked. He

was fabulous that day. Once everyone realised how good Liam was, the club sacked the reserve team manager because he had never let anyone know about Liam!'

RONNIE NOLAN
'Tuohy was quick, the best goal scoring winger ever. Wingers in those days didn't score, they stayed out wide and put the ball in. Tuohy could score from nothing. He was a great header of the ball too.'

'YOU DIDN'T EXPECT MUCH ELBOW ROOM'

With players like Coad and Tuohy providing the attacking flair to a richly talented side, the people of Dublin flocked religiously to Milltown every second Sunday. Country sides counted down the days until Rovers were due to pay them a visit, knowing that the Coad's Colts would provide them with a full house.

There was a wonderful innocence to the match day experience in the 1950s. It was before the era of television or mass entertainment. The game on Sunday was the highlight of the week – an occasion to look forward to and to spend the rest of the week discussing. Anyone who was ever in Glenmalure Park or Dalymount Park will appreciate what the spectacle of twenty or thirty thousand people crammed inside must have been like. The people of Ireland genuinely loved the League of Ireland and idolised the local lads who played in front of them ever week.

RONNIE NOLAN
'They were great days in Irish football. Most weeks in Milltown you'd have crowds of 12 – 20,000. It became a bit of a cult. If we were playing in Cork or Waterford there'd be excursion trains. Each train would hold 1,500 people but they'd often have to get two trains. You'd get 3,000 people travelling with us to see the games in the country. There'd never be any aggro on the trains, just a few singsongs and a few beers. People didn't have the money for boozing sessions – they were lucky if they had the train fare and enough to get them into the match.'

PAT O'DWYER
'I was born in the Liberties but there were no cars back then so I used to walk to Burgh Quay and get the "football specials". It was great craic on the buses; they'd always be full and everyone would be decked out in their Rovers scarves. The fifties was a great era. There wasn't much money around but they were great times. You certainly enjoyed your football back then, some great teams and great players. The crowds were unbelievable. There'd be queues all the way onto the roads and the Gardai would be out trying to guide the traffic, what little of it there was anyway.'

THEO DUNNE
'We played football on the streets. That's where some of the stars were found – on street corners. We'd play with a tennis ball. You went from a rag ball to a tennis ball to a bouncer and then onto a football. Every street would play against each other. We'd all be imitating League of Ireland players. There was such an interest in the game. They'd fit 45,000 people into Dalymount. It wasn't supposed to hold that many but they just kept letting everyone in.'

JIM PALMER
'There'd be lots of quips and things aimed at the referee but there was never any bad language

or fighting. There was no television and the cross-channel games were on Saturdays. You'd spend Saturday glued to the radio to listen for the cross-channel results and you'd spend Sunday at Milltown.'

PAT O'DWYER

'As you walked into the ground, the stand on the left was where you sat down. On the far side was where you stood, a bit of a Shed. The rest was open. I stood at the back of the goal. Being a small lad, I always got there early so as I could stand at a barrier. It was safer there because it was a massive crowd. You didn't expect much elbow room when you went to Milltown!'

JACK WILSON

'We got the train to away games. It would take four or five hours to get to places like Limerick. The trains would always have a big crowd on them. They used to put on three or four trains for Rovers away games. The train specials. You'd get a ticket for around three and six pence. My mother was on the social committee at Rovers and she did some bar work up there and made the tea for the players at half-time. It was a part of our life, we talked about nothing else at home.'

DICK DUNNE

'I remember playing Drums in Tolka Park and there were 21,000 people in the ground. They had to delay kick-off because the fans had spilled onto the pitch. There was no television and very little entertainment back then. Everyone went to mass and then to the match. Financially, they were bad times. Every penny you had you'd save for the match.'

MARIE CRADDOCK

'Back then the men went to the football and the wives weren't involved. My father was an ex-footballer and my brothers both played, so used to go to Rovers with them just to get some attention. The only way I could get a word in edgeways is if I knew something about football. Eventually, my father wouldn't stand with me at games because he didn't approve of my language! I even had the pleasure of kicking Sir Stanley Matthews. He was sitting in front of my at an Ireland v England game and I was shouting for our lads to get stuck into the English. He turned around to look at me and I jumped up and kicked him in the back by mistake.'

SONNY O'REILLY

'The crowds were so big back then and there was a great atmosphere. The ball would go down the pitch and everyone would be moving trying to see what was going on. Everyone would be shouting at each other, slagging everyone. I tell you, some of the things they'd say to each other!'

JIM PALMER

'I used to get the 46A bus from outside the Screen cinema. There'd be fleets of buses going to games, thousands of people would be making their way out from town. Then all the buses would bring everyone back into town afterwards. I'd sometimes get the 18 bus but you'd have to walk from Ranelagh and kids aren't great at walking. I'd be saying, "are we nearly there yet?"'

Coad's Colts (1950–1959)

'YOU WERE ON TENTERHOOKS'

Rovers reached the FAI Cup Final four times in a row during the 1950s, although they only brought the cup back to Milltown twice. The club already had a good name in the cup competition, having won it eleven times already, five of which were won in succession in the late 1920s/early 1930s. Today, the Hoops have won the cup 24 times, fifteen times more than their nearest rivals, Dundalk. Amazingly, if Rovers had not won another cup since 1945 they would still hold the record for most wins in the competition today.

The five-in-a-row success of the late 1920s and early 1930s had cemented the clubs association with the cup competition. Having won their eleventh cup in 1948, Rovers beat Drumcondra in 1955, but lost to their northside rivals in 1957 and lost to Dundalk in 1958. However, it was the cup final of 1956 that provided the moment for which the great Coad's Colts will always be remembered. Playing Cork Athletic in Dalymount for the cup, Rovers found themselves 2-0 down with only minutes remaining.

GERRY MACKEY

'I was marking Jimmy Delaney that day. He had a Scottish cup winner's medal with Celtic, an English cup winner's medal with Manchester United and a Northern Irish cup winner's medal with Derry, so now he was looking for an FAI cup winner's medal with Cork. They went 2-0 up and things weren't looking great. I'll always remember looking up at the clock on Phibsboro church and seeing that there were 12 minutes to go. Tommy Hamilton got one back and then Liam Hennessy scored a penalty to equalise. Suddenly, the game was turned on its head. In the dying minute we got a corner over on the right hand side right at the death. Everyone was up for it, it came over and I was at the back post and I was reasonably confident that I was going to get it. At the last second I heard Ronnie Nolan shout "leave it". I didn't go for it but I looked up and I saw Ronnie over my shoulder heading it in like a bullet. By Jesus,

Team shot prior to the 1956 Cup Final.

the place went mad. Within a minute the game was over. One of the Cork directors had gone down to one of the pubs on Doyles Corner to buy champagne and when he came back it was 3-2 to Rovers! He couldn't believe it, but fair play to him because he sent the champagne into us. If we did nothing else, we'll always be remembered for that day.'

NED ARMSTRONG
'There were 35,000 at that game and the excitement was unbelievable. Rovers were 2-1 down and Liam Hennessey got a penalty. You didn't want to watch it, but he took it very calmly – a hard shot in. But Nolan's winner – he was a classy player, top class ability in every way: heading the ball, tackling, placing the ball, passing. And that particular goal, it was a corner and he headed it at the back post. The excitement of it! You were coming back from 2-0 down – first one goal, then another one, you were on tenterhooks. Your team is losing by two goals in a cup final and comes back to win it! It was fantastic. The programme for that game is a treasured possession of mine.'

SONNY O'REILLY
'We were 2-0 down and I saw some Rovers lads leaving the ground because they couldn't stick it any longer. One of the Cork directors went down to the shops to get a bottle of champagne and when he came back in the lads on the turnstiles were telling him that Rovers had won. Rovers scored one, two, three, it was unbelievable. All Paddy Coad said to the team at half time was "keep playing football".'

RONNIE NOLAN
'People associate me with being a half-back but I was playing full-back that day. When we went 2-0 down, Coad switched myself and Liam Hennessy, he put Liam at full-back and myself at half-back to try and put a bit of pressure on them. We pulled two goals back and then Paddy Coad took a corner and I managed to get on the end of it. The ground erupted; it was a very special moment.'

'THE BEST LEAGUE OF IRELAND SIDE EVER'

In terms of trophies won, Rovers did not stand head and shoulders above the rest. Taking just the league and cup as a barometer of success, Rovers won three leagues and two cups over the course of the decade. This compares with three leagues and a cup for St. Pat's, a league and two cups for Cork Athletic, and a league and two cups for Drumcondra. The League of Ireland boasted an extraordinary strength during this era - players such as Shay Gibbons (St. Pat's), 'Bunny' Fullam (Drums) and Donal Leahy (Evergreen United) were household names throughout the country. However, the Coad's Colts had recaptured Rover's crown as the darlings of Irish football. In doing so, they cemented their place in history as the greatest League of Ireland side of all time.

GERRY MACKEY
'The thing is that, as great a team as we were, there were other great sides too – Drums, Shels, Waterford – so there was always competition. We were in four Cup finals but we were beaten in two. People sometimes say to me "How did you lose the other two finals?", but the teams we played were great sides. Drumcondra beat us once, Dundalk beat us on the other occasion. In fact, it was Hugey Gannon who scored the winning goal for Dundalk, he used to play for Rovers. Twenty-five years after that final, the two sides had a charity game in Dundalk. We won on that occasion!

There was a great camaraderie in that team. Even now, we all keep in touch. We meet up a few times every year and we've all kept up to date with each others kids and grandkids. Even now, people can list off that team. It's incredible really, you're talking about a team from 50 years ago. I find it extraordinary that I am still recognised. We've all had situations where we are sitting in a restaurant or a pool in Lanzarote or somewhere and a man will come up to you and say, "Excuse me but I was a Rovers fan in the '50s". It's incredible. I use the term lightly, but we seem to have become legends in our own lifetime. None of us can really understand it, there isn't a conceited bone in any of our bodies, no egos. To us,

Players and staff with the cup.

An array of trophies are displayed at the Rovers 1955 Christmas party'.

it was a wonderful journey and we're delighted that we gave so much pleasure to others.'
RONNIE NOLAN

'Liam Hennessy and I were totally different. We were wing halves, me on the right, Liam on the left. He was a cultured player, I was a rough and tumble player. I didn't have the natural ability that some of them had but I made up for it with energy and strength. Ambrose was a different sort of centre forward to others. The normal centre forward back then was a bustler who'd shove people. Ambrose was a footballer, he'd come back deep and lay the ball off. He later moved to inside-left, which was nearly what he was doing at centre-forward anyway.'

PAT O'DWYER

'I'VE ALWAYS SAID IT, I THINK THE ROVERS TEAM OF THE 1950S WAS THE BEST LEAGUE OF IRELAND SIDE EVER. THEY WON THREE LEAGUES AND TWO CUPS. YOU WERE GETTING 10–15,000 PEOPLE INTO MILLTOWN FOR THOSE GAMES. PAT'S WON THE LEAGUE IN '56 WITH A GREAT SIDE, SHAY GIBBONS AND OTHERS. SHELS AND DRUMS WERE THE BIG GAMES FOR US. PATS WERE THE BIG TEAM IN THE EARLY '50S, WITH SHAY GIBBONS AND 'GINGER' O'ROURKE. PATS PLAYED UP IN CHAPELIZOD BACK THEN, UP IN THE GREYHOUND STADIUM.'

MICK SMYTH

'Liam Hennessy was the penalty king of Ireland; he never missed. One of my favourite memories is of when I was playing for Drums and I saved two Liam Hennessy penalties in a match. Of course, the headlines the next day were "Hennessy misses penalties", nothing about me saving them! They were good saves too.'

JACK WILSON

'Prior to 1954, Rovers hadn't won the league in fifteen years. I'll never forget that day in '54 when they won it. There were wild scenes in Milltown, the players and the fans were ecstatic. To win it after a fifteen years absence was huge. Rovers always drew the crowds. Walking up the Milltown road would be packed with people. Crowds to Milltown would be at least 10,000, sometimes 20,000. For cup finals, we'd get the bus to town but we'd have to walk to Phibsboro from there because we wouldn't have enough money for the bus. But the crowds were unbelievable. For my first cup final there was 44,000 at it. You can imagine the atmosphere with 44,000 people in Dalymount Park. As kids, you'd have to make sure you got to the front of the crowd otherwise you wouldn't even see the match.'

★★★★

The Rovers faithful had witnessed an extraordinary decade. Rovers had changed the way the Irish nation viewed football and had been highly successful in doing so. In 1959 Paddy Coad returned to his native Waterford and many of his Colts also sought new challenges. When the side broke-up at the end of the decade many feared a return to the relative obscurity inflicted upon the club in the 1940s. However, just as the Coad's Colts took until 1953 to find their feet, by 1963 a new generation of Rovers players were setting the Irish domestic football scene alight. Along the way they would forge a fascinating rivalry with the club from Paddy Coad's home town of Waterford. They would also go on to complete what must be considered the most remarkable feat in Irish football history: the six in a row.

CHAPTER 5

THE SIX IN A ROW
(1963–1970)

As the 1950s rolled into the 1960s, the great Coad's Colts broke up. Although several players from the Coad era remained, the departure of players such as Gerry Mackey, Noel Peyton, Mickey Burke, Liam Tuohy, as well as Coad himself, meant that the great side that had enthralled Ireland for seven years was gone.

One of those who did remain was Ronnie Nolan, who had established himself as the best wing-half in Ireland. Nolan signed for Rovers in 1952 from schoolboy outfit Johnville, a junior club who provided Rovers with many players over the years. Nolan grew up on South Docks Street, which looks onto the Shelbourne greyhound stadium. It was not an easy place to grow up in 1940s Dublin: 'People had nothing back then. I was about 12 years of age before I saw an orange.' It was an upbringing, however, that gave Nolan the tough personality which he was later to become famous for.

'I used to kick football against the gable ends of houses', he says from his home in Kimmage. 'When I was a bit older, around 12, I used to go down to Ringsend Park. The dockers were all from Ringsend but they weren't working much because there were no ships coming in so they used to play football in the park. There'd be around twenty of them playing, big burly lads. I'd go down and stand at the goals and they'd invite me to join in. They'd kick the shit out of you, they didn't care if you were 12 or 32 – if you were in their way you got kicked! It was a great grounding for me when we had to go to Cork and places like that and you'd really have to stand up for yourself.'

Nolan signed for Rovers out of the schoolboy leagues and quickly found himself at the thick of the youth revolution at Milltown. After seven glorious years under Paddy Coad, Nolan was recognised as one of Ireland's brightest talents, earning ten international caps along the way, becoming Rovers' joint-third most capped player, behind Frank O'Neill (20 caps) and Paddy Coad (11).

When Coad left Rovers, all eyes were on Milltown to see who would be his successor. A bizarre turn of events would see former Irish international Albie Murphy take the reigns. Murphy, who was capped by Ireland in the 1950s, had been playing for Clyde in the Scottish

Nolan's medals.

League but supplemented his income by running a betting shop. At the start of the 1960s, the Scottish FA introduced a rule which forbade involvement in betting by professional footballers. Murphy was told to give up the betting shop or give up Clyde. He chose the latter and was promptly hired by Rovers, a club whose involvement in bookies stemmed right to the Cunningham family themselves.

'Albie Murphy came in after Paddy left', says Nolan. 'He was a lovely man. I remember he said to me, 'I don't understand the League of Ireland, over here the wingers tackle the full-backs!' He couldn't hack that, he was used to getting the ball and having a look around but the League of Ireland fellas were steaming into him. He was too nice, he didn't have the drive to be successful.'

Murphy took charge of Rovers in September 1960 and lasted just one season, guiding the club to sixth place in the table, their worst finish in a decade. As the season came to a close, Murphy was on his way out of Milltown. In his place came a man who would greatly impact upon both Rovers and the League of Ireland: Sean Thomas.

'Sean Thomas took over and he developed that '60s team', recalls Nolan. 'Johnny Fullam was very successful with Preston North End but he didn't like it in England and wanted to come home. Frank O'Neill was at Arsenal but the manager didn't fancy him and wouldn't give him a chance. So Sean snapped up both of them. They were both former Home Farm players and Sean Thomas had been at Home Farm so that is how he knew them.'

Just as Coad had taken the first three years of the '50s to mould his side, it was not until 1963 that Rovers re-grouped into a quality unit. Nolan and Paddy Ambrose were left-over from the Coad era and were soon joined by Pat Dunne, John Keogh, Pat Coutney, Tommy Farrell, Jackie Mooney and Eddie Bailham, together with O'Neill and Fullam. The crowning moment for Thomas was the decision of Liam Tuohy to return to Dublin after four highly successful years in Newcastle to captain Rovers.

The pundits began to speculate that the Shamrock Rovers of old was back. The 1963/64 season proved the critics right. That year Rovers won every domestic honour, with the exception of the Top Four Competition. With Tuohy and O'Neill pulling the strings, Rovers proved unstoppable, finishing five points ahead of Dundalk to claim the league title for the tenth time. Success in the Dublin City Cup, the President's Cup and the League of Ireland Shield was augmented by a 2-1 defeat of Cork Celtic in the FAI Cup final. Rovers had returned.

Although they could not know it at the time, it was the cup win that was to prove most significant. Having won the cup in 1964, Rovers would not lose a cup game until 1970. For six years the Hoops went unbeaten in the FAI Cup, smashing the 'five in a row' record set by Rovers in the 1930s. Ronnie Nolan was one of the few survivors of the Coad's Colts to play on the side of the 1960s. Having played on two of the all-time great League of Ireland sides, Nolan has memories of a playing career that most footballers can only dream of. On the wall of his home are several pictures of the two great sides he played on. However, pride of place on the wall is reserved for a newspaper clipping of the match report from the FAI Cup first round game against Dundalk in 1964. The Hoops were not fancied to get anything out of the game, but victory set them on their way to the first of six cup wins.

'We were second in the league, Dundalk were first and we got an offer to go over to Barcelona to play the Spanish international B team', he recalls. 'The game in Barcelona was on the Wednesday and we were playing Dundalk in the cup on the Sunday. The supporters were going ape over the fact that we playing in Spain a few days before such an important game. We flew over to Barcelona and were beaten 7-2 in the Nou Camp and got back into Dublin on Friday. Eddie Bailham had picked up food poisoning and a few of the lads weren't right but we played Dundalk and beat them 7-0! It was totally against logic.'

The remarkable 7-0 demolition of their closest rivals set Rovers on the way to a record six cup wins in a row, a record that no side has even come remotely close to beating.

'With eleven international caps, Frank O'Neill remains Rovers' most capped player'.

'The Cunninghams were Shamrock Rovers'

Defeat of Cork Celtic in the FAI Cup final underlined Rovers' resurgence. However, it took a replay to defeat the Cork outfit and events sandwiched between those two games were about to deal the club an unforeseen twist. Rovers and Cork drew the first game 1-1 in front of 35,000 spectators. However, Frank O'Neill, who had acted as an inspiration for the Rovers side for much of the season, had an off day. The Cunningham's wanted him dropped for the replay, which was to take place three days later. A furious row ensued between Thomas and the Cunninghams over who had ultimate control over team selection. It was a battle which Thomas was never going to win. Tony Bryne replaced Frank O'Neill on the Rovers side for the replay, which the Hoops won courtesy of two goals from Eddie Bailham.

Joe and Mary Jane Cunningham, who effectively ruled the roost at Milltown for forty years, were well known as colourful characters. They had assumed control of the club in the early 1920s. Previous to this, Rovers was a members' club, run on committee lines. The Cunningham takeover put Rovers in private hands, a situation that exists to this day. Stories abound of Mary Jane filling referees with whiskey the night before important games in an attempt to curry favour with the official. In an era when women were not prominent in Irish society, Mary Jane was a popular figure in Dublin for her brash and outspoken behaviour. It was not uncommon for Mary Jane to storm into the Rovers changing room as the players showered to give her opinion on the game.

However, the Cunningham's insistence that they maintain a degree of control over team selections had caused problems in the past. Paddy Coad was married to Margaret Cunningham, daughter of the club's owners, and was very much a part of the family. Prior to the 1940s, team selection was carried out by a committee comprising of the Cunninghams and the other board members – Capt. Tom Scully, Mattie McNevin and Charlie Fitzsimons. During the reigns of Jimmy Dunne and Paddy Coad, the manager was allowed to pick the team but only upon consultation with the Cunninghams. It was a situation that Sean Thomas was not prepared to put up with and the mastermind behind the all-conquering 1964 season stormed out of Milltown and joined Bohemians.

'The all-conquering Shamrock Rovers side of 1964'.

LIAM TUOHY

'Sean Thomas was doing very well but unfortunately he had a falling out with the Cunninghams. I was made manager after Sean left and I never had any problems like that with the Cunninghams. Maybe they learned their lesson because they'd lost a very good manager. It was sad because Sean had put together a very good team and we were winning everything. You shouldn't lose your manager after having a year like that.'

MICK LEECH

'If you look at clubs like Real Madrid, the President picks the team there. In theory the manager is the manager but it doesn't always work out that way. When people have money involved in it things change. Some managers won't put up with it though. I wasn't involved in the politics so I don't know, but the Cunninghams were Shamrock Rovers. I never had a problem with them. I'd say hello to Joe and to Mrs Cunningham and I'd respect them for what they were but I never dealt with them personally. I don't honestly know whether they did interfere with the team selection.'

TOMMY KINSELLA

'I thought the Cunninghams were great. People say a lot of things about Mary Jane but your wages were always there for you and if you needed new gear there were no questions asked. The dressing rooms in Milltown were only two wooden shacks. There was a bath and a shower but there was no privacy. Mary Jane would always walk in when the players were in the bath. It didn't bother us though.'

MICK SMYTH

'I don't know whether she influenced team selection but she did have her favourites, everybody knew that. Joe was a great man though. I remember going into Frank O'Neill when he was manager and asking for a two pound rise. He would only give me a pound but I told Joe and Joe says "Listen Mick, I'll give you the extra pound, just don't tell Frank". So I got my two pound rise.'

DICK DUNNE

'Mary Jane was a very nice woman, a real character. I remember playing down in Cork, we were winning 1-0 with around five minutes left and I made a good challenge to deny Donal Leahy a shot. After the game Mrs. Cunningham ran up to me and gave me a big hug! If she liked you, you were grand; if she didn't like you, you were in trouble.'

MICK MEAGAN

'Back before there were any cars on Irish roads, the Cunninghams used to arrive to the games in a horse-drawn carriage. After the game a large crowd would gather around the carriage and a hand would appear out of the side and throw a fist full of coins onto the ground and everyone would be scrambling around trying to pick them up! But they were decent people. I signed for Rovers in 1952 but Everton came in for me and the Cunninghams tore up my registration to allow me to go. That's the kind of people they were. There were a great football family.'

OSSIE NASH

'I thought they were very nice people. They paid me a signing on fee and agreed a wage with me but told me that I was to come back to them if I got on the first team and they'd increase it. The next year Joe says to me, "you never came back to me" and I said "but we didn't win anything". He gave me an increase and paid me back money too. They were lovely people.'

'Crowd favourite Mick Leech holds the 1968 FAI cup after scoring twice in a 3-0 demolition of Waterford'.

Although Liam Tuohy – who replaced Thomas as manager – had no problems with the Cunninghams, the Thomas affair was not to be the last time the issue arose. Five years after Thomas' departure, Arthur Fitzsimons resigned amid accusations that the Cunninghams were attempting to interfere with team selection.

'He was really rock 'n' roll'

Liam Tuohy assumed the reigns as player-manager at Rovers, setting in motion a coaching career that would span the next four decades. With largely the same group of players to work with, there were big expectations put on Tuohy's shoulders. Goalkeeper Pat Dunne was transferred to Manchester United and replaced by Mick Smyth, whilst the club uncovered a future star in Paddy Mulligan, who would in 1969 be transferred to Chelsea for £50,000.

However, for the first two seasons under Tuohy's command – 1964/65, 1965/66 – the Milltown outfit finished the league in second place, pipped by Drumcondra and Waterford respectively. Meanwhile, two successive cup final victories over Limerick ensured that the FAI Cup did not leave the Rovers trophy cabinet.

A poor start to the 1966/67 league campaign ensured that Rovers would finish in seventh place, their lowest league position since 1950 and the joint-second worst league finish in the club's history. By Christmas of that season, it was clear that new blood was needed in the side. Relief came in the form of a young St. Patrick's Athletic supporter.

The Six in a Row (1963–1970)

On New Years Day 1967, 18-year-old Mick Leech took to the pitch at Milltown for the first time. Dundalk provided the opposition on a bitterly cold January afternoon. Surrounded by established professionals who had for years been considered amongst the best in the league, Leech could have looked out of his depth but his early performances were of such a high standard that by the end of the season he was an established first team player. Although his peak at Rovers was short-lived – his first three seasons are considered his finest – Leech would write himself into the history of the club, and the league, as one of the most prolific and natural goalscorers ever seen in Ireland. In 1968, during his first full season in the League of Ireland, he equalled Drumcondra forward Dan McCaffrey's record of 56 goals in one season.

MARTIN MOORE
'Mick Leech is my all time Rovers hero. Frank O'Neill was a superb player but he wasn't as much of hero as Leech would've been because Frank was a bit older and he was a bit more serious. Mick was our George Best. He was really rock n roll – the hair on him and the gear.'

FRANK WHELAN
'I was at his debut. I remember he came on and little did we all know that this kid was going to go down in the history books as one of Rovers greats. Whenever Mick got injured he'd play a few games for the B Team and you'd see the B Team results in the paper and Mick would have scored six or seven goals! He had this great ability of being able to take on defenders in the box. Generally, you get forwards who are good in the box or good outside the box but Mick could take the ball and run at them, beat them all and round the keeper and walk the ball into the net.'

MICK LEECH
'I never felt any pressure going into a match. I could sleep in the changing room before a match I'd be so relaxed. The more important the game, the more relaxed I'd be. I responded to not having pressure on me. Some players would be really nervous or would go to the toilet but if I was getting a rub down before the game I'd fall asleep. They'd have to wake me up before the game. I found it harder to play in front of 200 or 300 people than in front of 40,000. In the later days when Rovers had started to struggle a bit, the crowds were poor and you could hear what people in the crowd were saying. When it was a full house you just saw the crowd and heard the noise and you got on with the game.'

MICK SMYTH
'Leech came on in his first season and he scored a few. Most of them were set up by either "Rasher" Tuohy or Bobby Gilbert. I'd kick the ball out of my hands, Bobby would knock it on and Leechy would be in like a flash. I remember on one occasion we didn't score a goal from one of my kick-outs and Ronnie Nolan says, "Jesus Mick, you're slipping up, you didn't make any goals today".'

FRANK ALLEN
'O'Neill would send in the crosses, Gilbert would flick them on and Leech would knock them in. It was like poetry.'

MICK SMYTH
'Leechy was so sharp in the box. The next season he scored 56 goals to equal Dan McCaffrey's record, I was actually playing with Dan at Drums when he got his fifty-sixth goal. But I never thought Mick was the same player after that season. He'd still score goals, 20 or so a

year, but he was a different player. He was deadly inside the box, sort of a Jimmy Greaves character, but he started coming deep to pick up the ball and he was never the same. If I was manager I'd have told him to get in the box and don't come out.'

FRANK ALLEN
'I was in Tolka Park the night he got the fifty-sixth goal and I remember the whole crowd rose to their feet to applaud him. '

LIAM TUOHY
'Mick could score goals for fun. He was simply outstanding. Once he was around the six yard box, he'd get his head or his knee or his toe to it. He really should have gone away [to England]. He had a talent and he had the ability to play at a higher level.'

Leech did have his chances to go to England. West Ham United, fresh from winning the European Cup Winners Cup, attempted to purchase the Rovers forward but their attempts were blocked by the Cunninghams. A few years later, Middlesborough manager Stan Anderson flew to Dublin to see Leech play, only for Rovers to deploy him in a midfield position. Anderson, in search of a striker, left the game at half-time.

'Winning the cup became such a formality'

Although Rovers regained their touch in the league, the great side of the 1960s would not win the title again, finishing fourth in 1968, second in 1969 and second again in 1970. It was for their cup wins that the side would go down in history. Cup Finals against St. Patrick's Athletic, Waterford and Cork Celtic would complete the club's record-breaking six-in-a-row. For Mick Leech, the new star of the Rover's side, the cup final of 1967 represented a special occasion. Not only was it his first cup final, it was against his boyhood club.

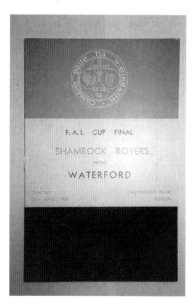

Programme from 1968 Cup Final v Waterford.

MICK LEECH

'MY FIRST CUP FINAL WAS AGAINST ST. PATRICK'S IN '67. MY FAMILY WERE ALL PAT'S PEOPLE SO IT WAS GREAT FOR THEM BECAUSE IF PAT'S WON THEY'D BE DELIGHTED BUT IF ROVERS WON THEY'D BE DELIGHTED FORM E. I'M SURE THEY WERE HAPPY ENOUGH WHEN ROVERS WON, BLOOD IS THICKER THAN WATER BUT IT WAS IRONIC THAT IT WAS AGAINST MY CHILDHOOD TEAM, ESPECIALLY BECAUSE I SCORED.'

FRANK WHELAN

'The Pats game [1967] was the first televised cup final. The crowd was quite poor because the fans stayed at home in their droves to watch it on TV. There was a novelty about having it on TV. There were only around 12,000 at it, whereas you would usually get well over 20,000. It was a great spectacle though, there were five goals in it and it was a very close game.'

****

The 1968 cup final is remembered as the most spectacular of the six finals Rovers were involved in. Having dispatched Cork Celtic, Shelbourne and Dundalk in the lead-in to the final, Rovers were attempting to equal the five-in-a-row record of the early 1930s. Although the players tried to keep the record out of their heads, everyone at the club was conscious of what defeating Waterford in the final would mean.

LIAM TUOHY

'There was a Rovers team in the '30s who won the cup five times in a row so we had that as a target. There'd always be a few old lads who would say, "I remember Bob Fullam doing this or doing that" so we were always conscious that there was a record there. We didn't start off to beat it but once we had three in a row we realised that there was a chance we could beat it.'

MICK SMYTH

'We weren't really conscious of the five-in-a-row record when we started out. In the later years we would have been trying to beat the record to a certain extent but once you go out on the pitch you're mind is solely focused on the game. I remember one year being very conscious of the fact that I hadn't conceded a goal until the final. I was trying not to think about it but the day before the final everyone was on the radio saying, "Rovers haven't conceded yet" so it was very hard not to be conscious of it. I was terribly superstitious back then, to the point of driving myself mad. I had to wear the same underpants as I wore the previous Sunday, the same jeans to the games, I used to watch out for 'H' signs on the street because it's 'H' for heaven, all this sort of stuff. I drove myself demented.

TOMMY KINSELLA

'It [winning the cup] became such a formality that the players would refuse win bonuses for cup games. Instead of getting a bonus after every cup win, we told the club to just give us a big bonus when we won it. That's how confident we were. It was very hard to beat Rovers in the cup because we had the tradition, so even when the chips were down we able to pull out that extra 10 per cent. We had enough players who could turn a game on their own. Myself and Frank [O'Neill] knew that if we crossed a ball into the box, seven or eight times out of ten either Bobby [Gilbert] or Mick [Leech] would score.'

With the pressure of the record hanging over their heads, not to mention the introduction of young players such as Mick Leech, Damien Richardson, Mick Lawlor, Mick Kearin and Frank Brady into the side, the odds were stacked heavily against Rovers defeating Waterford in the final. The club from the south-west had emerged as the best side in the country, winning the league in 1968 in what would ultimately be the first in their three-in-a-row title success.

MICK LEECH

'1968 was the big year for me. It was a real transition period for Rovers, there were a lot of young players coming through and we were struggling in the league. We got Waterford in the cup final and that Waterford side was superb – they won five out of six league titles in the '60s. They were an exceptional team and they really wanted the cup. The cup meant everything to Waterford. We played them in Dalymount in front of 40,000. That morning I left my house in Drimnagh and walked through the park down to where they had the special buses for the football. I got there and there were thousands of people waiting to get on the buses. I was strolling around and people were saying, "Jaysus, are you not playing Mick?" I was saying, "Sure, it's only half one" but they rushed me up to the top of the queue and put me on the first bus out to the ground.'

Against all the odds, on 21 April 1968 Rovers humiliated Waterford 3-0 in front of a crowd of 39,128 people at Dalymount Park. The Rovers team that day was: Mick Smyth, Jimmy Gregg, Pat Courtney, Mick Kearin, Frank Brady, Johnny Fullam, Frank O'Neill, Mick Lawlor, Bobby Gilbert, Mick Leech, Damien Richardson.

HAMROCK ROVERS.—Front, from left: Frank O'Neill, Damien Richardson, Johnny Fullam, Mick Lawlor, Liam Tuohy, Mick Kearin. Back: Billy Lord, Frank Brady, Jimmy Gregg, Mick Smyth, Pat Courtney, Mick Leech, Billy Dixon.

'Shamrock Rovers 1967/68: From left to right Back row; Billy Lord, Frank Brady, Jimmy Gregg, Mick Smyth, Pat Courtney, Mick Leech, Billy Dixon. (Front row; Frank O'Neill, Damien Richardson, Johnny Fullam, Mick Lawlor, Liam Tuohy'.

The Six in a Row (1963–1970)

FRANK WHELAN

'Waterford [1968] brought up a great crowd for the final. They were a huge club, they had Alfie Hale who was a legend. Rovers got a very young team together, loads of lads who were under 20, and they humiliated Waterford. Mick Leech got the third goal. He ran at Peter Thomas in the Waterford goal and went around him and slid the ball into the goal but before he went around him he patted him on the head! Peter Thomas was a big name but Leech just humiliated him.'

FRANK ALLEN

'I WAS AT fIVE OF THE SIX CUP fINALS. THE ONE THAT STICKS OUT IS THE fINAL AGAINST WATERFORD IN 1968. THERE WAS CLOSE TO 40,000 AT THAT GAME, WHICH SHOWS HOW POPULAR IT WAS. THERE WAS HUGE COMPETITION BETWEEN ROVERS AND WATERFORD BECAUSE WATERFORD HAD A GREAT LEAGUE RUN IN THE '60S. THAT BECAME A REAL GRUDGE GAME.'

In 1969 Rovers began their defence of the cup with a 3-0 victory over Dundalk, followed by defeat of Ringmahon Rangers and Shels to set up a Cup final against Cork Celtic. John Carroll put the Cork side in front and with the clock ticking down it appeared as if Rovers' cup run was coming to an end. Salvation, however, came in the unlikely form of John Keogh, the ex-Rovers defender who had recently signed for Cork.

FRANK WHELAN

'The cup final against Cork Celtic [1969] was great. Celtic went a goal up and they looked like they'd hold onto it. The crowd was really heaving trying to push Rovers on and with about ten minutes to go John Keogh, who played with Rovers for years before going to Celtic, put in an own goal. The Corkonians were convinced it was a fix! We won 4-1 in the replay. Mick Leech wasn't fully fit in the first game and he came back and scored twice in the replay.'

MICK LEECH

'I'd been out for six weeks prior to the cup final against Cork Celtic with knee ligament trouble. I didn't think I'd any hope of playing but I went to a specialist and he told me to go out to the Magazine Hill in the Phoenix Park and run up and down it. On Saturday Liam rang me and asked me how I felt and I told him that I felt alright but all I'd done was run up and down a hill. On the Sunday he told me that I was playing. It was a dry, April day and the pitch was hard and bumpy and I just couldn't get any sense of coordination. I was replaced half-way through the match by Hughy Brophy. We played the replay the following Wednesday and it had rained all day so the more flexibility there is in the ground the easier it is on the knee and I went out and played what I consider to be one of my best games.'

MICK SMYTH

'Games against Cork were always strange – my God, they hated us with a vengeance down there. We were quite lucky in the first game to get the draw but we completely blew them away in the replay. We were superb that day.'

'I STOOD ON THE TERRACE AND CRIED'

Undefeated in cup competition since 1964, Rovers had gone 32 cup games without defeat. The last time Rovers had tasted defeat in the cup was against Shelbourne, when they went down 2-0 in Dalymount Park in the 1963 semi-final. When the draw was made for the first round of the cup in 1970 it was Shelbourne who were drawn to play the Hoops.

Shels had finished in tenth place in the league the previous season, only managing two league victories and ending the season just two points ahead of bottom club Bohemians. In terms of Dublin football, Shels had been completely overshadowed by Drums, Rovers and even St. Pat's. While pundits were eagerly awaiting Rovers slipping up in the cup, an easy passage into the quarter-finals was expected. The Rovers line-up that day was: Mick Smyth, Billy Dixon, Pat Courtney, Damien Richardson, Christie Canavan, Mick Kearin, Frank O'Neill, Mick Leech, Eric Barber, Mick Lawlor and Jimmy Gregg.

Rovers took the lead after twelve minutes, Barber heading in a Mick Lawlor cross, but Shels piled on the pressure and, after scoring two second half goals, ran out the winners. Rovers phenomenal cup run was over. As the final whistle blew, not even the Shels fans could believe it. Milltown stood in silence as all around struggled to take it in. The feeling on the terraces was one of utter disbelief.

Jimmy Conroy

'It was hard to cope with that because we just didn't lose cup matches. It's funny: we beat Shels in '66, '67, '68 and '69 and then they beat us in '70 and that's always the one that's remembered. In '71 Drogheda knocked us out, beating us 5-2 in Milltown, which was absolutely incredible, but no one talks about that.'

Frank Whelan

'We began to think that Rovers were invincible, that they'd just keep on winning the cup. When Shels knocked Rovers out of the cup in 1970 I stood on the terrace and cried. I couldn't believe it. I'd never seen Rovers beaten in the cup. That was the start of the decline of Rovers. It all went downhill after Shels knocked us out of the cup in 1970. Brendan Place, who was a legend with Shels in the '60s, headed a goal with around ten minutes left. I'll never forget that goal. We were stunned. After the game people were still standing on the terrace in silence. We hadn't lost a cup game in six years.'

Mick Smyth

'Our first defeat in the cup was in my last year there when Shels beat us 2-1 in Milltown. I actually wasn't too disappointed because we'd beaten Shels every year in the cup, often undeservedly, so I thought they deserved a bit of luck. And so that was the end of our cup run. It was strange to lose a cup game after so many years, but the advantage was that we had the odd Sunday off!'

Mick Leech

'I think that I would have much preferred to have played for ten or fifteen years before winning the cup because I'd have appreciated it more. It happened to quickly – "ah look, we've won the cup again". The night after we beat Cork Celtic all the players left the changing room and we left the cup behind by mistake. The Cork lads came in and took it and actually went off celebrating with it!'

Shels were beaten by Bohemians in the next round, with the Dalymount club going all the way to winning the competition, rounding off a truly bizarre FAI Cup.

'The Cup belongs to us'

The cup exploits of the 1960s has led to an attachment to the cup which supporters of the club still have to this day. Despite not winning the trophy since 1987, Rovers have won the cup 24 times, nearly three times as many as Dundalk who, with nine cups to their name, are Rovers' nearest rivals. While other clubs are eventually catching up on Rovers' record of fifteen league title wins, the club's record in the cup stands head and shoulders above the rest.

JOHN BYRNE

'Our attachment to the cup probably has a lot to do with the Irish mentality. We like the do-or-die element. If you look at the GAA, no one gives a toss about the league, it's all about the cup. Even as a kid, the cup games were always special. I'd seen Rovers play in eight cup finals before I saw them lose one, and that was a replay so technically speaking it wasn't a cup final.'

FERGUS MCCORMACK

'From an emotional point of view, the cup is the one Rovers want. It's ours. I went to the Bohs – Longford cup final and we had good seats right beside Bertie Ahern and the FAI lot. They had the cup with them and it was just sitting there at their feet. I was thinking, "We have won that cup 24 times, it is ours". I was so tempted to just walk up and say "Sorry, I believe that belongs to us" and walk off with it. They would have had no right to stop me walking away with it. I don't even know what the league trophy looks like, but to me the FAI cup is as famous as the FA cup or the World Cup. And it belongs to us. To Rovers, the cup is way more emotionally important than the league.'

'Rovers draw 5-5 with West Ham, Dalymount Park 1967. Johnny Fullam, Mick Smyth and Tommy Farrell are the Rovers players, whilst England World Cup hero Geoff Hurst looks on'.

JIM PALMER

'The Six in a Row was fantastic. Think about it: winning six cups in a row!'

JIMMY CONROY

'Even after the decline in crowds set in, we still got big crowds for cup games. It's hard to explain, but the cup is very special to us. It's ours and we want it back.'

'I HAVE LOADS OF RUNNERS-UP MEDALS'

Despite the heroics in the cup, Rovers were unable to build on their league form after winning the title in 1964. As fantastic as the Rovers side was, the league in the 1960s belonged to Waterford, who, if it wasn't for Rovers success of 1964, would have won the title an unbelievable six times in a row. Try as they did, Rovers simply could not match the men from the south.

LIAM TUOHY

'Waterford were an outstanding side. On one occasion we were seven or eight points ahead of them but they pulled it back and won it. They were a great football team, we loved playing them because they'd always be great matches. They say that the team that wins the league is the best team, so fair play to them.'

RONNIE NOLAN

'It was a very good time to be involved in the League of Ireland because it was a respected league back then. People went to the games and were happy with the standard. Waterford had a fantastic side, Shelbourne had a good side, Cork and Dundalk were always good. The team who were mostly at the bottom of the league was Bohemians, they were just an amateur club until the 1970s.'

MICK LEECH

'The fact that Waterford were nearly full-time gave them the advantage over the season. There were days when you'd go to Limerick or Sligo and you'd be playing on a bog of a pitch and the full-time training would have helped Waterford in those situations. Coming into the last 20 minutes of a 0-0 game, Waterford would have the advantage. People say that the league evaded us but we finished runners-up four times. The problem was that Waterford were so good back then.'

MICK SMYTH

'I've loads of runners-up medals. In the seven seasons I was at Rovers we finished runners-up four times. I ended up winning the league four times – with Drums, Athlone and two with Bohs – but people still come up to me on the street and say "Mick, I remember all those great cup games with Rovers". No one seems to remember that I won the league four times with other clubs!'

TOMMY KINSELLA

'I played on the last two years of the Six in a Row side. I'd always been a Rovers fan and I'll never forget my debut. I remember walking out onto the pitch at Milltown and the hairs on my neck were standing up. I was running out on Milltown dressed in the hoops – my dream had finally come true. There was no feeling to compare with running out onto Milltown in the green and white hoops. It made you feel eight foot tall.'

The Six in a Row (1963–1970)

JIMMY CONROY

'I am a northsider but back in the '60s the two best clubs were Rovers and Waterford and Waterford was obviously too far away so it had to be Rovers for me. Probably the two best sides I have ever seen. It was bizarre that Rovers were so successful in the cup but never had the luck in the league. They won the league in '64, then they blew it in Dundalk in '65. In '66 they were done by Waterford when there was the biggest ever crowd in Milltown during the run-in. It was really weird, even in the late '60s I remember we beat Waterford 3-0 in the cup final and then the following year beat them 4-2 down there and 4-1 in Milltown but they still won the league. Mick Leech scored 56 goals but we still didn't win the league. We should have won at least two leagues.'

RONNIE NOLAN

'We all worked full time and had to play over 60 games a season. It amuses me to see these full-time pros in England getting rested after playing two or three games. We played something like sixty-four matches that season ['63/'64] and only lost four. The season started with the Presidents Cup, then the City Cup, then the Shield - which was a one round league - then the league, then the FAI cup, the Leinster Senior Cup, European matches, then exhibition games against English clubs, inter-league games, the odd international match. The year you were playing the English league at home you'd play the Scottish league away. You'd play the Irish League in Belfast on Easter Monday and in Dublin on St. Patrick's Day, so there were four inter-league games a year, and we also played the Hessen League in Germany a few times. We were kept busy!'

FRANK ALLEN

'My absolute hero was Frank O'Neill. As a boy you try to imitate your heroes when you're playing football and I remember trying to do the Frank O'Neill shuffle. Frank O'Neill was good enough to play on any Irish team of the past forty years. He was a very cultured winger.'

MICK SMYTH

'I made my debut against Drogheda and Frank actually collapsed during that game and got sick on the pitch. That was probably the best game he ever played, he was knocking in balls from everywhere. He was brilliant.'

TOMMY KINSELLA

'Frank was a funny character. I was a natural right winger but they played me on the left because Frank was out the right. He never wanted me to have the number 7 jersey. We were playing a charity seven-a-side one time and we were in the dressing room when Liam tells us all that Frank is running a bit late. I thought I'd have a laugh by getting the number 7 jersey then but Liam saw me looking for it and says to me, "don't bother looking Tommy, Frank knew he'd be late so he called around to my house last night and took the number 7 jersey"!'

MICK LEECH

'The '60s was the golden period of Irish football but also of world football. If you look at lists of the world's greatest ever players, a huge number of them are from the '60s and early '70s. All the great musical artists were from that era – the Beatles, the Stones, Dylan – and I think football expressed itself in the same way. It was really the liberation of a young generation. The '50s was a sort of dull time and all of a sudden the '60s came along and the world opened up. That reflected in the players as well because the great players from that era – Cryuff, Best, Beckenbaur, Pele – they were all great individual players.'

FRANK WHELAN

'You'd get the bus from just outside the Screen cinema. There'd be around ten buses lined up to take Rovers fans to the game and they'd all be full. If you tried to get a bus on the way – in Ranelagh or Dolphins Barn – you wouldn't get on because it would be full. I remember a cup game in Dundalk and twenty-eight buses went up! They'd only ordered twenty buses and I remember the lad shouting "We need another eight"! We were beaten 2-1 in that game.'

JACK WILSON

'The hassle started in the '60s. Before that there was never any trouble, but I remember a few fights on trains to Cork and Waterford in the mid-60s. I stopped going by train after that, I drove everywhere. I remember coming back on the train from Cork and the Gardai had to come on and take around ten lads out in Kilkenny. We didn't get back to Dublin until 4:30am and I had to walk home because I couldn't afford a taxi.'

ALAN O'NEILL

'I lived on the northside but I'd always been a Rovers fan. I used to go to Milltown regularly on the "football specials" from Hawkins House. I remember when I first started playing with Bonnybrook Boys Under-12s that Frank O'Neill, Damien Richardson and Mick Smyth presented us with prizes one year. They were real heroes at Rovers at the time, little things like that stick with you.'

TOMMY KINSELLA

'The fans would have to turn up two and a half hours before the kick-off. They'd be lifting the kids over the stiles. On one occasion a neighbour of mine asked could himself and his son get a lift to the game. I gave them a lift and took them into the ground with me for free. The next week, he shows up at my door with two other kids looking to get in. Every week his family got bigger, in the end the hatchback was completely full! I got into the dressing room and Tuohy gives his team talk, he says, "ah, here's Tommy, we had to get a traffic cop to get all his passengers into the game today!" Ah, the craic!'

MICK SMYTH

'Quite a few of us used to get called up to the Ireland squad. I made my international debut on the night Joe Wickam, President of the FAI, died. It was quite funny in a way because he always said that I'd play for Ireland over his dead body!'

★★★★

Supporters of Shamrock Rovers had enjoyed two decades in which hardly a season passed by without a trophy finding its way to Milltown. In the twenty years between Paddy Coad taking over Shamrock Rovers in 1949 and Liam Tuohy resigning as manager in 1969, Rovers had won four leagues and eight cups. It was an era when players such as Frank O'Neill, Ronnie Nolan, Mick Leech, as well as Tuohy and Coad themselves, had enthralled thousands around the country. Although the famous cup run had come to an end, Rovers supporters were convinced that it was merely a blemish and that success would return. However, behind the scenes dark clouds were gathering. Within the space of two years, a remarkable sequence of events would conspire to halt the Hoops' march and condemn them to the bleakest period in the clubs' history.

CHAPTER 6

THE DEATH AND REBIRTH: 1971–1983

If the 1960s had offered Rovers continuous success, the 1970s was to stand in stark contrast. A decade of glory was to be replaced by ten years of dramatic underachievement. However, the league positions obtained by the club throughout the 1970s hid the true story of what was going on at Milltown. On the field of play, Rovers were enduring their worst ever decade. Behind the scenes, however, the 1970s was perhaps the most fascinating in the clubs' history.

The decade began badly, with Rovers losing their stranglehold over the FAI Cup. The defeat to Shelbourne marked the end of the glorious cup era of Rovers. However, the team picked themselves up and finished the 1970/71 season on 35 points, equal with Cork Hibernians and one above Waterford, who had pipped Rovers to the league for the two years previous. Rovers were desperately unlucky not to win the title outright given that Mick Leech had a perfectly good goal disallowed by the referee when the Hoops met Cork Hibs in a crunch fixture at Milltown. The game ended 0-0, but it could have been so different had Leech's goal stood.

JIMMY CONROY
'We had an awful start to the season and were near the bottom of the league in October. Then, suddenly, we went on this run and only lost one more match all season. They really went for it, played mad football. Waterford were going for the four in a row but we played them in Milltown and beat them 2-0. I had great view of the goals because since I was a kid I was put right down the front. Mick Leech and Paul Martin scored that day. We only lost one more match that year but that match that we did lose, against Sligo, was painful. We were 1-0 up and should have been 6-0 up but conceded two careless late goals and lost the game. That defeat did us in the end. We played Cork Hibs in Milltown in the run-in to the end of the season and there was the famous disallowed goal. The goal was disallowed

'The 1970s – when hair came in all shapes and sizes. From Left to right, Back row; Sandy Smith, Jimmy Gregg, Damien Keogh, Pat Dunne, Terry Daly, Eddie Byrne. Front row; Mick Lawlor, Frank O'Neill, Denis Stephens, Mick Leech, Damien Richardson, Eamonn Gregg'.

for dangerous play but it was a perfectly good goal. Leech was just so sharp. That proved to be very costly.'

MICK LEECH
'When we played Cork in the league I had a perfectly good goal disallowed. Joe Grady was the Cork goalkeeper and I was standing around five yards away from him but the way Joe used to kick the ball he'd throw it way in front of him first. He went to kick it out and threw it right out to me so I lobbed it back over his head and into the goal. The referee didn't know what had happened and he didn't know what to do, so he gave a free out but there was no way it was a free out. I did get some goals where I'd kick the ball out of the goalie's hands but I did nothing wrong in that particular incident.'

Having finished level on points, Rovers and Hibs met in Dalymount on April 25th 1971 in a play-off for the title. A total of 28,000 people flocked into the Phibsboro stadium to witness the sides battle it out. However, Rovers' pre-match build-up was thrown into disarray when players and directors clashed over win bonuses. The Rovers team that day was Dunne, Fagan, Courtney, Dixon, Canavan, Kearin, O'Neill, Leech, Richardson, Byrne and Lawlor.

MICK LEECH
'The play-off against Cork was the beginning of the end for Shamrock Rovers as I knew

them. The league had gone on for two extra weeks because of the play-off and the club said that they would pay us our wages for those two weeks but that we weren't entitled to anything for the game. There was a standoff in the changing room and the players weren't going to play. It was eventually decided that we'd get £25 win bonus but you could see that the player's hearts weren't in it. The goings-on in the changing room affected some players and I think once we went behind some of the lads let their heads drop. We were beaten 3-1 and half-way through the following season the Cunninghams sold-out. For me that was the beginning of the end of Rovers.'

JIMMY CONROY

'Rovers were dreadful in the play-off. I remember Mick Leech had a very good game, he got the goal and he had another disallowed, but the team didn't play well at all and lost 3-1. The Cunninghams stayed for another season before they left but I always thought that what happened before the play-off was the beginning of the end for them. Losing the league play-off is still my greatest disappointment.'

JOHN BYRNE

'The moment I knew I was Rovers was when we lost the play-off in '71 against Hibs. I was only 11 and I made up a little placard saying "Up Rovers", which I still have at home. But we lost that game and I cried my eyes out on the way home. I was so upset. A play-off for the league, 28,000 people in Dalymount, I was just sick. When you feel the pain, that's when you know you're Rovers; it has pierced all exteriors and it is right inside you.'

'YOU'D READ IN THE PAPER ABOUT THEIR BUSINESS EXPLOITS'

By the early 1970s, Joe and Mary Jane Cunningham had more or less retired from Rovers, and had handed the club over to their sons, Arthur and Des. Family commitment to the club had waned and it wasn't long before Des and Arthur were looking to get out. Three brothers from Dublin offered to take the club over and Rovers was soon sold. Paddy, Barton and Louis Kilcoyne now ruled the roost.

JIMMY CONROY

'The Rovers supporters had a real love-hate relationship with the Cunninghams. They were real dictators, very much the old style football directors. Milltown was alright, but it had become a bit run-down and they weren't putting any money into it. By the time the Kilcoynes took over, the ground was a mess. We'd never really heard of the Kilcoynes. You'd read in the paper about their business exploits and they seemed very ambitious, so it was seen as a positive thing.'

MICK LEECH

'I thought it was good for the club [when the Kilcoynes came in]. Joe had left the club to his sons and they didn't have the same commitment. They sort of let the club go. The Kilcoynes are despised now but they came in and got the club running again. If they hadn't have stepped in there is a possibility that the club could have gone under. The improvements they made to Milltown between '73 and '83 were immense.'

SONNY O'REILLY

'Some people say that the Cunninghams should have put more money into the club, but no matter what way you look at it the Cunninghams kept Rovers as a top club. But it was getting harder to run League of Ireland clubs because it was harder to get the crowds in.'

JOHN BYRNE
'The Kilcoynes were ambitious but there was probably a degree of vanity too: "Hey, we own the biggest club in Ireland".'

'THE MILLTOWN ROAD WAS DESERTED'

The Kilcoynes had witnessed decades of huge crowds flocking to Irish football and had sought to take-over Rovers primarily for business reasons. Although all three brothers took over Rovers, it was Louis, the youngest at just 31, who handled the day-to-day running of the club.

Irish football, however, was about to change. Within the space of five years, the crowds were to disappear from Irish football grounds. Televised football from England played a huge role in the dramatic decline of interest in the domestic game, but internal factors also played a huge part. Two of the most successful clubs of the 1950s and '60s, Drums and Cork Hibs, both disappeared virtually overnight. Rovers, the club which had always captured the public's imagination more than others, underwent massive change at board level and the new owners began their reign by implementing serious cutbacks. The Cunninghams, who personified Rovers, were gone, as too were the great players of the previous era. Shelbourne and St. Patrick's Athletic were also struggling, leaving Bohemians – a club with little tradition of success – as the only power in Dublin football.

The Football Association of Ireland had yet to see the glory days of the international side and so did not have any serious finances. However, the association must take some blame for standing back and allowing the domestic league to enter into a period of serious decline. Up until the early 1970s, League of Ireland football attracted regular crowds of over 15,000, yet when the numbers started to fall off there was no guidance or aid from the country's football leadership. As a result of continued neglect on behalf of the FAI, Irish football has yet to recover from the devastation of the early 1970s.

JOHN BYRNE
'The '70s was a strange decade because Irish football completely collapsed. Even in 1971 we got 22,000 people at a league game but within five years crowds just disappeared. It was a time of massive social changes – Ireland started opening up, getting British TV and men stopped thinking of their houses as the place where dinner was served. You also had things like Drums going out of business overnight in '72. They were the big rivals at the time. Seven years before they went out of business, they beat Bayern Munich 1-0 in Tolka. Then, suddenly, they were gone. Within two years Hibs were gone too. From Rovers point of view, we'd just won the six-in-a-row and how do you follow that? So you had all that going on, as well as the socio-economic changes in the country. I mean, the '70s was the start of the twentieth century in Ireland.'

MICK LEECH
'Lifestyles changed, the world became smaller and people began to see the bigger picture. All of a sudden people knew who was playing for Real Madrid and Manchester United and could contrast that with the local league. If you look at Gaelic football, one of the reasons why Gaelic has retained its greatness in Ireland is because there is nothing else to compare it with. You can't compare your local side with a side in Spain or England. Gaelic football

'Rovers players train in China during a tour of the Far East'.

in Ireland is the best Gaelic football in the world! When people could compare League of Ireland to English football, the lukewarm people drifted off.'

MICK SMYTH
'The crowds started dropping off, although as players you don't really notice it that much. People started watching matches on the telly instead of going to live matches.'

MARTIN MOORE
'When the crowds started to go downhill a bit in the early '70s, as a kid the first thing you think is, "there's more room". In 1969, when I first started going, Milltown would be packed. They said that the ground only held 18,000, but I remember seeing at least 22,000 there.

SONNY O'REILLY
'Society started changing. You had English football on television and condensing games into highlights makes them seem exciting. I even saw it in my own local football club. After the game, I'd go off to Rovers and they'd be saying "Are you not staying for the game on television?" The amount of sports shops that opened up didn't help either because suddenly all the kids were wearing English jerseys.'

RICHIE PHILPOTT
'Irish football really began to die in the 70's. The crowds were awful and a lot of that had to do with Match of the Day. People started watching Match of the Day on their colour televisions and started saying "Well, the standard here just isn't as good as the standard on the telly, so sod it". It took an awful nose-dive.

FRANK WHELAN

'It was weird because I remembered the good times, but suddenly I was walking to a game and the Milltown Road was deserted. In the mid-70s, I stood on the terraces of Milltown and there would only be a handful of us there. It was completely unknown for Rovers.'

'ROVERS HAD REALLY HIT ROCK BOTTOM'

As the Kilcoynes faced into their first season in charge, hopes were high that Rovers would challenge for the title. However, Waterford were to prove too strong and Rovers could only manage fifth place.

JIMMY CONROY

'They started quite well in '72/'73. We won the President's Cup and weren't a million miles off being a good team. We had the fiasco in the cup that year when we played four cup matches in five days. We played Athlone and drew there, the following Sunday we beat Waterford 3-0 in the league, then played Athlone in the replay on the Wednesday. We drew 0-0 after extra time so they ordered a replay for the following night. Drew that again after extra time so they ordered another replay for the following night and we finally beat them 3-1. I ended up on top of the dugout when we got the third goal. So the players rested on Saturday and played the quarter final against Limerick on Sunday. We lost 1-0 but it was a bit hard to take considering how wrecked the players were. There was a major riot in the Limerick that day, thousands of Rovers fans went down on the train. It was a particularly mad day.'

MICK LEECH

'We'd played on Sunday, Wednesday, Thursday and Friday, two of which went into extra time. We then had to play Limerick on Sunday and I remember getting up on the morning and barely being able to move. I don't know how I got down to the train. I almost had to be helped stepping onto the train! Limerick beat us but we couldn't raise a gallop that day. We were odds-on to win the cup that year but what they put us through was inhumane.'

Faced with dwindling crowds, the Kilcoynes tightened their belts even further. Frank O'Neill and Mick Leech were transferred to Waterford, leaving goalkeeper Pat Dunne as the sole link between the 1970s and the all conquering side of the 1960s. For the following two seasons – 1973/74 and 1974/75 – Rovers finished seventh and eighth respectively, under the managerial guidance of Mick Meagan and Theo Dunne. At this point, the Kilcoynes decided to starve the club of all money, selling senior players such as Eamon Fagan, Tony Ward and Tommy McConville, and replacing them with players bought from junior football. Cherry Orchard – one of the country's most established junior clubs – became the main feeder club for Rovers. The team was young and inexperienced, although they did show potential. On a tour of Japan, Shamrock Rovers defeated the Japanese national side 3-2 in front of 60,000 spectators at the Olympic Stadium. However, Meagan and Dunne were forced to field a side of 18-year-olds with no experience of League of Ireland football. The result was that Shamrock Rovers finished bottom of the league in 1975/76 for the first – and only – time in the clubs' history. There was only one division at the time and so Rovers had to re-apply for admission into the league.

MICK MEAGAN

'The great era at Rovers was over by the time I joined the club. Myself and Theo [Dunne] were really thrown in at the deep end. I think it was more a case of just keeping the ship afloat until Johnny Giles came home. I think that was always on the horizon and in the meantime there was no point throwing money at the club. Young players can't just walk into the league, it takes a few years, but we did our best with what we had. In many ways, it would have been a black-mark against the league if we'd have done well. You shouldn't be able to win matches with a team of young lads and I think what happened to Rovers proves that the League of Ireland is better than people will give it credit for.'

JOHN BYRNE
'It was dire. They were just a bunch of kids competing in a mans league. We went from being a side that was capable of challenging to a side that had to apply for re-election for the first time ever. That was a real shock. The Kilcoyne's didn't even get that much stick over it, people just stopped going to games. In 1977 we played Athlone on Grand National Sunday and there were 63 people there. That's still recorded as Rovers lowest attendance, although I know at least 5,000 people who claim to have been there!'

ALAN O'NEILL
'THE WHOLE TEAM AT THAT TIME WAS BASED ON YOUTH WITH JUST A SPRINKLING OF SENIOR PLAYERS LIKE PAT DUNNE AND A FEW OTHERS WHO WERE IN THE TWILIGHT OF THEIR CAREERS. THE BALANCE WASN'T RIGHT AND WE STRUGGLED BADLY.'

JIMMY CONROY
'Rovers went into serious decline. It was embarrassing. In '75/'76 we played a yellow-pack team and only won four matches. We beat Limerick twice, beat Cork Hibs once and also beat Bohs, which was incredible because they were league champions. There wasn't much anti-Kilcoyne feeling on the terraces purely because there wasn't anyone on the terraces. People always look back on Milltown and think everything was rosy but it was a particularly bad time then.'

JOHN BYRNE
'Behind the Gonzaga End in Milltown they used to have a board where they would slot in the letters to write out the teams. There was a slogan underneath that said "With cigarettes you just can't win". Someone took out Mick Megan's name and put it in front of "cigarettes" so it read "with Mick Meagan you just can't win". I also remember that someone had a banner, basically a white bed sheet, with Shamrock Rovers written on it, but they put an "e" in Shamrock so as it read "Shamerock Rovers". I presume it was down to them being semi-illiterate rather than attempting to be poignant.'

MARTIN KEATING
'I started following Rovers in 1975. It was the worst possible time to start following the club because they had just applied for re-election and we may as well have been supporting Cherry Orchard.'

MARTIN MOORE
'I've seen Rovers at a low ebb, but that was the lowest ever. In '77 we were kept off the bottom by Limerick, who were an awful side. They were completely rubbish but they came to Milltown and beat us 4-0. It was 3-0 and I was walking out, but I stood at he top of the steps in Milltown and I saw the fourth goal going in. We made them look like Real Madrid that day.'

FRANK WHELAN
'They were only kids and it was too much of a step up for them. An awful lot of lads fell away. I know a lot of lads who never went back to Rovers. They'd just read about Rovers and talk about them in the pub but they never went.'

MICK LEECH
'I went to Waterford and ended up scoring the only goal of the game when Waterford played Rovers in the FAI Cup. I was completely silent after I scored. At the end of the day, I was a Rovers man and I'd just knocked them out of the cup. It was a game I'd rather not have played in but it's just one of those things that happened.'

MICK MEAGAN
'There was no money back then. Myself, Pat Dunne and Theo were the only people at Rovers getting paid. The young lads were just given expenses. Rovers had a boiler that was heated by a stove. Before a game one day, one of the lads went across to the shop to get a bag of coal but they wouldn't give him one because Rovers owed the shop money. We had to go breaking up sticks and throwing old boots into the stove to get the showers working! We used to rob cooking oil from our houses and rub the players down in it because we had no olive oil. We didn't tell the players it was cooking oil though!'

'IT WAS A GREAT FEELING'

Faced with an impossible task, Mick Meagan and Theo Dunne resigned from the club and were replaced by Sean Thomas, who had guided Rovers to every domestic honour in 1964. The Kilcoynes made a limited amount of money available and Thomas re-signed former Rovers greats Mick Leech and Johnny Fullam, together with John Conway from Bohemians. The presence of experienced players helped take Rovers off the bottom-spot, but the club still finished the 1976/77 season in eleventh position.

However, the club was to be given a major boost by capturing the League Cup, the first piece of silverware to come to Milltown since the FAI Cup in 1969. Mick Leech's two hundred and fiftieth career goal proved the difference as Rovers beat Sligo 1-0. The Rovers line-up was O'Neill, Doran, McNevin, Wyse, Synnott, Fullam, Leech, Conway, Meagan, Lyons and Gaffney.

MICK LEECH
'The goal against Sligo in the League Cup was probably the best goal I ever scored. It was the last minute of the game and I picked up the ball ten yards outside the box and hit it – next thing I knew it was in the back of the net! Most of my goals came from inside the box so I think people were quite taken aback to see me score one from 30 yards.'

ALAN O'NEILL
'LEECHY WAS RENOWNED FOR SCORING WITH TOE POKES, HITTING THEM OFF HIS KNEE, OFF HIS HEAD, OFF HIS BUM, BUT THIS ONE WAS A BALL THAT BROKE WELL OUTSIDE THE BOX AND HE BURIED IT RIGHT INTO THE TOP CORNER. I REMEMBER THE EXCITEMENT AFTERWARDS WHEN WE WON BECAUSE IT WAS STILL A YOUNG SIDE AND IT WAS GREAT FEELING TO WIN SOMETHING AT LEAGUE OF IRELAND LEVEL.'

MICHAEL KEARNS
'My earliest memory of real satisfaction was when Mick Leech scored to win the League Cup. That was the first time I'd ever seen Rovers win anything. I was hooked from then.'

If society's changing values had conspired to send League of Ireland crowds plummeting, supporters of the game also noticed another major change: the emergence of football hooligans. Although there had been sporadic violence at football matches prior to the 1970s, trouble was rare. The 1970s saw a sinister change, with groups of young males travelling to football purely to cause trouble. Although hooliganism has largely been associated with England, Ireland was also affected.

The idealistic 1960s were over and were replaced by a decade of negativity. Huge housing estates were being constructed in urban areas, giving birth to an entirely new demographic of under-educated and under-resourced youths. Thousands of young people found themselves in a bleak society with very limited opportunities. They became violent and football became their outlet.

John Byrne

'Rovers had a sizeable group of hard lads, the Bridge Boot Boys they were called. They were tough lads. Rovers was a beacon for mad people. It was basically somewhere you could go to create mayhem. I don't know whether they were Rovers fans as such, they were basically just thugs. After games in Dalymount we'd all march back into town, a few hundred of us. It was all terribly sexy when you're 13. But the '70s was a very violent decade in general. I remember being in town in the middle of the day and seeing people beating the crap out of each other. Dublin was an extremely violent place and that reflected itself in Rovers.'

Robbie Foy

'You'd always see "BBB" – Bridge Boot Boys - and "SRFC" written on jackets, especially on the northside. That whole area on the northside around the bridge in Donnycarney, that was the first batch of skinheads in the '70s. Lads would be waiting for you when you went down the country. If you got the train down to Waterford, you'd have to walk over the bridge into the town and lads would be waiting for you. I remember one lad getting thrown over the bridge, and that is a very dangerous river. Limerick, Athlone, Cork, it was all the same story. One my mates got battered by Cork Hibs fans wearing war paint. Drogheda fans would stand on the bridge and throw rocks at the buses. I worked with guys from Dundalk and they said that their fans used to go into Oriel Park the night before the game and bury things under the ground to use as weapons. Sligo fans had swords and saws and things like that. They'd produce this stuff and you'd like be like, "What the fuck is that?"'

Martin Moore

"Sligo was bad enough, they'd be waiting at the train station for you, but in Limerick they'd be waiting on the tracks. Waterford too. You'd almost hope Rovers would lose, just to avoid trouble. I remember once Rovers were hammered three or four nil in Waterford and they were still waiting for us. I was thinking, "Jesus, what more do you want?" I remember Limerick came to Milltown and ambulances were coming in and out of the ground all day. There was one particularly mad game in Dundalk when their fans went insane. We got back on the bus and every single window was gone. And we were on the third bus, the first one was nearly on fire!'

In July 1977 Rovers supporters had to pinch themselves after hearing news beyond their wildest dreams: Irish football legend Johnny Giles was returning to Dublin to

'The Giles era begins: From left to right, Back row; Noel Synnott, Pierce O'Leary, Mark Meagan, Alan O'Neill, Steve Lynex, Robbie Gaffney, Ray Treacy. Front row; Eddie O'Sullivan, Mick Gannon, Johnny Fullam, Eamon Dunphy, John Giles, Larry Murphy'.

manage the club. Giles – a brother-in-law of the Kilcoynes – had quit his post at West Bromwich Albion, where he had achieved promotion to the top flight, to take over the reigns at Milltown. Suddenly, having starved the club of money for five years, the Kilcoynes implemented a full-time policy at the club and unveiled plans to build a 50,000 all-seater stadium at Milltown. Rovers would be turned into a school of excellence for Irish football, sweeping up all domestic honours and, ultimately, competing for European honours. For the supporters, the bleak years at the club seemed to be at an end.

JIMMY CONROY
'There were huge expectations when Giles came in. He was doing well with West Brom and there was talk of him going to Spurs, he was the big thing at the time. He came in and started talking about European Cups. We did win two cups that year – FAI and Tyler – but not the European one.'

MICHAEL KEARNS
'All of a sudden Rovers were the darlings of League of Ireland again – back where we belong. It changed from going to Milltown and there being no one there, to going to Milltown and there being a buzz around the place.'

FRANK WHELAN

'It was the news that every Shamrock Rovers supporter wanted to hear. John Giles – an international legend at Rovers - I couldn't believe it! I was in work when it came over the radio – "breaking news: John Giles to take over Shamrock Rovers".'

MARTIN MOORE

'Giles' first game for Rovers was away to Dundalk. The match kicked off at seven and the last train back to Dublin was at eight, but we decided to go anyway. We got the train up and Rovers won one-nil, Mick Leech getting the goal. There was this drunken bloke going around singing the good auld days are here again. We were saying, "He's right. Obviously we'll do the double this year, no question. Two or three years, the European Cup is ours". So we got out of Dundalk about 9:40 and had no way of getting home, so we just started walking. We were going to walk the whole way, which is around 60 miles, but eventually we got a lift.'

'IT WAS LIKE BRAZIL PLAYING IN YOUR BACK GARDEN'

As well as donning boots himself, Giles signed up Irish internationals Ray Treacy, Eamon Dunphy and Paddy Mulligan. For young players, such as Robbie Gaffney and Kieran Maher, it was an unbelievable chance to prove themselves alongside international stars. However, Giles' full-time policy did not suit everyone and it wasn't long before Mick Leech and Pat Dunne departed Milltown.

'John Giles takes in a training session and Glenmalure'.

MICK LEECH

'I was 29 at the time and turning professional didn't interest me. Giles decided who he wanted to keep and I wasn't one of them, but that is a manager's prerogative and I don't hold any grudges. Giles mightn't have been my favourite person but he was acting in the interests of the club and I understood that.'

ROBBIE GAFFNEY

'Myself and some of the younger players thought it was great but only expected to be on the fringes of the action, so to find myself in the team was amazing. I was playing alongside these lads who I'd only ever seen playing for Ireland and I was actually voted Player of the Year by the supporters! I'd arrive to games and there'd be big cars outside the ground, I'd always get the bus up!'

KIERAN MAHER

'Giles was so methodical in everything he did. He brought in Frances Burns, who was 33 and had played with United and won a European medal with Celtic. Myself, Harry Kenny and Richie Bailey were playing beside him, we were all around 17 or 18 and we learned so much from him. Suddenly, we became the team that everyone wanted to beat, which is the way it should be at Rovers.'

ALAN O'NEILL

'The excitement at the club and with the supporters was immense. The younger players were very much in awe of Johnny, although he never intended it. We were part of a new full time professional set-up – even the part-timers started training four or five times a week. We'd meet the morning of a match, have a light training session, you'd be taken off to a hotel before the game and then back for the game – it was just totally different to what we were used to.'

LIAM BUCKLEY

'I was playing youth football with Shelbourne but Giles offered me full-time football with Rovers. I had a few other options – I could have gone to Ipswich, for example – but Giles convinced me that staying in Ireland was the best thing to do. It was a very exciting time at Rovers, we had great young players – Pierce O'Leary, Alan Campbell, Ronnie Murphy – and some great senior players – Paddy Mulligan, Ray Treacy, Eamon Dunphy.'

ROBBIE FOY

'It was unbelievable – it was like Brazil playing in your back garden! These were international superstars, at least you thought they were. Paddy Mulligan, Ray Treacy, Johnny Giles, Eamonn Dunphy – you'd seen them playing for Ireland and the next thing you know they're taking a throw in beside you at Milltown!'

FRANK ALLEN

'Initially, the crowds came back when Giles took over. People had faith in his plan and admired his ambition. Perhaps, looking back, there was a bit too much youth in the side. A youth policy needs time to develop and all the other clubs had seasoned League of Ireland professionals.'

FRANK WHELAN

'People like Dunphy and Treacy were probably a little past their sell by date but by League of Ireland standards they were big, big stars. To this day I still say that John Giles was the best

Four young players
(Gaffney, O'Neill,
Maher & Beglin).

player I've ever seen in a Rovers shirt. It's strange because Rovers fans will still talk about Giles the manager, but never about Giles the player. In the League of Ireland you don't get any time on the ball, but Giles had this great ability to hold onto the ball and make space for himself. That was a big change for League of Ireland fans.'

KIERAN MAHER
'I came through the youth system with Alan Campbell, Terry Byrne and lads like that. We played under John Wilkes for the Shamrock Rovers schoolboy team, but we had players like Alan Campbell and Richie Bailey so the average score for a game would be 12-0.'

FRANK ALLEN
'I used to teach at Pearse College and one of the classes I had was a Shamrock Rovers class. They used to send their apprentices to college for one day every week. It was based on the English model whereby the clubs would give the players an education so as they had something to fall back on. It was a wildly ambitious plan.'

ALAN O'NEILL
'Eamon Dunphy played with us for a season or two, and then he just decided to give it up. When he went into journalism I remember reading some of the articles he'd written and they weren't too complimentary about the League of Ireland. If you look at what Johnny Giles

had done – he came home and tried to put something back into the game. But Eamon lasted two years and then spent a lot of time just slagging us off.'

MARTIN MOORE
'Dunphy was responsible for forming the first Rovers supporters club. I remember he made a great speech to the fans about how our voice should be heard too. But since then he has never missed a chance to slag off Rovers and Rovers fans. He always defended Louis [Kilcoyne] and got very personal with Rovers fans, basically calling us scum. He was looking for a career in journalism and was trying to make a name for himself. He used to do the match previews for the Tribune and every game he would predict Rovers would lose: "Rovers, very overrated" This was in the '80s when we were winning four-in-a-row! When Bohs beat Rangers [in 1984] he described Bohs as "champions elect" - Rovers won the league by a mile that year!'

JOHN BYRNE
'St. Pat's brought Gordon Banks over just to play against us. That's how Micky Mouse the whole thing was. "Oh, Rovers have Giles, well we'll get Gordon Banks". Banks had just lost an eye in a car accident and I remember all the Rovers fans singing "Gordon, show us your eye". Fair play to him, he took it well and pretended to take out his eye and show it to us. George Best played a couple of games for Cork Celtic, even though physically he looked more like a darts player; Geoff Hurst and Trevor Brooking played for Cork; Bobby Charlton played for Waterford. It was a complete joke. Uwe Seller played one game for Cork Celtic against Rovers in '76. He scored two goals that day. Of course, Rovers got six so it didn't matter too much. God know how old he was at the time.'

'I WAS SHIVERING I WAS SO HAPPY'

Rovers began the 1977/78 season well and confidence was high that the club could challenge for the title. However, the side would soon fall away, ultimately to finish the season in fourth place, four points behind league winners Bohemians.

Giles was not to finish his first season empty handed though. A Ray Treacy inspired 3-2 extra-time victory over Finn Harps in the FAI Cup first round paved the way for a quarter-final clash against Dundalk. A Steve Lynex goal put Rovers into the semi-final, where they faced the still-mighty Waterford. Mark Meagan and Steve Lynex scored in front of 18,000 spectators in Dalymount to give Rovers a 2-1 victory and send the club into it's first FAI Cup final in almost a decade.

ROBBIE FOY
'The cup run in'78 was unbelievable. For the replay against Finn Harps in the first round, I bunked off school on the Thursday and got the second half. Same with Dundalk, bunk off school and get the second half.'

MARTIN MOORE
'We beat Waterford in the semi, that was another big game. The thing about Waterford that year was they had this English guy called Syd Wallace. The Rovers fans hated him and he hated the Rovers fans. So when we won, it was all like, "Sydney, Sydney, What's the Score?" Of course, he scored a last minute winner against us in the following year's semi-final. I saw normally very calm people trying to climb over a fence to try and get him that day.'

'Ray Treacy and Eamon Dunphy after the 1978 Cup Final victory' (Photography: Bobby Best).

Sligo Rovers were the opposition when Rovers took to Dalymount Park on 30 April 1978. The Rovers team that day was: Alan O'Neill, Mick Gannon, Pierce O'Leary, Noel Synnott, Johnny Fullam, Eamon Dunphy, Johnny Giles, Mark Meagan, Larry Murray, Ray Treacy and Steve Lynex, with Eddie O'Sullivan making a substitute appearance.

As the clock ticked into first half injury time, referee John Carpenter gave a penalty kick to Rovers for a foul on Steve Lynex. Ray Treacy scored from the spot in what would prove to be the only goal of the game. The cup was coming home to Milltown.

ALAN O'NEILL
'It was my first cup final and there was huge pressure on the team. We're Rovers, Giles is the manager, we're in the cup final, we simply have to win. It was probably one of the worst cup finals ever because it was an awful day. It poured out of the heavens all day. It was an absolute monsoon. Sligo fans still dispute the penalty. Whenever I'm in Sligo since we all have bets on how long it will be before someone mentions the penalty. The feeling after the game was strange though – it was more a sense of relief because of the pressure we were under.'

MICHAEL KEARNS
'I was standing in the Shed and Treacy took the penalty down the far end. I'll never forget

that day. I got the number 23 bus home and I was sitting on the bus literally shivering I was so happy.'

JOHN BYRNE
'Guys in Sligo will still come up to you and say, "that was never a penalty". Sligo County Council passed a vote of censure against John Carpenter for his refereeing performance.'

MARTIN MOORE
'The night of the match, there was a do in the Hoops Club in Milltown. Myself and another lad tried to go in and join the celebrations but they wouldn't let us in because we were too young. So we walked down the street and who was coming down the street only Steve Lynex, the man who'd got the penalty for Rovers, so we tried to get in with him. We walked up to the door and they wouldn't let him in because they thought he was with us! The three of us ended up climbing over a fence at the back of the building to get in. Of course, they threw myself and my mate out nearly straight away.'

'THE GAME STARTS 0-0, SO WHY CHANGE IT?'

Having brought silverware back to Milltown during his first season, Giles now attempted to challenge for the league title. However, in the four seasons between the cup win of 1978 and finishing second in 1982, Rovers only managed two fourth place finishes and two fifth place finishes, a highly disappointing return for a full-time side containing such an array of talent.

JIMMY CONROY
'The style of football didn't appeal, it was far too technical for Irish eyes. To Giles, a 0-0 draw to Cork Albert away was a good result.'

JOHN BYRNE
'Irish people like fast sport; they like the ball being battered up to goal. Look at the GAA, it's all about hoofing the ball up to the forwards. We don't appreciate subtly. Under Giles the football was very, very dull. The game starts 0-0, why change it? I remember once in Cork there were around 12,000 people at the game and the football was just terrible. And that's 12,000 people who don't want to watch Rovers again.'

KIERAN MAHER
'His tactics were defensive but his whole philosophy was that if you kept the ball you couldn't concede a goal. Now that I'm 40 years of age I can understand that, but when I was 18 I just wanted to get the ball and run towards the goal.'

PAT BRADY
'The joke at the time was that Rovers would need three men to take a corner kick. As a fan you are tolerant and you give things time to see if it works out, but fans reach an end of their tolerance. He was terribly inflexible: he had Plan A and Plan B was to revert to Plan A.'

ALAN O'NEILL
'If you look at how football is played today, maybe he was ahead of his time. The way football has gone since has vindicated Giles.'

ROBERT GOGGINS

'It was possession football – one step forward, two steps back. Having said that, under Giles we were always there or thereabouts. With the exception of the Four in a Row era, the Giles era compares very favourably with what has gone on since.'

MARTIN MOORE

'We played Galway Rovers in 1978 and the game was so boring that the fans, as a protest, turned around and watched a schoolboys rugby game that was being played in Gonzaga at the far end of Milltown. None of us knew the rules of rugby, but it was still more interesting than the Rovers game.'

SONNY O'REILLY

'We were being beaten 2-1 in a cup game and time was running out but Giles was still playing defensive football. When the final whistle went I couldn't for the life of me understand what he was at. It disappointed me a lot. I couldn't understand that match, I wanted to jump onto the pitch myself and say "what are you doing?"'

ROBBIE GAFFNEY

'Not only did we not dominate the league, with the exception of one year we didn't even challenge for it. I've never understood that. We had fantastic players, yet we were regularly getting hammered by clubs like Athlone. You could think that maybe some of the lads who came back from England weren't really up for it, but if you saw them in training you wouldn't think that.'

NED ARMSTRONG

'I wouldn't say it was an attitude problem, they were very keen to win things, but players like Giles and Dunphy were past it. Everyone thought Rovers would go back to the top, but it didn't work out. These things happen, I suppose.'

KIERAN MAHER

'We had a pitch to die for. When you look at pitches like Marketsfield or St. Mels, they were farming land. No disrespect to the clubs, but they were dreadful. If you look at Richie Bailey, he was a phenomenal player at Milltown, a really beautiful footballer, but bring him to St. Mels or the Showgrounds and he disappeared. The result was that the league never saw the best out of the team.'

ALAN O'NEILL

'He had his own style of play. He didn't want to play the conventional League of Ireland way, but the pitches weren't conducive to his style. You could play that way in Milltown, but not down in Terryland or Cork, and his whole method was you played at home the same as you played away.'

JOHN BYRNE

'There was no such thing as professionalism back then. Pitches down the country were full of daisies, for God's sake. It was as if they'd just taken the cows off for the game. Some of them didn't even have markings on them. This was back in the day when there was only one division, so it meant that inertia was the order of the day. It was easier to do nothing, so there were only a certain amount of clubs with any ambition.'

'THE ENTIRE DREAM WAS OVER'

After five disappointing league campaigns, Rovers finished the 1981/82 season in second spot. Giles opted to give it another chance and began the 1982/83 season hoping to go one further than the previous campaign. However, having fallen eleven points behind league-leaders Athlone Town, the legendary midfielder decided to pack it in. On 3 February1983 John Giles resigned as manager of Shamrock Rovers.

ROBBIE GAFFNEY
'Fans weren't happy because Giles was managing Rovers, Ireland and Vancouver and people felt that Rovers wasn't his top priority. I think the results reflected that to an extent. We were in pre-season training when we heard that he was resigning from the international team, which we all thought might be good for Rovers. In the end, it was only a few months before he resigned from Rovers too. The players were gutted because we knew that everything he was trying to do was now over. It wasn't just that the manager was leaving, the entire dream was over.'

ALAN O'NEILL
'I was naturally very disappointed when I heard that Giles was leaving. I arrived up the night it was announced and there were lots of reporters outside, but no one knew anything. I got a phone call from Giles two days later. He met myself and Noel Synnott and he explained his reasons and thanked us for our contribution and just said, "that's football, you have to move on". People tend not to see the human side of Giles, but he's a very decent person. I think that's been proven over the years in the way he's looked after different people, Dunphy being one of them.'

ROBERT GOGGINS
'Giles was appointed coach of the Vancouver Whitecaps and their season used to start before ours, so he used to miss the start and end of our season. It wasn't an ideal situation. In his last season, we were playing Pat's and there was a lot of disquiet amongst the fans that Giles wasn't there. The fans had turned against Giles. When that happens, it's time for a manager to go. Once the manager loses the confidence of the fans, he is not going to get it back. Even if he wins a cup or a league, it only papers over the cracks – if you lose the fans it's only a matter of time before you have to walk.

FRANK ALLEN
'When Giles left it was confirming to the fans that the dream had failed.'

KIERAN MAHER
'I think if Giles had stayed things would have got better. We pushed Dundalk very hard for the league [in 1982] and I think we would have won it eventually had he stayed. It was only a spit in the wind between ourselves and Dundalk that season.'

MARTIN KEATING
'League of Ireland was just so different to what he was used to. He came from a highly professional set-up into the League of Ireland, which was a Mickey Mouse set-up in the '70s. He left half way through a season, which I thought was very poor. You should stick it out until the end of the season at least. He also became the only manager to sell a player to himself when he sold Pearce O'Leary to Vancouver. That was a bit bizarre.'

FRANK WHELAN

'Giles had no knowledge of League of Ireland football. He didn't realise that you have to change your game when you play away. You didn't get time on the ball in places like Limerick and Galway and, as a result, Rovers were beaten a lot. He never adapted the team to the circumstances. It ended in a nightmare, to be honest.'

PETER ECCLES

'I loved working with Giles. He was way ahead of his time. If you look at what they're trying to do now in the league, Giles was trying to do that twenty years ago. Even if you look at the brand of football teams are trying to play now, that's what Gilesy wanted back then.'

KIERAN MAHER

'Giles was the ultimate professional. He was a winner in everything he did – in five-a-sides, in training, he was just a winner. He was the best thing to happen to the League of Ireland because he made everything turn. As a result of Giles the league set up a grounds inspection committee, so grounds had to be of a certain standard. That improved the standard of football, which is better for the players and also better for the spectators.'

ALAN O'NEILL

'Johnny as a manager was incredible. He didn't get the credit he deserved because he tried to do something different. He tried to bring in a full-time set-up, which has only begun to happen over the past three or four years. I've nothing but the utmost respect for Johnny. He had a major influence on the game here, especially in the way people prepared for games. If you look at the pitches in Ireland now, they are all superb, and it was Johnny who started all that.'

JIMMY CONROY

'I always found Giles to be a very nice man, he got on very well with the fans and was always willing to have a pint after the game or to sing a song at a social event. In '78, the night we won the Tyler Cup, he got up and sang Don't Cry For Me Argentina, which was funny because that's the year Ireland didn't make the World Cup. Good singer too.'

CHAPTER 7

THE EUROPEAN BATTLES

'WE RAN OURSELVES INTO THE GROUND'

By the mid-1950s, football was already a global sport. Across Europe millions flooded into stadiums every week to watch teams compete in domestic competitions. Although UEFA was more concerned with starting an international tournament, the organisation soon adopted a blueprint for a European-wide club competition. In 1955 the European Cup was born.

The first year of the competition involved fourteen clubs from across Europe. Although Hibernians of Scotland took part – and managed to go all the way to the semi-finals – no representatives from Ireland or England were sent. Manchester United took part in 1956 – thrashing Anderlecht of Belgium 12-0 in their European debut – but it was not until the 1957/1958 season, the third year of the competition, that an Irish side entered into the European Cup. That side was Shamrock Rovers.

Rovers had won the League of Ireland title in the 1956/57 season, pipping city rivals Drumcondra to the title by five points. A decision was made to enter into European competition and everyone involved in the club awaited the draw eagerly. As the UEFA delegates plucked the names of the fourteen competing clubs out of a hat, a fascinating tie was produced: Shamrock Rovers against Manchester United.

In the greater scheme of European football, this tie meant little. Matt Busby's United were fast emerging as one of the continent's greatest sides and they were expected to demolish their Irish opponents with ease. Yet, to those accustomed with the Irish game, the parallels between Rovers and United were unmistakable. Both Paddy Coad and Busby had changed forever the face of their domestic leagues, relying on young, exciting players. Both sides are still regarded as the greatest ever produced in their respective countries; both sides had restored their clubs to the domestic supremacy which their supporters believe to be their divine right. When the Coad's Colts and the Busby Babes went head-to-head, it was a fixture that had football fans salivating.

The first leg – the first ever competitive club game involving a non-Irish side to take place in Ireland – was hosted in Dalymount Park. Due to its ability to hold numbers far greater than Glenmalure Park or Tolka Park, the northside venue played host to all club European matches, as well as FAI Cup finals and Irish international matches, right up until the 1980s. People flocked from all over Dublin to see the Rovers – United clash, with 46,000 paying customers recorded at the gate. The attendance remains the largest to ever witness a club game in Ireland. In modern times, the Irish public regularly turn out to support English clubs when they play friendlies against Irish teams. However, when Manchester United came to town in 1957, they faced a highly partisan crowd urging Rovers to victory. The sides responded by providing plenty of goals. Unfortunately, they were all in the Rovers net. Entering the final ten minutes Manchester United led 3-0. At this point, the difference between full-time professionals and part-time semi-professionals became clear. Rovers crumbled and conceded a further three goals, ending up losing by half a dozen to nil.

GERRY MACKEY
'We were the first side to play in a European competition, when the Busby Babes beat us 6-0 in Dalymount. We ran ourselves into the ground that night, they scored three of their goals in the last ten minutes when we just couldn't stand up anymore. Liam Whelan, who played schoolboy football with most of us, scored twice that day. He wasn't known for scoring goals and he got a lot of stick after, I remember lads saying, "Jesus Liam, you picked a great time to start scoring". We were disappointed to lose by that much but we'd played well and it was nothing but physical exhaustion.'

SONNY O'REILLY
'Rovers were brilliant against Manchester United, despite the fact that they lost 6-0. Their mistake that night was that they ran themselves into the ground in the first half. They still played good football in the second half but the steam had gone from them.'

There is no doubt that United were the better side. The scoreline didn't lie, even if it did flatter. Initially, it looked as if United were going to pull off a repeat performance in the second leg, going 2-0 up within twenty minutes. However, Maxie McCann pulled one back and, shortly after Dennis Violett had made it 3-1, ex-United player Tommy Hamilton pulled another one back.

GERRY MACKEY
'That game was as good a game as we ever played, we even got a standing ovation coming off the pitch. We were delighted with how we performed in Old Trafford.'

NED ARMSTRONG
'UNITED WERE JUST THAT BIT TOO GOOD FOR THEM IN THE HOME LEG. BUT IN THE RETURN MATCH THEY DID WELL, THEY LOST 3-2 BUT THAT WAS VERY GOOD OVER THERE. I DON'T REALLY REMEMBER THE SCORE IN THE HOME LEG, THEY WERE BEATEN BY A BIG SCORE AND I TEND TO BLOCK THOSE RESULTS OUT. BUT THEY PRODUCED IT IN THE RETURN LEG.'

MARIE CRADDOCK
'My first ever trip on a plane was when I went to Manchester for the Rovers game. We flew in on this rickety old plane and flew back again the same night. Old Trafford was completely different then to what it is now. The team lost but it was a very good night.'

PAULINE FOY
'My biggest memory is of seeing Tommy Taylor, he was a stand-out character. A big, good looking man, the girls loved him. He was far more attractive than that David Beckham.'

SONNY O'REILLY
'When they went over to England they changed their tactics and slowed it down in the first half. They only lost that game 3-2 and the crowd gave them a great reaction.'

JACK WILSON
'I got the boat to Hollyhead and travelled from there up to Manchester. We had been beaten 6-0 in Dublin but they played fantastic over there, Paddy Coad was brilliant. The United fans were great to us, it was a very enjoyable trip.'

The poignancy of that fixture was made clear just six months later when the United team suffered a tragic plane crash in Munich, killing 23 people, including five of the team who played against Rovers: Roger Byrne, Duncan Edwards, David Pegg, Tommy Taylor and Liam Whelan. The crash happened later on in that European Cup campaign, after a quarter final clash in Belgrade. For supporters and players of Rovers, who had struck up a bond with the Manchester club so recently, the crash was a huge shock.

GERRY MACKEY
'I'll never forget that day. I was just finishing up work at around five o'clock and someone came rushing into the offices with the news. It was such a shock. That United side was so good though, if the crash hadn't happened that would have been the all-time great English side. People like Duncan Edwards were just phenomenal.'

MARIE CRADDOCK
'I was actually down in Milltown on the night of the crash. The news broke when I was in work but I had to go down to a meeting in Milltown that night. It was a very sombre atmosphere there, especially because Tommy Hamilton had just come back from United to play for Rovers so he would have known all the lads very well. We were all completely shell-shocked.'

PAULINE FOY
'You couldn't even get out to Cabra for the removal of Liam Whelan. We left early in the morning and eventually got to the church, I remember the entire floor was covered in floral tributes.'

'WE NEVER EXPERIENCED ANYTHING LIKE IT'

Four months before the 1960s began, Rovers travelled to southern France to play OGC Nice in the European Cup. Against United, exhaustion had been the sides' downfall; against Nice, the extreme heat would conspire to do the Hoops in.

At the height of the August heat, Rovers took to the pitch with the temperature standing at an unbearable 98°F. Paddy Coad had left the Hoops the summer previously and the Coad's Colts had broken up. In addition to Coad, gone too were O'Callaghan, Mackey, Burke and Peyton. Nice were the top club side in a country which had just one year earlier finished third in the World Cup. Everything suggested a drubbing. Yet, after 18 minutes Tommy Hamilton stunned the French crowd by putting the Hoops in front. Nice pulled two back before half-

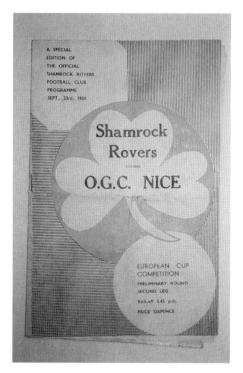

Programme from game v Nice.

time – one of which was a highly disputed penalty - and Rovers re-emerged for the second half with just ten players, Liam Hennessy having collapsed from sunstroke. The game finished 3-2, Tuohy getting Rovers' second.

In the return leg, one month later and a few degrees cooler, 32,000 people crammed into Dalymount to urge Rovers on. Hennessy put Rovers ahead, only for Nice to equalise. As Rovers laid siege to the Nice goal, they couldn't find a way through the defence and the game finished 1-1. Nice lost to eventual competition winners Real Madrid in the quarter finals.

SONNY O'REILLY
'We played Nice away and we only had nine players for some of the game because the heat was too much to take. There was over 30,000 at the game in Dalymount. These days, you wouldn't be sure if everyone would be up for Rovers but that night the whole crowd got behind them.'

RONNIE NOLAN
'We played a mid-week game against St. Pats and I got a severe twist in my ankle. I couldn't walk. We played Nice a week later and I did play but I wasn't 100 per cent fit. It was the first time that we'd gone away and experienced such heat. It was almost 100° F and we'd never experienced anything like it.'

NED ARMSTRONG
'ROVERS DID VERY WELL AGAINST NICE. THAT WAS ONE OF THE fIRST EUROPEAN GAMES, SO THERE

was a lot of excitement in the build-up to it. A very close match, a draw. I thought Rovers deserved to win it, they played excellent football. Hennessey scored, he always scored important goals for Rovers.'

Having been entered in European competitions twice, Rovers had been convincingly defeated by Manchester United and narrowly defeated by OGC Nice. When the draw for the 1962/63 Cup Winners Cup pitted the Hoops against Botev Plovdiv of Bulgaria, there was a sense that the break-through could finally be made. Unfortunately, this tie was to be the first of many real European disasters for the club. In the 1960s, Bulgaria was still firmly behind the Iron Curtin. For the Irish players, the game was a chance to experience a world that was otherwise shut off to them.

Ronnie Nolan
'Going out to Eastern Europe in those days was just unbelievable. The food was awful, nobody had anything. You'd go into a shop and there would be literally nothing there. There'd be six people behind the counter selling nothing.'

Unsurprisingly, there is collective amnesia about the game itself, which saw Rovers crash out 4-0 in Dublin and 1-0 in Bulgaria. At this stage, Rovers had begun their great cup run, which would see the club win the FAI Cup six times in a row. Cup success brought European football to Rovers every year and over the next three years Rovers lost 3-2 on aggregate to Valencia, 5-0 in an ill-tempered clash with Rapid Vienna and 3-2 to a great Real Zaragoza side. The Valencia side which defeated the Hoops had won the Fairs Cup (now called the UEFA Cup) the previous two years and were stunned when Rovers went 2-0 up in Spain. However, having already beaten Rovers 1-0 in Dublin, the Spaniards clawed two goals back and narrowly made it into the next round.

'Rovers in action in Bulgaria against Botev Plovdiv in the European Cup Winners Cup'.

Above: 'Rovers took on Botev Plovdiv in the Cup Winners Cup, but would lose 1-0 in Bulgaria and 4-0 in Dublin'.

Right: 'Rovers prepare to board the plane prior to their Fairs Cup clash against Valencia'.

MICK SMYTH
'Zaragoza were the top team in Spain at the time, they were all current Spanish internationals. We drew 1-1 with them in Dublin. It was lashing down that day; in fact I was convinced that the game would be called off. When we went over to Spain, we were getting the bus to Zaragoza and we were taking it in turns to stand at the front of the bus and sing. Johnny Fulham was up singing The Street Where You Livewhen he looked out the door and screamed – we were driving on cliff fronts and the driver was speeding around! We all thought it was hilarious until we realised what he was screaming about!'

'THE WARLOCK GOT IT WRONG'

After six attempts, Rovers finally made their European break-through in 1966, defeating AC Spora of Luxemburg 8-2 over two legs. If the draw for the first round had been kind to the Dublin club, the second round pitted them against one of the greatest sides the world has ever seen. In the summer of 1966, Germany famously lost to England in the World Cup final held in Wembly Stadium. Four months later, Bayern Munich, a side which contained household names such as Gerd Muller and Franz Beckenbaur, came to Dalymount Park to take on Shamrock Rovers. Urged on by 20,000 spectators, Liam Tuohy's men took the game to the Germans and, after Billy Dixon cancelled out Koulmann's effort, the tie finished 1-1.

MICK SMYTH
'We were very unlucky in that tie. We probably could have won if it wasn't for the crowd. Just after we got the equaliser Bayern were really nervous, even Beckenbaur was rattled. Some gobshites in the crowd started throwing things at the goalkeeper so the match was held up for five minutes which gave them time to compose themselves. When it restarted it was the old Bayern Munich again.'

FRANK WHELAN
'What a game! Dalymount was packed that night. That was a great occasion, just getting to see some of those lads play was brilliant. Rovers equalised and then the game was stopped for a few minutes. When it restarted, Bayern got back into it and Rovers couldn't get a second.'

Rovers securing a draw against the mighty Bayern Munich was a remarkable feat. Even more remarkable was what happened a few weeks later in the Olympic Stadium in Munich when the sides met for the second leg. It was the biggest stage the Dublin lads had ever played on and there were nerves in the Rovers camp before the game.

RONNIE NOLAN
'When we played Bayern Munich in Munich there was ice on the ground. The teams were lined up in the tunnel to come out onto the pitch and the Germans had silk stockings on them! We couldn't believe it, we were thinking "What the hell is this all about?" But when we got onto the pitch we realised. They were all wearing tights.'

Things appeared to be going to script when Brenninger scored after just five minutes and Olhauser made it 2-0 seven minutes later. Two-nil down at half-time, there were mixed emotions in the Rovers dressing room at the break.

MICK SMYTH
'Billy Dixon was playing for us but he'd played against Bayern a few seasons earlier for

Drums. I asked him, "What was the score in your match against them at half time?" "Nil all", he said, "but we lost 6-0", I was thinking "holy Jesus, they could murder us yet".'

LIAM TUOHY
'We went in at half-time two goals down but I told the lads that if we could pull one back we would really rattle them.'

Less than ten minutes into the second half, Bobby Gilbert made it 2-1. Five minutes later, Liam Tuohy, playing one of his finest games in a Rovers jersey, rounded a defender and slotted the ball into the back of the net to make it 2-2. The tie stood at 3-3 on aggregate but Rovers were now leading on the away goals rule with half an hour of play remaining. Very few Rovers supporters had made the trip to Germany, most were on the edge of their seats at home listening to Philip Greene's commentary on RTE.

FRANK WHELAN
'Philip Greene was commentating on RTE. At half-time it was 2-0 to Bayern and it looked over. Suddenly, they get it back to 2-2 and Philip Greene is saying, "if they hold onto this they will go through on the away goals rule". Everyone was so excited because Bayern were one of the top sides in the world!'

MICK SMYTH
'The team and Philip Greene had met a Warlock, a Gypsy of sorts, the day before and she'd predicted we'd lose. So, with a few minutes to go in the game, Greene in his radio commentary starts saying "the warlock got it wrong" and people at home were telling me after that they hadn't a clue what he was talking about.'

Coming to the end, Rovers were setting their stall out to defend. The Germans were throwing themselves at the Hoops but couldn't break through the defence. After 83 minutes, Liam Tuohy was caught offside in the Germans half. Beckenbaur surveyed the field for his options.

MICK SMYTH
'Beckenbauer takes the free kick but we had everything nice and tight at the back – Ronnie was with the centre-forward, Mulligan was with Muller and the two full backs were out wide. Beckenbauer floats it in and Mulligan leaves Muller and runs over beside Ronnie, "yer man gets up and knocks it to Muller who drops it with his left foot and I swear to God he hit it so fast that I hadn't a clue where it was. I literally heard a whistle going over my head and it was in. I reacted to the whistle but at that stage the ball had already come back out of the net. It was the hardest shot I've ever seen; from the time it left his boot I didn't see it. His thighs were like tree trunks.'

Gerd Muller – 'Der Bomber' – had rescued Bayern. The great Bayern Munich side of the 1960s had gone within seven minutes of being knocked out of the European Cup Winners Cup by eleven part-timers from Dublin.

LIAM TUOHY
'We were very disappointed to go out because we'd come so close. I still say that the Bayern Munich game was our biggest achievement in Europe. We were only part-time players and we were playing against some of the world's leading full-time professionals.'

MICK SMYTH

'It was still the best display by an Irish team in Europe. We were in the changing room getting ready to leave when we got a telegram from the Irish Ambassador saying that we'd done more for Irish sport than anyone else could have. On one hand we were delighted but on the other hand we were disappointed that we didn't beat them. Their goalkeeper, Sepp Maier, was a great fella. Before the game he asked me to swap jerseys with him when it was over. I used to wear an old black jersey of Billy Lord's, so I went down to him and he saw me taking it off he said "you keep, you keep" and just gave me his. I don't blame him.'

FRANK WHELAN

'It was getting so close to the end that we thought we'd done it. Everyone was so excited because Bayern were one of the top sides in the world! It was a real sickner when they scored again, it really would have gone down in history if we'd beaten them.'

Bayern Munich went on to establish their credentials by winning the European Cup Winners Cup that season, defeating Glasgow Rangers in the final.

'WE SORT OF TOOK IT FOR GRANTED'

Rovers were in the Cup Winners Cup for the following three seasons. In 1967 they faced a Cardiff side who were more than holding their own in the English top flight, but went out 3-1 on aggregate. The following year it was the turn of Randers Freja of Denmark to knock out the Hoops, again on a 3-1 aggregate scoreline. In 1969, in what would ultimately be Rovers last European adventure for a decade, FC Schalke of Germany ran out 4-2 aggregate winners in their clash with Rovers.

MICK LEECH

'Cardiff were a good side back then, they were no Liverpool but they were good. The following season we played Randers, that was a game we should have won easily. They got a late goal but I missed around six good chances. I could have had six goals, I could have broken the records for European competitions that night.'

MICK SMYTH

'When he played Randers Freja we were 1-0 down at half time and Tuohy took Mick Leech off, which was a real shock. Tommy Kinsella was taken down and Johnny [Fulham] scored from the free to make it 1-1. But Tommy was limping and complaining that a stone or something had hit him in the leg. Rasher was telling him to run it off and get on with it but Tommy couldn't go on and so he came off. Tuohy slagged him from a height but it turned out that Tommy had broken his leg just below the knee. I felt sorry for Tuohy because he was so apologetic to the lad.'

RONNIE NOLAN

'Because we were winning things every year we were always in the European Cup or the European Cup Winners Cup. We had some great games but we sort of took it for granted though - we expected to be in Europe every year.'

MICK LEECH

'We played Schalke, the German champions, and beat them in Dalymount. I don't know how the fans saw anything that night because I was on the pitch and the fog was so bad that

I couldn't see anything! It was incredible, if you were standing on the half way line you couldn't have seen both goals. How the game went ahead I don't know.'

MICK SMYTH
'When we played Shalke 04 the fog was so bad that I couldn't see anything outside the box. I heard a cheer and I asked one of the defenders what was going on. "Leechy just scored", he said. We got another goal and then I was just standing around the goal minding my own business when I got a shout – their winger was sprinting right at me, practically on top of me. He scored too but we won 2-1. We stayed in a kip of a roadside hotel on the return leg, bloody trucks going by all night. It was terrible.'

The club had featured in European competitions in ten out of the past twelve seasons but had only once managed one aggregate victory. However, as the club entered the bleak 1970s, Milltown wouldn't see another trophy for eight years. The glorious, if not very fruitful, European era of the club was over.

'I COULDN'T WAIT TO GET OUT OF THERE'

In 1977 Johnny Giles returned to his native Dublin to take over Shamrock Rovers. Giles vowed to make the glory days return to Milltown and stated his ambition to turn Rovers into a side capable of competing with the best in Europe. After winning the 1978 FAI Cup, he was given his first test when Apoel Nicosia of Cyprus came to town.

The Nicosia game was the first European game to be held in Milltown and the event was given the perfect start when Giles himself put Rovers in front. Stevie Lynex got a second to give Rovers a 2-0 win and it was Lynex who scored for Rovers in the away leg, securing a 3-0 aggregate win. Banik Ostrava of the Czechoslovakia proved too strong for Rovers in the second round, running out 6-1 aggregate winners.

Four years later, Rovers took apart Fram Reykjavik in the UEFA Cup, winning 3-0 and 4-0, which remains the biggest ever winning margin by an Irish club in Europe. However, yet again, it was an Eastern European side, this time Universitatea Craiova of Romania who ended Rovers European exploits. Under Communism, each football club was sponsored by a different arm of the state. In theory, the players were part-time footballers and worked full-time jobs for state bodies. However, the reality was that there were no such jobs. They were full-time professional footballers in all but name.

ROBBIE FOY
'We beat Nicosia home and away. In the away leg, the home fans were so outraged that they threw their seat cushions at the players. We played Banik Ostrava in the next round but they were in a different class. All those teams from Eastern Europe were unbelievable in those days. Tactically they were superb.'

PETER ECCLES
'Giles' style of play was probably more suited to European football. Over here, it was more about stopping teams play rather than two sides trying to play against each other. In Europe, teams would try and play against you instead of just stopping you, so we could show that we were better than them. In the League of Ireland, you had the top four sides and then the others would just try and stop you playing and hope to score one themselves.'

Harry Kenny and Kevin Brady in Cyprus.

JOHN BYRNE

'In fairness to Giles we did well when we got to Europe. We beat Apoel Nicosia home and away without conceding a goal. In '82 we played Fram Reykjavik and beat them 3-0 away and 4-0 at home, a scoreline which would be unthinkable now. We had Banik Ostrava of the then Czechoslovakia in '78 and they were just too good for us, too technical. Likewise, when we got Universitea Craiova in '82 they were just too good. We were unlucky to lose 3-0 over there, but 5-0 over two legs doesn't lie.'

ROBBIE GAFFNEY

'Beating Fram Reykjavik was a great achievement for a League of Ireland club. Celtic had only managed a draw in Reykjavik the year before. Universitea Craiova were one of these army clubs and they were full of professionals. This was Romania before the fall of the Berlin Wall, it was a weird place. I couldn't wait to get out of it, to be honest.'

ROBERT GOGGINS

'After we beat Reykjavik, we played Craoiva. That was a real eye-opener for me because they were so much fitter, so much faster. Rovers were chasing shadows all night.'

PETER ECCLES

'I played in the away leg [against Fram Reykjavik] but in the home game Michael Giles, Johnny's son, played at right-full. I was 18 and suddenly playing in the UEFA Cup, it was fantastic. I was used to playing in junior pitches around Dublin and suddenly I was being flown to Iceland to play Fram Reykjavik! We hammered them too.'

MICK SMYTH

'The food in Romania was diabolical, I was convinced it was all dog meat. I only heard one dog bark in the three days we were there, which was suspicious. I was playing for Athlone before I came back to Rovers and one of the directors there owned a jeans factory so we'd often get cheap jeans. When we went to Romania I didn't bring any money with me I just brought the jeans and sold them to the chamber maids in the hotel. We were sitting in the lounge and this lad goes up to Jim Beglin and says he wants to buy his clothes. Jim said he wasn't selling but I told him I had a few pairs of jeans. I offered them to him for 1000 of whatever their money was and he says, "I'll give you 600 and you can have that girl". She was a lovely looking bird but we settled on 800 and he kept the girl.

On another occasion, I went out with Alan Campbell, Liam Buckley and Jacko McDonagh to change some money. I had a bit more experience so the lads got me to do the bartering. We were offered a good rate and so we gave him over around £20. I was watching him like a hawk but he gave me a bundle of money and ran off. I opened it up and it was all newspapers wrapped up in one note. The lads never forgave me for that."

'YOU COULD CUT THE TENSION WITH A KNIFE'

Rovers were out of European competitions until 1984, when four straight league successes gave them another sustained spell of European football. The four European trips of this period produced three games which, although for very different reasons, were all completely surreal. The other fixture – against Honved Budapest in 1985 – was run-of-the-mill only because it afforded an Eastern European club – albeit captained by the inspirational Lajos Detari - the opportunity to humble Rovers 5-1.

A total of 69 people lost their lives as a result of the Northern Irish 'Troubles' in 1984. It was against this backdrop of violence that Shamrock Rovers were drawn against Linfield of Belfast in the European Cup. Linfield are traditionally a Protestant, unionist club and no one on the island of Ireland was under any illusion that the political situation in Northern Ireland would add extra spice to this European Cup tie. This was a fixture that, given the choice, everyone at the FAI, IFA and UEFA would have avoided.

Two weeks earlier, Glasgow Rangers had travelled to Dublin to play Bohemians in the UEFA Cup. Rangers supporters – both from Glasgow and the many loyalists who had travelled to the game from Belfast – set about causing an orgy of violence throughout Dublin before, during and after the game, which Bohs famously won 3-2. Having both Glasgow Rangers and Linfield travel to Dublin within the space of a month was a security nightmare for the Gardai as both games had the potential for serious violence.

JIMMY CONROY
'It [Linfield away] was very tense. A lot of us went up, even though the Kilcoynes had said that they didn't want us to go. We all went up in small groups and stayed on the Falls Road. None of us had ever been to Windsor Park before but on the way we saw a flute band marching along wearing Linfield scarves. So we got in behind them and marched to the ground, that's how we found it! Obviously, we weren't wearing colours. When we got to the ground they started looking for money off us for loyalist prisoners so we had to run in pretty quickly.'

The sides played out a 0-0 draw in front of a highly partisan and hostile crowd. For the supporters who did travel from Dublin, an uneventful game was probably the best result. When the sides met in Dublin Rovers were limited through injury and were forced to play Peter Eccles, a centre half, up front. Amid a record level of security, the Rovers players found it difficult to concentrate on the job in hand and drew the game 1-1, sending Linfield through on the away goals rule.

'Pat Byrne exchanges pennants prior to the European Cup meeting with Linfield in Windsor Park'.

PAT BYRNE
'We let ourselves down against Linfield. We simply didn't perform on the day. We got through the away leg, which we thought was the hard bit, but we came down here and there was so much tension. The atmosphere surrounding that game was the worst I've ever experienced. You could cut the tension with a knife. Our preparations were all wrong because we were all so tense, whereas the lads at Linfield were used to it. That said, the Linfield players were a smashing bunch of lads. As a club they treated us excellently and they joined us for a few pints after the game. But the atmosphere definitely affected us more than them.'

PETER ECCLES
'Jacko [McDonagh] took a shot and the keeper knocked it onto the bar but I managed to get to the rebound. It was a very special moment for me, but we were shockingly disappointed to lose that game. I had a chance in the second half but Liam O'Brien ran into the back of me and the chance was gone.'

MARTIN MOORE
'There police checkpoints all over the Milltown Road. Rovers never got going that day. We were well on top, we just couldn't score.'

NED ARMSTRONG

'A lot of people were very annoyed about losing to Linfield, but I don't think we deserved to win. They didn't play well in that particular match. They didn't play as well as usual.'

FRANK ALLEN

'The tension was unbelievable. I didn't like to see Linfield go through to the next round but sport has to be put in perspective. It is sport and I don't think people should get too hot-headed about it.'

DAVID BYRNE

'I was only 12 at the time so my mother was very nervous about letting me go to the game. My dad ended up taking a half-day from work in order to bring me. I'll always remember the noise of the Linfield fans coming down the Milltown Road surrounded by police. To a 12-year-old it was very frightening. I didn't understand the politics of it, I was just gutted not to beat them.'

PAT BRADY

'The Linfield game was probably the biggest disappointment of that era. I remember the Rovers fans were taunting the Linfield fans by singing "there's only one team in Ireland" at them. Then, of course, Rovers were knocked out and the Linfield fans started singing "there's only one team in Ireland", so they became temporary Republicans for the purposes of getting at the Rovers fans.'

'IT WAS A VERY UNIQUE GAME'

Two years later, in 1986, the draw for the European Cup could not have produced a tie in greater contrast to the Linfield game. When the names came out of the hat, Rovers were paired off against Glasgow Celtic. It was a dream fixture for both clubs. Against Linfield, the atmosphere had been one of hatred, bitterness and hostility; against Celtic it was like two brothers being reunited after years apart.

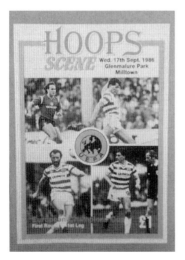

Programme v Celtic.

ROBERT GOGGINS
'I was at Milltown on the Tuesday and I overheard two of the Celtic players talking and one said to the other that it was a terrible shame to be playing football on that surface because it was so perfect.'

JOHN BYRNE
'We played Celtic in what would be the last ever European match in Milltown. Rovers were superb that night but just didn't get the breaks. Dermot Keely was player/manager at that time and when Rovers got a corner with 7 minutes to go he pushed everyone up and he stayed on the half way line. Keely was carrying an injury at the time and when the corner broke to Celtic he was completely skinned for pace: 1-0 Celtic. We lost because we went for it and there was a certain comfort in that. We had a very depleted side for the second leg; had our chances but we needed our full team.'

JIMMY CONROY
'The only black mark on the four in a row team was that they never performed in Europe. We used to play in Europe the same way as we'd play in the league, whereas we should have adapted to European competition. The Celtic game summed it up, we were going all out for the win and then they hit us on the break and beat us 1-0. As soon as that ball broke, I knew they'd beaten us.'

MARTIN MOORE
'There was some gobshite Celtic fan with a papal flag, I don't know what he was doing with it in Dublin. Rovers were brilliant though. The only problem on the night was that Mick Byrne was trying to score a flashy goal for television. If he'd have just put them away we would have won two or three nil.'

PETER ECCLES
'We should have beaten them in Milltown. We had a corner with two minutes to go and Mick Neville took a short corner but Murdo McCloud broke away and scored. It was very disappointing to lose that, but I suppose we were all Celtic fans anyway.'

PAT BYRNE
'Losing to Celtic 1-0 in Milltown was my biggest disappointment in football. We were so dejected in the dressing room that no one could even speak. I remember walking down the Milltown Road on my own and just being so disappointed. We should have won that game easily and put ourselves in a very strong position going to Parkhead. We played them off the park in front of 18,000 people but it just didn't happen.'

Having been highly unfortunate to lose the home leg to a late goal, Rovers travelled to Parkhead for the second leg. However, Celtic proved too strong and ran out comfortable 2-0 winners.

PAT BYRNE
'I got a knock in the Celtic game at Milltown and I shouldn't have played the next league game but I did so I ended up missing the game in Parkhead. I remember sitting in the directors box at half-time and looking around the stadium. It was unbelievable, the entire stadium in green and white and all the supporters congratulating each other, exchanging scarves. I'd say that 99% of Rovers fans support Celtic too; you had the

Dermot Keely v Celtic.

Rovers fans singing We love you Celtic and the Celtic fans singing We love you Rovers. It was unbelievable. It was a very unique game.'

PETER ECCLES
'It was a great experience to play in Parkhead. We came onto the pitch and we went over to the old Jungle [Celtic's terrace] and the place went crazy. Murdo McCloud blessed himself in front of the Jungle and it went beserk. One of the Celtic lads told me to do it, so I blessed myself in front of the Jungle and the place erupted.'

MICK BYRNE
'A disappointing thing about the game in Parkhead was that we wore yellow jerseys and blue shorts. Louis must have got them on the cheap because they were so horrible that the Celtic players didn't want to swap jerseys. They were the worst jerseys in Europe.'

ROBBIE FOY
'We lost the game 2-0, Moe Johnston scored both goals. A lot of Rovers fans went to the Jungle, which I thought was ridiculous. I'm Rovers first, last and always.'

MARTIN MOORE
'The Celtic fans all applauded the Rovers fans when we were coming in on the buses and I remember one of the lads was leaning out the window giving them the fingers and going,

"You won't be applauding us if we beat you, ye bastards!" I know a lot of Rovers fans follow Celtic, but they almost seemed proud to lose. As far as I'm concerned, if they're playing Rovers, they're the enemy. End of the day, they beat us 2-0 and I wasn't happy. To take an extreme example, we were playing Man Utd in the '80s in a friendly and one Rovers fan – he's not right in the head – pulled a hatchet and he was milling Rovers fans. He kicked me around outside the ground and as he was kicking me he said, "Sorry about this Martin, but I'm up for United tonight!"'

If the majority of Rovers fans didn't seem too bothered that Celtic had progressed at their expense, Rovers next European outing saw the overwhelming majority of their support actually cheer for the opposition. Coming off the back of the Celtic defeat, Rovers managed to win the league for the fourth time in a row. However, this achievement was soon dashed by the news that Glenmalure Park was to be sold. By the time of the next European game, against Omonia Nicosia of Cyprus, Rovers were playing in Tolka Park and the club was in a state of civil war. The supporters had made history by withdrawing their support en masse from the club and boycotting all home games in a bid to starve the chairman, Louis Kilcoyne, out. Even when competing in Europe, the supporters stayed outside. Rovers lost the home leg 1-0 and then earned a 0-0 draw in Cyprus, crashing out of the tournament on the away goals rule. A total of 2,489 people paid into Tolka Park for the home leg, although most of these were interested neutrals as the vast majority of Rovers' supporters stayed away. The attendance was the smallest crowd to ever witness a Rovers European game. Despite not attending the game in Tolka Park, a small group of supporters did make the trip to Cyprus for the away leg.

MARTIN KEATING
'We went over to Cyprus and stayed in a holiday resort. Myself and another lad got t-shirts printed up saying "Keep Rovers At Milltown". We went to the match and managed to get into the changing room at half time. Kilcoyne called security and threw us out, but we made our

KRAM members in Cyprus.

point. The players couldn't believe it, I think it probably changed a lot of the players attitudes to what was going on. I think they knew then that we were right. There were only around 12 of us on the trip but for the whole match we just sang "Louis, Louis, Louis, Out, Out, Out". The strange thing was that we'd travelled all that way and we actually wanted Rovers to lose. I was delighted when they were beaten. The whole idea of the boycott was to starve Louis out of the club and if we'd won the game it would have meant more income for him.'

'WE WEREN'T HAPPY'

Having won the league in 1994, the majority of the team were sold the following summer, leaving the club with a depleted squad to take on Gornik Zabrze. It was to be one of the biggest humiliations in the club's history.

TERRY EVISTON
'It is best forgotten. We went on tour to America pre-season and it was quite gruelling. We came back to Ireland shattered and a lot of the players put the Gornik result down to that tour.'

DAVID BYRNE
'I was on holiday in Gran Canaria when Rovers went to Poland. I was away with two Bohs fans and a Shels fan and I was dying to get the result of the game so I rang home from this dodgy phone on the beach. It was a really bad line and I couldn't make out what he was saying. All the lads were asking me what the score was and I said "I think he said it was 1-0 to Zabrze". I was thinking, "Jesus, that's alright, we'll be in with a shot in the return leg". Then, all of a sudden, the line cleared and he said "7-0". All my mates heard it perfectly and they fell about laughing. My heart sank.'

RICHIE PHILPOTT
'A few of us headed over to Poland for the week and that was some experience. We got a complete hiding in the match though. Seven-nil. I couldn't wait to get out of the ground. Their fans got so bored at one stage that they started fighting amongst themselves.'

JOHN BYRNE
'My money was quite tight at the time so when they made the draw I decided to keep my money for the next round. I thought we could easily do Gornik Zabzre, which shows you how optimistic football fans can be. Seven bloody nil.'

JIMMY CONROY
'They had this massive scoreboard in the ground, but six different players scored against us and the big fear was that if they got another goal they wouldn't be able to fit it all on the board. It was a great trip but it did leave a bad taste. We weren't happy with Ray Treacy [manager] at all.'

ROBBIE FOY
'The minute the team came onto the pitch in Poland you knew it wasn't going to be a good night. A few of the players looked overweight and it all went wrong. We took a nine hour bus ride to get there. That Gornik game changed the relationship between the fans and the management for the worse.'

It was to be another four years before Rovers got the chance to put their European nightmare to rest. In 1998 they were drawn against Altay Spor of Turkey in the Inter-Toto Cup.

FERGUS DESMOND

'The fact that the game was on in the middle of the World Cup no doubt put some people off the idea of travelling; the media at home all but ignored the game. We put up a poster in one of the Irish bars advertising the game Sunday hoping that a few people would come along. Of course, come Sunday not one Irish holidaymaker turns up, although plenty were interested in the result after. Typical Irish so-called football fans. When it came to the game, a lot of Rovers fans got taxis to the wrong stadium and by the time they reached the right one Rovers were 1-0 up. We were given tea and biscuits at half-time!'

Rovers lost the away leg 3-1 but defeated the Turks by the same scoreline in Dublin, sending the game into extra-time.

JOHN DORNEY

'The World Cup semi-final between France and Paraguay was on the same day as the Altay Spor fixture so the neutrals stayed away. We went in at half-time at 1-1 and were swamping the Altay goal in the second half. With twenty minutes to go, Tony Cousins belts in a goal for Rovers. The Hoops fans explode. Altay are visibly rattled. One of their players, abused taking a throw-in, loses his head and starts ranting at the crowd. Some Hoops responded with cries of "Greece, Greece!" With Marc Kenny running the game, Rovers piled on the pressure. Needing one more goal to draw level on aggregate, Rovers get a corner in the last minute and Paul Whelan blasts it into the net. Pandemonium breaks out. Sadly, in extra time it all went downhill when Marc Kenny took a swing at an Altay player and got sent off. Exhausted and without their playmaker, Rovers conceded a sloppy goal. The Hoops won 3-2 but lost 5-4 on aggregate. For the record, France had more luck. They were also missing their playmaker – Zidane - through suspension, they also got a late goal from a centre half – Laurent Blanc - but they won the World Cup. Jammy bastards.'

'WE WERE AS ONE'

Four years later, Djurgardens IF of Sweden knocked Rovers out. The following season, however, saw Rovers progress to the second round for the first time since 1982. Rovers were drawn against Odra Wodzislaw and many fans feared a second Polish drubbing. Rovers won 2-1 in Poland and 1-0 in Dublin before being knocked out by Slovan Liberec of the Czech Republic.

DAVID BYRNE

'For all the titles we won when I started going to see games, my most amazing experience was being in Poland for the Odra match. It really bonds the fans. We didn't expect to get anything out of the game but we roared them on from the start. Then they got a goal with twenty minutes to go and we thought it was going to be the same old story. But Stephen Grant got the equaliser and a few minutes later Tony Grant got knocked the second in. It was the only time that I have seen a goal in the flesh when it went in slow motion. I went to jump on this big white fence in front of us but I slipped and my head went down between two spikes and I thought I'd impaled myself. But I got on the fence and I'll never forget that feeling. An unbelievable feeling of emotion. People were hugging each other and crying with joy.'

JOHN BYRNE

'Apart from the performance and the result that night, when the players came back onto the pitch after the game it was unreal. The bond between player and fan was incredible. We were as one.'

FERGUS MCCORMACK

'We arrived in Bratislav and these local skinheads came up to us and said, "Are you the Shamrock Rovers Ultras". We said yes and they brought one of the lads up to their house and made him tea, showed him Ultras videos, gave him scarves. He was waiting for some lad to jump out and batter him but they were so friendly because they'd seen our internet site and they had respect for us.'

THOMAS FREYNE

'Our fans are absolute loopers, it's that simple. We took 150 fans to some backwater in the Czech Republic the size of Athlone, it was just unbelievable. When we played Odra in Poland the Rovers fans made the front pages of the Polish papers and got a special mention from the UEFA representative at the game.'

JOHN DORNEY

'Being in Europe gives a club a chance to compete against continental sides. For League of Ireland fans, winning in Europe is more than just winning, it is a vindication for the entire league. It's showing everyone who slags us off that we can play.'

Rovers have played twenty-four different sides from nineteen different countries in European competitions. Out of a total of forty-eight games in Europe, the club has managed just nine victories and eight draws, ending up on the losing side thirty one times. Defeat is a regular occurrence; victory, when it does come, is greeted with euphoria. Victory against Odra was a special moment for anyone who witnessed it. At the end of that season, the Rovers team was broken up for financial reasons. During the last game, against Shelbourne in Tolka Park, the Rovers supporters, knowing that it was to be the final time they would see that team perform together, displayed a simple banner: "Odra 1 Rovers 2 – We thank you".

CHAPTER 8

THE FOUR IN A ROW
(1983–1988)

To many people the 1980s is a decade to forget. Wild haircuts, extravagant clothes and cringe-inducing music is the image the decade usually conjures up. However, behind the surface lay much deeper problems: a stagnant economy, widespread unemployment and mass emigration defined the Irish 1980s experience. Yet to the Rovers supporter, the 1980s will also conjure up images of success beyond their wildest dreams. It was a decade in which the club recovered from a spell of virtually uninterrupted mediocrity to reclaim the title of 'kings of Irish football'; it was a decade in which Shamrock Rovers achieved a level of dominance never before seen in the domestic game, winning four leagues and three cups in a row.

Despite the success and glory, there remains a darker side to the 1980s. It was also a decade which sowed the seeds of the virtual destruction of Rovers as a force within Irish football. A decade which began poorly, only to reach an almighty crescendo, before crashing to earth in the most spectacularly devastating fashion. The 1980s ensured the immortalisation of Shamrock Rovers in the modern era, but also brought the club to the verge of complete extinction. It all began with the appointment of Derryman Jim McLaughlin as manager of the club.

'He had the Midas touch everywhere he went'

When John Giles threw in the towel on his Rovers experiment in February 1983, the club initially turned to Noel Campbell, an eleven-times capped Irish international who had played with St. Patrick's Athletic and Fortuna Cologne, to guide the club. However, whilst Campbell finished the 1982/83 season off, leading the club to a sixth place finish, the association between club and manager ended suddenly that summer when Jim McLaughlin agreed to take over the reigns.

McLaughlin had made his name as manager of Dundalk, completely transforming the fortunes of the Louth outfit. Dundalk had not finished outside the top two in four seasons and Louis Kilcoyne hired him to perform a similar miracle at Rovers. Having pumped money into the club during the disappointing Giles era, Kilcoyne decided to give it another

Alan Campbell.

Liam Buckley.

go and made money available to McLaughlin to buy the players he thought he needed. The bank balance was boosted significantly by the sale of Jim Beglin to Liverpool.

McLaughlin responded to the circumstances and either sold or let go almost the entire squad he had inherited from Giles, retaining the services of Peter Eccles, Harry Kenny, Liam Buckley and Alan Campbell. In their place he brought in Jody Byrne and Noel King from Dundalk; Mick Neville from Drogheda; Terry Eviston, Kevin Brady and Liam O'Brien from Bohemians, Anto Whelan from Manchester United; and Neville Steedman from Thurles.

In order to make way for these signings, most of the Giles squad were shown the door. The most controversial departure from Milltown was that of Alan O'Neill, a fans' favourite who had been with the club for a decade.

Alan O'Neill

'I have always maintained that both Jim and myself misread the situation. From a personal point of view, I had to re-assess where I was going. I had been with Rovers for ten years and maybe I had become too comfortable at the club and maybe Jim sensed that. Considering all he won, I don't think you can say he made a mistake. I can laugh and joke with Jim about it now. I remember just after he left Rovers, having won three leagues and two cups[1], we were heading away for a game with the Olympic squad and he stopped me and said, "I'm after winning three leagues and two cups and the first question Philip Greene asks me is why did I let Alan O'Neill go?"'

John Byrne

'The fans thought that Campbell was treated quite badly, but they brought Jim McLoughlin in and suddenly the dancing girls were on, as they say. It just clicked. He did a big clean out, the only player that he shouldn't have gotten rid of was Alan O'Neill. But he basically bought a national league eleven. He brought in the six or seven players we needed to totally dominate the league.'

Robbie Foy

'The first thing Jim McLaughlin did when he came along was got rid of two Rovers legends, Alan O'Neill and Noel Synnott. We were all very upset over that.'

Jimmy Conroy

'I thought Campbell did alright but they got rid of him in much the same way they'd done with Sean Thomas when Giles came in. McLaughlin became available and they had to take him. The fans had no problem with that, we knew McLaughlin was the best manager in the country.'

Jack Wilson

'McLaughlin had the money available and he handpicked the players he wanted. They offered more money than the other clubs and so they attracted the best players.'

Robert Goggins

'I was quite surprised when the club got rid of Campbell. I was just an ordinary fan on the terrace so it came as a surprise to me. Campbell subsequently took the club to the High Court for unfair dismissal, which he won, so it obviously came as a surprise to him too. There was a great air of excitement when McLaughlin came in because he brought in so many new signings. People had good expectations, it was like the Giles era starting all over again. McLaughlin was very well respected and had a great reputation, he had revitalised

Dundalk and turned them into the team to beat. So now he's come to Rovers and the club are spending big money on the team, so there were expectations.'

MICK SMYTH

'I re-signed for Rovers shortly before Giles left but I decided to leave before McLaughlin had the chance to get rid of me. I would have stayed if Campbell had stayed on. He was the only qualified Bundesliga coach in Ireland and he had great ideas. His mistake was that he didn't change things, he left things more or less the same as they were under Giles. I liked Gilesy, I liked Campbell but I didn't like Jim. No one who spoke their mind got on with Jim.'

PAT BRADY

'I started going regularly in 1981. It was a good time to start because you saw the bad times, we got a few hammerings in those years, and then that led into the golden period. McLaughlin transformed things. He made a lot of changes, but he had the Midas touch everywhere he went. He was just a great manager. We got big crowds when he first took over, I remember there being 8-10,000 at a game against Athlone. And there were no prawn sandwich fans at Milltown, that's for sure.'

MARTIN MOORE

'McLaughlin is without a doubt the best manager I've ever seen. He's the absolute master of the part time game. I remember when he was manager of Dundalk they went away to face Celtic in Parkhead, losing 3-2. I was working in a warehouse at the time and there was a delivery the next morning. And who was driving the delivery van only Jim McLaughlin! Straight up for work the next day, that was Jim McLaughlin.'

ROBERT GOGGINS

'McLaughlin was given money to spend but he spent that money very wisely and the players had enormous respect for him. You have to speculate to accumulate. People were surprised that the Kilcoynes were putting so much into the team, but it was a business decision.'

PETER ECCLES

'McLaughlin had a great air around him. His record stands for itself. He came in and basically got rid of everyone except myself and Harry Kenny. I always had confidence in my own ability so I was never that worried. We went up to play Ards in a pre-season game and I remember watching that game and thinking, "Jesus, this is a special team".'

'THE MORE WE PLAYED, THE BETTER WE LOOKED'

The Rovers side that took to the field on the opening day of the 1983/84 season bore little resemblance to the side that had competed in the league the previous season. Having beaten Drogheda 2-0 in that first match, there was an air of confidence around the club. By Christmas, Rovers were flying high and suddenly it appeared that the club could be on the verge of their first league title since 1964.

Liam Buckley and Alan Campbell were scoring goals for fun, whilst a midfield orchestrated by Pat Byrne and Noel King was proving match-winning. As the mid-way point in the season arrived, McLaughlin made one final addition to his side: Dermot Keely. The uncompromising centre-back proved to be the final card in 'McLaughlin's Aces'.

Pat Byrne with 1984
league title.

ROBERT GOGGINS
'I hadn't set my heart on winning anything that season, I was just thinking "let's get to the other side of Christmas and see how we get on". But the more we played, the better we looked. We took everyone by surprise that first year, no one thought it would happen so quickly. Rovers were a class above the rest.'

JIMMY CONROY
'We started off that season playing great stuff but were beaten 3-1 up at Finn Harps in what was, ironically, one of our best performances. Then he signed Keely, which really proved to be the final piece in the jigsaw. All great football teams need to be tough and Keely came in and he meant business. A hard player, he'd run through a brick wall. We never would have had that level of success without Dermot Keely.'

MICHAEL KEARNS
'McLaughlin came in and turned the club around. The difference between himself and Giles was that McLaughlin knew the domestic game inside out.'

JOHN BYRNE
'People say McLoughlin was a chequebook manager who just bought the league title but he was great at getting inside players' heads. When McLaughlin came in, Alan Campbell

had no confidence at all and was really struggling. Suddenly, McLoughlin comes in and Campbell becomes brilliant again, winning the Player of the Year award in '84. McLoughlin made the speech before Campbell got the award and I remember him saying, "When I came here Alan Campbell had no confidence but I got into his head". Maybe it was just his way of saying that it was only because of him that Alan Campbell was brilliant, but the way he talked about getting inside the mind of a player and turning him around was very impressive. He knew Campbell was brilliant but just needed the confidence. Campbell went on to play top-level football in Europe.'

PAT BYRNE
'It's not fair to just say that McLaughlin handpicked his players. There were some players at Rovers – John Coady and Alan Campbell being two – who were on their way out because they hadn't gotten into the team. Campbell hadn't featured at all but he played pre-season and struck up a good relationship with Liam Buckley and they just started scoring goals. McLaughlin was able to get the best out of them and they both had very successful careers.'

RICHIE PHILPOTT
'When McLaughlin took over there wasn't any sense that we were on the verge of anything big. He brought in a lot of players and moulded the team, and suddenly we were winning matches left, right and centre and playing great football too. Seven players from that team – Pat Byrne, Kevin Brady, Terry Eviston, Anto Whelan, Neville Steedman, Liam O'Brien and Jacko McDonagh – all played for Bohs at some stage, which was really funny because they never won anything with them.'

JOHN BYRNE
'My first child was born in 1986. Rovers won 2-1 in Cork that day, but I was stuck in hospital! After Stephen was born, I rang up one of my mates and he says, "What's it like being a father?" "Well", I says, "sort of like winning the league in '84". He understood immediately.'

Rovers clinched the title on 1 April 1984 when a 3-1 defeat of Shelbourne and were presented with the trophy fourteen days later when they faced Limerick in Milltown. Billy Lord, who had served as club trainer and physio since the 1940s, led the sides onto the pitch that day, as Rovers ended their twenty year title famine. Lord was approaching his ninety-fourth birthday and it was fitting that he got to see the club win the title one last time before his death in 1985.

   Lord was known as one of the characters of the Irish game and served Rovers for over forty years. A chain-smoker, Lord would smoke Woodbines whilst rubbing the players down prior to games, with many players recalling that ash from the cigarettes would inevitably get rubbed in on top of the oil. One player interviewed for this book recalls falling to the ground injured during a game, only for Billy Lord to run onto the pitch with his physio bag to help. By the time Lord had made it to the player, the pain had subsided but the player was told to fake the injury for a minute: 'I'm after running all the way out here, now you'll stay down until I get my breath back', Lord told him.

'WE'LL WIN THE DOUBLE NEXT YEAR'

The league title won for the first time in twenty years, Rovers made it to the final of the FAI Cup, where they faced UCD. The University side had only been admitted into the League of Ireland five years previously and, although they had just finished sixth in the league – their best finish yet – they were considered massive underdogs.

For two UCD players – Alan O'Neill and Robbie Gaffney – the tie pitted them against their former club. Both O'Neill and Gaffney grew up as Rovers fans but had both been victims of McLaughlin's purge.

ALAN O'NEILL

'I signed for UCD for one reason and one reason only – Dermot Keely. However, half-way into the season, Dermot leaves for Rovers, whom we subsequently met in the cup final later that season. I got such a great reception from the Rovers crowd that night. When I was at Rovers each player had their own chant. As we were warming up, this chant goes up from the Rovers fans, which I presumed was for Alan Campbell but it was actually for me. It meant an awful lot. It meant that the ten years I had spent with Rovers meant something to the fans too.'

ROBBIE GAFFNEY

'Once you've played for Shamrock Rovers, the only way your career can go is down. Myself and Alan O'Neill went to UCD and I used to often sit there and think, "What have I done?" It was always strange playing against Rovers, it was a fixture you'd dread, to be honest, because both myself and Alan were Rovers men.'

JOHN BYRNE

'I got married shortly after the '84 cup final. I remember on the day of the game I was in the Wexford Inn and I realised I'd left my ticket at home. I called my soon-to-be wife and asked her to bring it into me. I was waiting outside for her with a hell of a lot of drinking left to do, I'm sure my father-in-law was very impressed: "Thanks for the ticket, I'm off to the pub, see you whenever'."

A disappointing crowd of just 8,000 turned up to Dalymount Park to witness the two clubs battle it out. The game ended in a 0-0 draw and so a replay was held in Tolka Park one week later. This time, UCD managed to pull off a huge shock, Ken O'Doherty getting the winning goal deep into injury time to give the university a 2-1 win. Rovers were stunned.

ROBBIE GAFFNEY

'Beating Rovers in the cup final in '84 was a strange feeling because you want to do well for your new club – you have to give it your best - but you don't want to do anything that might damage Rovers. I always felt sort of bad about winning the cup that year because it deprived Rovers of four cups in a row.'

RICHIE PHILPOTT

'The '84 Cup Final against UCD was an absolute sickner. We were convinced we were going to win it but Rovers just froze. Then in the replay I remember Buckley missing an absolute sitter and we went on to lose. It was one of the biggest disappointments I've ever had. But then we won Cup the next three years so that helped make up for it.'

MARTIN MOORE

'We were all wearing suits into Tolka Park because it was the Rovers Player of the Year afterwards in the Gresham that night. It was strange: we'd just won the league but everyone was down in the dumps because the double was gone. Jim McLaughlin made a speech,

"We're going to win the lot next season" and he was carried off on people's shoulders. And the next three seasons we won the double!'

JOHN BYRNE
'We lost the cup when UCD scored a very dodgy goal around three years into injury time. There was the Player of the Year awards that night in the Gresham and I remember Noel King standing at the bar saying, "Fuck it, we'll win the double next year". There was just this great air of confidence. If you believe you can do something, you'll do it; any doubts and you won't.'

'ROVERS WAS LIKE A FAMILY'

McLaughlin and King were correct: Rovers won the double for the next three seasons. Following the league success of '84, the clubs' two star strikers, Alan Campbell and Liam Buckley, were transferred to Santander of Spain and Waregem of Belgium respectively. Supporters feared that the departure of the free-scoring forwards might spell the end of the clubs' success. However, McLaughlin signed Mick Byrne from Shelbourne and lured Noel Larkin out of retirement and the new front-pair proved just as successful as their predecessors.

MICK BYRNE
'Alan Campbell was leaving and it was in the papers that I was one of the possibilities that McLaughlin was considering. I was very flattered to even have my name linked with Shamrock Rovers. I was playing with Shels and they had about four good players whereas Shamrock Rovers had fourteen good players. I had to sign before a certain date if I was going to play in Europe. It was the last day and I still hadn't even spoken to Jim McLaughlin yet. I was in the Marble Arch pub in Drimnagh and a friend of mine was actually talking to me about the speculation that I was going to Rovers. Next minute, Jimmy Shields [club secretary] comes in and taps me on the shoulder and says "Jim wants to see you in the car". I couldn't believe it. It was around ten o'clock and I had around six pints down me. I jumped in Jim's car and very little was talked about money, the only question I had was "Where's the pen?" It was a massive club, a club who wanted to win everything.'

Byrne and Larkin fitted into the formula for success. Players of the era recall that it was the professional attitude of the club that brought such success. It is recalled that even the groundsman wore a suit to work every day, such was the professional image of the club. McLaughlin fostered a family atmosphere amongst the players and forged a close-knit unit.

MICK BYRNE
'Rovers was like a family. There were no cliques because the older players – Pat Byrne, Kinger, Dermot Keely – just wouldn't allow it. If one player went for a drink, we all went for a drink; if one player was going for food, we all went for food. It was very tight knit. We'd often sit around for an hour after training just chatting, which doesn't tend to happen with players these days. In the time I was there we won three leagues and three cups and it was mostly with the same group of players. You knew going out on that pitch that if you didn't perform to the best of your ability then you wouldn't get back in the team. We set very high standards for ourselves and that's why McLaughlin had it so easy in one respect because he would often pick the same eleven players for ten weeks in a row without having to change it. As a manager, it's a great position to be in.'

Mick Byrne.

PAT BYRNE

'I always look at teams in terms of pairing. It's all about having players that complement each other. At centre half we had either Jacko McDonagh or Peter Eccles alongside Dermot Keely, so we had one who could play and one who was quick; we had John Coady and Kevin Brady on the left hand side, both of whom could inter-change with each other, likewise with Harry Kenny and Neville Steedman on the right. In the middle, there was Noel King and myself, Noel could kick people but of course I never kicked anyone! Up front there was Campbell and Buckley in the first year and then Mick Byrne and Noel Larkin after that. Those pairings were as close off the field as they were on the field. Off the field is a huge aspect.'

LIAM BUCKLEY

'We [Buckley and Campbell] scored our fair share of goals over the few years we were there together. I was particularly good in the air and he was particularly quick, so we complemented each other, which is so important for a team. In Ireland there were – and still are – some great individual talents but I transferred to Belgium and it was noticeable that players there are better at complementing each other than Irish players are.'

LIAM O'BRIEN

'It was a great team. They were great individual players first and foremost but there is not point in having great individuals if they don't play well together. Nothing is handed to you in football, you have to work for everything. We worked very hard but we did have some great players and we gelled perfectly.'

PAT BYRNE

'We earned little or nothing through football but money never came into the equation. We loved the game and we wanted to play. Our whole week was ruined if we lost. It rarely ever happened, but losing was a nightmare. On one occasion, a player had gone to a wedding the night before a match and indulged in a few pints. It was obvious looking at him the next day that he had been drinking. We got away with the result but we had a team meeting on the bus on the way home and he was told in no uncertain terms that if he ever did that again he would never play for Rovers again. He had jeopardised our chances of winning a game by suiting himself and that simply wasn't going to happen ever again.'

PETER ECCLES

'He [McLaughlin] had myself and Jacko playing in the centre and it was going well but then one day I hear that he's signed Dermot Keely. Jacko and Dermot became the first choice but I'd regularly play. Keely was older than myself and Jacko so I'd learn a lot off him. When I played with Jacko, I'd look after the right side, he'd look after the left, but Dermot would play as a sweeper so I'd play as an out-and-out centre half. Keely was the best partner I ever had. He wouldn't shut up, that was his whole game. He couldn't play football but he could organise like no one else. Myself, Jacko and Dermot had a great relationship and that really went throughout the entire team. We all socialised together and we played as a team. Team spirit is one of the key ingredients. We still all meet up the odd time and reminisce.'

PAT BYRNE

Dermot [Keely] kicked a tractor in training one day because he didn't see it, although I'm sure the tractor came off worse. He wasn't a good 5-a-side player and because the standards were so high he wouldn't play in the games. We all had our jobs in the team, Dermot could run and he could organise but he couldn't pass water. On one occasion the ball fell to him in a match against Finn Harps and he whacked it up field, it could have gone anywhere but it fell right to John Coady's feet. Dermot goes to me, "See that? How's that for a fuckin' pass?" On another occasion, he had the ball and there was no one around him at all. He kicks it and falls to the ground – he'd kicked the ground first and broken his ankle! That sums up Dermot: tried to kick a ball and broke his ankle.'

MICK BYRNE

'The standard in the 5-a-sides was so high. I'd say most of the injuries to players over the years were caused in 5-a-sides because they were taken so seriously. I walloped John Coady in the back in training once and he was out for eight games. We trained as we played, there was no messing around.'

'THE OTHER TEAMS DIDN'T HAVE A CHANCE'

Although some players left the club and others joined, the playing personnel remained much the same throughout the Four in a Row. Jody Byrne was the goalkeeper; the defence was comprised of any combination of John Coady, Kevin Brady, Dermot Keely, Peter Eccles, Harry Kenny and Jacko McDonagh; Pat Byrne and Noel King were stalwarts in the centre of midfield, with Neville Steedman, Liam O'Brien, Paul Doolin and Mick Neville competing for the positions on the wings; whilst Liam Buckley and Alan Campbell made up the original striking partnership, only to be replaced by Mick Byrne and Noel Larkin. It is a group of players which supporters will always remember as the squad which delivered four league titles and three FAI Cups to Shamrock Rovers between 1984 and 1987.

John Coady with the cup on
his head.

JACK WILSON
'The side of the '80s was the best side I ever saw, even better than the '50s or '60s sides. You knew they were going to win. Players like Mick Neville and Pat Byrne were amongst the best I've ever seen. Mick Neville couldn't make a mistake even if he tried.'

JOHN BRYNE
'Bringing Pat Byrne back to Ireland was a fantastic coup because he was a current international. Only for Liam Brady he would have got 50 caps. He was far too good for our league. Even during the first of the Four in a Row seasons, there was something missing so McLaughlin brought in Keely and that was the final link in the chain. Suddenly, Rovers became invincible in the back. Couple that with a midfield led by Pat Byrne - who was our Dartanion - and Campbell and Buckley up front. The other teams didn't have a chance.'

FERGUS McCORMACK
'What summed Pat Byrne up was his pass to Noel Larkin in the '87 cup final. Sublime. No one in the league has come close to Byrne. Even when he played at Leicester and Hearts, he was a fans' favourite at both those clubs. He was just sheer class. Byrne was definitely the best player, but John Coady was my favourite. He was a Hoop through and through. He looked a bit lazy, like he didn't really give a bollox, but then he'd just score a goal out of nowhere. He never got tap-ins either. Mick Byrne was famous for his tap-ins, but Coady always got the spectacular goals. And every time he scored, he'd be straight over to the fans with his fist clenched.'

135

Pat Byrne with 1984 league title.

ROBBIE FOY
'John Coady was great. When he scored at Dalymount he nearly did whole lap of the pitch. He was a real Rovers man – a fan on the pitch.'

MICHAEL KEARNS
'Campbell and Buckley were superb. Campbell was a poacher and Buckley was excellent in the air. But, for me, Larkin and Byrne were even better. Noel Larkin would stick his head in a mincer if he thought there was a goal for Rovers in it. He was the best culchie to ever play for the club. We didn't think that Noel King was contributing too much at one stage. The fans were getting on his back a bit. He went out injured and suddenly we noticed what Kinger was doing. Without him, Pat Byrne wasn't receiving the ball as much.'

RICHIE PHILPOTT
'My all time favourite Hoop was Liam Buckley. He was the best player in the air that Rovers have ever had. I remember I was at a Rovers – Bohs match in Dalymount once and I was just walking in past a load of Bohs fans when Buckley scored after around 30 seconds. We actually went on to lose the game but it was great giving the Bohs fans loads as I walked in.'

DAVID BYRNE
'Pat Byrne and Mick Neville won us the last Bohs game a Milltown. It was 3-2 and it was probably my favourite memory of Milltown. We were 2-1 down with around ten minutes to go and we got two unbelievable free kicks to win it. Byrne got an equaliser direct from a free kick and then a few minutes later we got another free kick from the same area. This time Byrne laid it off to Neville who scored an absolute screamer. It was pandemonium on the terraces. I remember my uncle falling to his knees, eyes to heaven. I was only a kid and it was the first time that I realised that I hated Bohs and I really wanted to win.'

NED ARMSTRONG

'THAT TEAM PRODUCED LIAM BUCKLEY, TERRY EVISTON, NOEL KING, PAT BYRNE, DERMOT KEELY AND MICK BYRNE, ALL SIX OF WHOM WENT ON TO BE FUTURE MANAGERS OF THE CLUB! THEY WERE A CLEVER TEAM. TAKE PAT BYRNE FOR INSTANCE, HE WAS A VERY TECHNICAL PLAYER, A COMMANDING PLAYER. WHEN HE GOT THE BALL HE DIDN'T LOSE IT VERY EASILY, BUT HE ALSO HAD VERY GOOD PLAYERS ALONGSIDE HIM. THEY WERE NEARLY HOUSEHOLD NAMES. PETER ECCLES, PAT BYRNE, LIAM O'BRIEN, LIAM BUCKLEY, JACKO MacDONAGH – THESE WERE ALL FULL INTERNATIONAL PLAYERS.'

ROBERT GOGGINS

'Pat Byrne was the best player I've ever seen at Rovers, no doubt about that. My God, did he know how to nag a referee. He never stopped, the refs used to laugh at him.'

JIMMY CONROY

'Jody Byrne was an amazing signing. Think of all the big games over those four years and can anyone tell me one howler Jody Byrne made in any of them? He didn't let in a goal in three cup finals.'

FRANK ALLEN

'I played with Pat Byrne, Kevin Moran and Gerry Reilly on the Drimnagh Castle school team and even then they stood out. Pat was a year younger than me but he was still on the team. I would put Byrne in the same category as Giles and Brady when it comes to Irish midfielders. Such a cultured footballer.'

JOHN BYRNE

'I remember one day Pat Byrne walked into the place I worked and I couldn't believe it. I couldn't believe that the Skipper had just walked in, I jumped out of my seat and I just started pointing at him saying, "That's Pat Byrne. My God, that's Pat Byrne".'

DAVID BYRNE

'The first player I really noticed was Jacko McDonagh. He had a Spandau Ballet haircut and I remember all the hard lads in school had the same style - he looked like my idea of a footballer.'

PAT BRADY

'Pat Byrne was undoubtedly the best League of Ireland player I ever saw, an absolutely superb player. Kevin Brady, in my mind, was one of the best defenders never to have left the League of Ireland. Dermot Keely was famous for shouting at his teammates. He would always shout for them to "bite", meaning to tackle, although in Dermot's case you always felt he might have meant a bit more.'

KITTY MELON

'McLaughlin used to say that Rovers played as a unit and that's why they won everything, but they were phenomenal individual players too. We drove up to Newry to see a Rovers match once and when the teams kicked off Mick Byrne ran on his own from the centre circle, beat all the players and scored a goal. I'd never seen that before, it was so quick.'

JAMES COOKE

'It was around that time that Rovers became like an obsession to me. I remember getting my religion book in school and "decorating" the pictures: Jesus became a Rovers fan,

Nazareth was turned into Milltown, Judas was given a Bohs jersey, and John the Baptist became Dermot Keely, which was strange because he did actually look quite like him. Unfortunately, it never occurred to me that the Christian Brothers might take a rather dim view of my version of Biblical times!'

MARTIN MOORE

'Pat Byrne was the man. The greatest player I've ever seen in the League of Ireland. Pat Byrne won Ireland caps. And it wasn't like a token thing, like now with Crowe. He captained Hearts in the Scottish Premier Division, he captained Leicester when they got promoted to the old Division One in England. That team had Gary Lineker in it.'

ROBBIE FOY

'We beat Man United twice, beat Arsenal, drew with Liverpool, who were European champions at the time. The second time we beat United Ron Atkinson was saying in the papers, "I'm back here for revenge". Beaten again.'

'IT KILLED THE LEAGUE STONE DEAD'

Rovers enjoyed four years of unprecedented success, becoming the first Irish club to win four league titles in a row, a record which still stands. In the one hundred league games played between August 1983 and April 1987, Rovers lost just eleven, winning a total of seventy-four.

However, it has often been claimed since that Rovers were too successful for their own good. Such was the strength of the side that there was very little competition in the league, which ultimately led to a lack of interest. In 1984 they finished six points clear at the top, the following year that was widened to nine points, while in 1986 they narrowly pipped Galway by just two points, before finishing nine ahead of Dundalk in 1987.

Attendances throughout the league were extremely poor, with crowds at Milltown rarely surpassing the 3,000 mark. Sceptics claim that the Rovers dominance killed any interest in the league and set the cause of football in Ireland back.

1987 team shot.

FERGUS MCCORMACK

'People say that the Four in a Row was bad for the league, but we couldn't see that. We got so used to winning over those years. No matter who came to Milltown, Rovers won. Whether it be Arsenal, Man U or Bohs, Rovers would win. They were just that good. But it did get to the stage when you weren't really bothered going to all the games because you knew Rovers would win. What we go through now has really put the whole successful period into context. My God, we win a corner now and we're ecstatic. I suppose we thought it would go on forever.'

JAMES COOKE

'I began to think that it was getting a bit boring, until some older Hoops reminded me that they had waited 20 years for this and it could well be another 20 before we had this type of success again. How right they were.'

RICHIE PHILPOTT

'It almost got predictable after a while. You'd go out to Milltown and Rovers would stroll to a 4-1 win and you'd leave happy as Larry. They were amazing days but in some ways it got kind of boring.'

JOHN BYRNE

'It got to the stage where people saw no point in going because Rovers had the game won before it even started. If the other team scored first, we'd all be looking at each other saying, "Jesus, these guys are asking for it now". Rovers would wipe the floor with them. Clubs coming to Milltown had a choice: do you want a 1-0 defeat or a 6-1 hammering? Choice is yours because we're going to win either way. Just don't make us angry. We didn't realise it at the time but Rovers were too strong for the league. It was one of the best part-time teams in European

Noel Larkin with 1987 Cup.

football history. If the attitude in the league was better, other clubs would have seen us up there and looked at us as a benchmark, something to aspire to. But instead it gave other clubs an excuse to do bugger all. That's not Rovers' fault.'

ROBERT GOGGINS
'I don't believe that the dominance of that side had a negative impact on Irish football. ITV started showing live English football during McLaughlin's first season and even at the time I remember thinking that the live English football had seriously affected our crowds. Clubs had their heads in the sand. There was no marketing strategy, no one realised that the clubs had to be sold to the public. Similarly, clubs didn't try to emulate Rovers' success. Clubs were very conservative, there were lots of old guys running the committees and they weren't progressive. Everyone was happy to just plod along. When Giles came in and made everything professional, other clubs should have tried to follow his lead but they didn't, and it was the same under the McLaughlin era.'

JIMMY CONROY
'There were some good sides in the '80s – Galway, UCD, Bohs Dundalk - so you can't belittle what Rovers achieved.'

DAVID BYRNE
'During the four in a row days you never expected Rovers to lose. The club won doubles for the craic. Back then you went to games expecting Rovers to win so you didn't really take the satisfaction from games that I suppose we should have.'

MARTIN MOORE
'In those four years, they lost twice at Milltown in the league. Twice. They lost to Pats and Home Farm. The two times we lost, we were almost amused. It was nice to see someone putting them down. But that four in a row team in one way killed the league stone dead. The crowds really started to die after that because it was so uncompetitive.

ROBERT GOGGINS
'The four in a row era will haunt any manager who comes to Rovers. The great history of the club leads to great expectations.'

ROBBIE FOY
'If you ask people in our age group – 35-45 – at other clubs when their support slipped, they will all point to that era as when it all went wrong. Our side was unbeatable.'

While the consequences of the Four in a Row were questionable for the league, for Rovers the era proved even more costly. Louis Kilcoyne, the clubs' chairman, had pumped money into the team, although he also received large transfer fees when four Rovers players made highly successful big-money transfers: Jim Beglin to Liverpool, Liam O'Brien to Manchester United, Alan Campbell to Santander and Liam Buckley to Waregem. Shortly after winning the fourth league title in 1987, Kilcoyne made an announcement that was to stun everyone associated with the club. The chairman argued that he had put too much money into the club and was receiving nothing in return. To address the problem, Kilcoyne had a solution which would all but kill Shamrock Rovers: he was going to sell Milltown.

CHAPTER 9

THE SALE OF MILLTOWN

'I'LL NEVER FORGET THAT DAY'

Milltown had seen some glorious years, none more so than the great 'four in a row' achievement of the mid-1980s. However, following the title success of 1987, a bombshell was dropped: Milltown was to be sold to property developers.

PETER ECCLES
'I was on my way to training and I picked up the paper and the back page said that Milltown was sold. I couldn't believe it. I still can't believe it.'

TERRY EVISTON
'Milltown was like a billiard table, it was an unbelievable surface. Even when I was with Bohs, you'd love going to Milltown because of the atmosphere in the ground. I wasn't playing with Rovers when it was announced that the ground was to be sold but I went to a few of the protests anyway. It was a complete disgrace.'

ROBBIE GAFFNEY
'I was at Pats when Milltown was sold and all the Pats players were gutted. No matter who you played for, you loved going to Milltown. Not only had I played on it for a few years, but I'd stood on the terraces as a fan too.'

FRANK ALLEN
'I was dumbfounded. I remember saying that I didn't believe something like that could be allowed to happen. The ground had such a history and a tradition, it was almost like Newgrange or Kilmainham Gaol, these are places that you just don't pull down because they are part of our history. It was basically one family destroying a hundred years of history. I'd seen so much magic in that ground and to think that they could pull it down and build

houses on it made me sick. I know that football is a business but supporters have a part-ownership of clubs. Football isn't just about money, it's about aspirations and dreams. It's what holds communities together.'

PAT BRADY

'There is that dilemma that lots of clubs have moved grounds and prospered. A lot of people would have stepped back and thought "is this a good idea", but it was recognised that there was a different agenda. It wasn't about Shamrock Rovers, it was about the money.'

JIMMY CONROY

"There was a story in the [Evening] Herald early in the year and everyone laughed at it, dismissed it out of hand. I went for a few pints one night and a lad who used to work for Healy Homes told me that the Kilcoynes were selling the ground. I thought it was a joke and sort of forgot about it, but then it was in the paper the following Friday and I knew instantly that it was true. It was a complete bombshell."

ROBBIE FOY

I'll never forget the day the Milltown story broke. Friday morning, I bought the Irish Press and I saw the story: "Rovers will play their last game at Milltown". It came out of nowhere.'

ROBERT GOGGINS

'A few of us were in Milltown in January 1987 and a journalist with the Evening Herald came up to us and asked whether we'd heard anything about Rovers selling Milltown. That was the first we'd heard of it, but we decided to go straight to Louis and ask him. Of course, Louis told him that there was absolutely no truth in the rumour at all. So we went through January, February and March and we never heard anything about Milltown being sold. Then, the Friday before Rovers were due to play Sligo in the second leg of the cup semi-final, I walked into a shop on Capel Street and I picked up the Irish Press and blazoned across the back page was "Milltown to be sold". I knew then that it was true.'

RICHIE PHILPOTT

'The whole thing was a like a nightmare, you kept thinking someone was going to come along and stop it. It was the most sickening thing that has happened in my life. We knew that if Milltown was sold that the club would be in huge trouble. They came out with this story about moving to Tolka but no one bought that for one second.'

MICHAEL KEARNS

'I was living in Australia and I got a phone call from a friend who says "Milltown is gone". I was in disbelief.'

FRANK WHELAN

'I'll never forget that day, I was coming home from work and I picked up the Press and there was a beautiful picture of Milltown on the back and it said "Milltown to be sold". I couldn't believe it. It was so unexpected.'

JUSTIN MASON

'I was only ten but I was devastated. I was in school and during break time one of the lads says "Have you heard?" He told me but I didn't want to believe him. It broke my heart.'

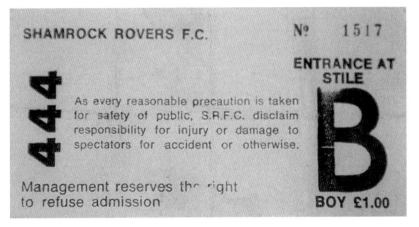

SHAMROCK ROVERS F.C.   N? 1517

ENTRANCE AT STILE

As every reasonable precaution is taken for safety of public, S.R.F.C. disclaim responsibility for injury or damage to spectators for accident or otherwise.

Management reserves the right to refuse admission

BOY £1.00

Ticket stub v Sligo.

'It was like being at a funeral'

On 14 April 1987, Rovers played Sligo in the semi-final of the FAI Cup in Milltown. At half time the supporters held a demonstration on the pitch. Demonstrating the huge importance of Milltown to the entire League of Ireland, the Sligo fans joined their Rovers rivals on the pitch in protest at the sale.

Pat Byrne
'That Sligo game was so strange. It was like when you know someone is going to die and you're going to pay your last respects. As players, we were just focused on winning the game, but we were all praying that something would stop the sale.'

Peter Eccles
'The Sligo game was strange. The supporters were protesting before, during and after the game. Fair play to them, they got on the pitch at half time. If I wasn't playing the game I would have done the same myself.'

David Byrne
'It was a lovely sunny day and it was so surreal to look around and think that it was the last time you would ever be there. It's all I knew as a football fan. Sad, sad day.'

Robbie Foy
'The Sligo game was like being at a funeral. It genuinely was.'

Macdara Ferris
'I dug up a bit of the pitch, as many people were doing, and stuck it in a crisp bag. I kept it in a Chinese takeaway dish for around three years. I used to water it regularly so it was still growing and I put little Subetteo men on it. Unfortunately, one day I dropped something and it hit the shelf that I kept the grass on and a part of Glenmalure Park flew across the room and fell into countless little bits. I tried putting it back together but it was gone.'

Above and below: Protest v Sligo.

MARTIN MOORE
'The Sligo game was just weird. I still didn't believe that the ground would be sold. Then there was a press conference on the Monday and Louis said that Milltown was going and that Tolka was the stadium of the twenty first century. So then we knew. It was gone and there was no coming back.'

JOHN BYRNE
'Rovers fans have had a lot of respect for Sligo because of the support their fans gave us on that day. The Sligo fans were magnificent.'

JIMMY CONROY

'We beat Sligo and then played Dundalk in the cup final in Dalymount. The Rovers fans went out on the pitch at half time but, of course, the Dundalk fans disgraced themselves by throwing missiles at us. There was a riot after the match. We hammered them 3-0 anyway. We were very annoyed at that game because in the programme it listed Tolka Park as our home ground. It was a huge insult from the FAI. A lot of Rovers fans tore up their programmes in disgust. We weren't going to be playing in Milltown the following season, but we'd played in Milltown all that season so it was very petty, they shouldn't have done that. But at least we knew where we stood with the FAI.'

Above and below: Protest v Sligo.

JOHN BYRNE

'It was hard to take when you looked at the programme and saw Tolka Park listed as our home ground. I saw some fans actually pissing on their programmes they were so disgusted.'

ROBBIE FOY

'The Sligo lads had been great, they'd seen the bigger picture and joined us on the pitch for the protest. The Cup Final was a different story. Rovers fans went on the pitch at half time and they went down to the try to get the Dundalk fans to join them but they got rocks and bottles thrown at them. But that got sorted out after the game anyway. They got a kicking off the Rovers fans outside the ground and then when they tried to get away the Dublin fans, who were coming back from Croke Park having played Kerry, gave them a hiding too.'

DAVID BYRNE

'I remember a few Dundalk fans getting their jerseys ripped off their backs and the jerseys being burnt on sticks'.

MARTIN KEATING

'The programme listed Tolka Park as our home ground. I think he did it for effect but it was a lousy thing to do. Milltown was still there, we'd just finished what turned out to be our final season there, and two weeks later "home ground: Tolka Park". It was absolutely disgraceful.'

'THE BATTLELINES WERE DRAWN'

JIMMY CONROY

'The season ended and we formed KRAM [Keep Rovers At Milltown]. We had a general meeting in Liberty Hall and it was decided to set up an organisation to save the ground. Louis [Kilcoyne] was invited to that meeting but he left the room at one stage because he said he had nothing to offer us. The silence was deafening. At that stage, the plan was to put at stay of execution for one year on the ground, give us one year to see if we could resolve it. Of course, he turned that down point blank, so the battle lines were clearly drawn. It got very vicious, it wasn't nice at all.'

NED ARMSTRONG

'It was a dreadful thing to do. There were lots of meetings and writing about Milltown, but the Kilcoynes just went on and sold it anyway and there was nothing the supporters could do about it. They just made their financial decision to sell the place, they made their money and that was the end of it. There was no comeback. Milltown was our home.'

PAULINE FOY

'There was a lot of opposition in this area [Milltown / Ranelagh] to the selling of the ground. There were big protests outside the ground and we'd all go up with our placards. Ordinary people, even if they weren't into football themselves, were very upset because they felt that they were losing a great amenity for their children. There is still an awful lot of bad feeling in this area about what happened.'

ROBERT GOGGINS

'All the Rovers fans were protesting outside of Buswells Hotel at the league AGM in 1987. I remember Paddy Kilcoyne came out and he said "Sure, what are you protesting about, haven't you got the best team in the league, what more do you want?" That summed it up for me.

KRAM in Germany.

They thought that just because we were winning leagues that we didn't care about Milltown.'

MARTIN KEATING
'I was involved in KRAM from the beginning, although I was more involved in the supporters club. KRAM held fundraisers - race nights, golf outings, quizzes, collections. We would collect on the trains going to away games. Linda Martin gave me £2 on the train to Cork. I brought my KRAM banner everywhere - I brought it to Germany with Ireland and it ended up being on one of the biggest selling Irish team posters, the Keep Rovers at Milltown banner in the background.'

FERGUS MCCORMACK
'Everyone in school had KRAM badges and all the cars had KRAM stickers. We just thought that there was no way the sale was going to go ahead. I was 17 at the time and maybe I was just too naïve. We just thought that the righteousness of our case was enough to win. At 17 you think that just being right is enough to win. It was a cruel lesson in life to learn and a lesson that I still haven't come to terms with.'

KITTY MELON
'We had an all-night vigil outside the ground. We always said that if Rovers lost their home it would be the end of them, it was an absolute scandal.'

MARTIN KEATING
'We slept outside Milltown twice. Looking back at it, it was a crazy time, sleeping outside football grounds and things like that. Locals would bring us tea and food. That's why I always think it's strange when people say that the neighbours wanted Milltown gone. I did a petition all around that area and I got a great response – all around Windy Arbour,

Rosemount and Milltown. Even seven out of ten of the people in the houses directly opposite the ground supported us.'

JIMMY CONROY

'We'd hang banners at the end of his [Kilcoyne's] road too. We'd have rallies at the ground and have brass bands marching up the Milltown Road. It was hugely embarrassing for him. We got good at propaganda; we learned to use the media well. We won an awful lot of the battles, but he was always going to win the war.'

JACK WILSON

'I was on the committee of KRAM and at that stage we thought we could save the ground. We made a very good offer for Milltown but they sold it to the highest bidder.'

JIMMY CONROY

'We drove the FAI crazy. There were one-man pickets some nights, posters on the door, handing in letters. We used to go to the AGMs and I remember once a prominent member came out and told us that he wouldn't open our letter because we didn't represent a constituent body in Irish football. That always got me, the arrogance of them. They'd sneak Louis in the back door. He wormed his way back in and eventually became President. That was such a huge insult.'

GERRY MACKEY

'Looking at it with hindsight, we really had no chance of saving Milltown. We got the people who owned and ran Wembley Stadium over to have a look at it and they were interested but the problem was that it was too small, they wanted room to build a running track and things like that.'

MARTIN KEATING

'We raised around £90,000 and we could have borrowed around three times that, but it would have been way short of what Brent Homes paid for it, which was around £900,000. Had he given us enough time we probably could have raised the money. A lot of the lads involved don't go to games anymore for whatever reason, which is sad really.'
'WE WERE PREPARED TO PULL THE PLUG ON THE CLUB'

When Rovers kicked-off the 1988 season, they did so in Tolka Park. The Supporters Club called for a boycott, which was observed by the vast majority of Rovers fans. The supporters were determined to starve Kilcoyne out of the club before the sale of Milltown had gone through. It was the lowest moment in the club's history. A mere handful of fans paid into games and dozens picketed outside, whilst the majority stayed away altogether, in many cases never to return.

MICK BYRNE

'It was awful arriving at Tolka Park every week. The fans were outside and our families didn't want to go anymore. It affected us all, both on the pitch and at home.'

PAT BYRNE

'I had a year to run on my contract and I saw out that year playing in Tolka. That was the worst year of my career. As a footballer, you need an audience to show off your skills. Everybody has an ego, I suppose, and you need to perform in front of people. At Tolka,

KRAM at the Mansion House.

there was no one to entertain. Rovers have superb supporters. They have some arseholes but the vast majority are superb and so loyal to the club. The people outside of Tolka were real supporters, they loved their club. They'd grown up in Milltown, some of them were 60 years of age and had probably gone to Milltown since they were 6. It was a way of life for them and it just changed overnight.'

JOHN BYRNE
'I joined the picket but I didn't last the whole season. I just couldn't cope with the situation. I was never going to go into Tolka, but I just stayed away altogether. We were prepared to pull the plug on Rovers. If a loved one is on a life support machine, sometimes you have to make that decision and we were prepared to pull the plug on the club. It was an awful time.'

JIMMY CONROY
'We were the first supporters to ever withdraw our support en masse from a club. We knew it was the right thing to do. There were more important considerations than winning the league or the cup. We looked at the bigger picture, and I believe that the last 17 years have proven us right. We knew that if we lost Milltown we were in big trouble.'

MARTIN KEATING
'Louis only had a 16-month lease for Tolka, nothing more. In other words, we were leaving Milltown and not going anywhere else. At the last game in Tolka Park there were 45 people at it. I know the figure because we sang "1, 2, 3...." at every person who went in to embarrass them. I never abused anyone, all I said was "Please support the boycott, this guy as a 16 month lease on Tolka and he is putting houses on Milltown". Some people gave abuse to people going in, but it was a very emotive issue. Some who went in left again because

they felt so embarrassed at being there. It really divided families. We have to move on now, but it's very difficult when people you know pass you on the picket line.'

JACK WILSON
'We boycotted all the home matches and went to all the away matches. It was a terrible thing to have to do. Kilcoyne sold up and left us with nothing but jerseys and two players.'

JIMMY CONROY
'Some fans broke the boycott and went in to Tolka and I think they showed great courage in doing so. I was on the picket and there was a lot of bitterness at the time, but it shows a lot of bottle to go against the vast majority. Mates of mine went in and we just don't talk about it now. The media tried to portray us as thugs, which was grossly unfair. We ran the club down. Totally destroyed them, but we had to do it.'

JOHN BYRNE
'Rovers fans didn't go into the ground and we asked away fans not to go in. But you had lads travelling down from Derry and you couldn't fault them for going in. The away fans were generally very good, they'd come up and chat with us and tell us that they supported what we were trying to do. On the other hand, Bohs fans didn't do that. We were standing outside and we asked them not to go in and they just laughed at us and strolled in. That raised tensions between Rovers and Bohs a lot. Rovers hammered them that day and it was us laughing when they left the ground.'

MARTIN KEATING
'Dermot [Keely] supported Louis but I think he was a bit naïve. I think he apologised afterwards. I remember I was standing with three other lads and I went head-to-head with Keely, which I didn't really like because he's a tough guy and the other three disappeared pretty quickly! Dermot was giving it loads and I was looking around and the lads who had started it were suddenly at the other end of the road! The press gave us a hard time too. We were very passionate and some of the lads would be giving Kilcoyne a lot of abuse and the soccer writers generally took his side. They'd be writing about the "hooligans" outside the ground. Maybe we were a bit boisterous but we were losing our home – what would they do if they were being kicked out of their home?'

'WHY IS THIS HAPPENING?'

While Rovers played in front of empty terraces in Tolka Park, the terraces of Milltown were still intact. Although the club moved out of the ground in 1987, it was 1990 before Milltown was finally torn down. In the meantime, the ground was left in a state of disrepair.

MICK BYRNE
'I went away to Holland for a year and when I came back they still hadn't done anything to Milltown. I drove over to see the ground and I couldn't believe it. The grass was two foot off the ground. I went up to the stand and I just sat there thinking "Why is this happening?"'

JIMMY CONROY
'Louis wasn't a Rovers man, he had no feeling for Rovers, he proved that when he burned all the old pennants and the photos of the old teams. In the bar upstairs in Milltown they used to have the photos of all the old teams, but it all got burned. I rescued a few things. I have the

'Keep Rovers At Milltown: fans apply the pressure'.

pennant from the 1959 European Cup game against Nice hanging off my bed, along with the one from the 1974 game against Betis and the 1978 one against Academico of Portugal. I also have the trophy that was presented to the club in 1965 by Real Zaragosa. I found it in the long grass behind the goal in Milltown, it was very sad really. The fact that all that history just got thrown out really showed a lack of feeling towards the club. Why didn't he give that stuff to the fans? It would have been common decency. During the boycott season in Tolka, he still wanted to make money out of Milltown so he had them selling Christmas trees inside the ground. That was hard to take. He sold used cars from the ground too – it was like something from "Steptoe and Son".'

ROBBIE FOY
'Some of the lads managed to get their hands on a few old cups and things like that before they were thrown out. I only lived around the corner from Milltown so I used to just go into the ground sometimes and literally just watch the grass grow.'

MICHAEL KEARNS
'In January 1987 I went to Australia and I came back on 21 December. I went up the Milltown Road the next day and the ground was in rack and ruin. It had been left in total decay – turnstiles hanging off the wall, the pitch covered in weeds. It was just so wrong. I sat on the terrace and I asked myself "How could one family inflict this on a football club who have been playing here since 1926?" I stood on the terrace on my own and I cried.'

MARTIN KEATING
'Some pennants from European games were found them in the undergrowth in Milltown. When the builders came in, he threw everything out. If he had any decency at all he would have handed them over. I've just no time for the man.'

MARTIN MOORE

'A few of us got into the ground and the offices and we couldn't believe the place. It was completely gutted. Everything that couldn't have been sold was just thrown around on the floor, completely wrecked. It was tragic.'

PAT BYRNE

'We'd always hoped that someone would step in and save the ground. Eventually I heard that they were going to take the stand down and so I drove over and I watched them tear it down. It was so surreal.'

'I DIDN'T WANT TO PLAY FOR ANYONE ELSE'

Against this background, the players decided that they no longer wanted to play for the club. The four-in-a-row team, a team which is still sung about to this day, was broken up.

MICK BYRNE

'As players, our own family group broke down. I saw my contract out and then went to Holland. I probably wouldn't have gone to Holland if Milltown hadn't had been sold. I didn't want to play for anyone else but Shamrock Rovers. Ten years after Milltown was sold, six players from that team were still playing. From a personal point of view, selling Milltown deprived me of another two or three medals.'

PAT BYRNE

'The players understood the supporters' view and we responded in kind because we didn't want to play for the Kilcoynes anymore. We were still contracted but most of us just saw the contracts out and left. That side was good enough to win another two or three league titles. Five of that team went to Derry and won the league there the following year.'

KRAM at FAI offices.

JIMMY CONROY

'Dermot Keely unwisely came out early that season and spoke against the Rovers fans, but he resigned at the end of the season and that was seen as a great triumph for us. Things got very bitter with Keely, but he gave an interview for the Sligo Champion years later and he admitted that he got it wrong – it takes a big man to do that and I've always respected him for it.'

ROBBIE FOY

'After the ground was sold, Derry won the league, then Shels did, but it was the Rovers team, they'd just all moved clubs.'

'THE CLUB ALMOST WENT'

With no ground, no players and no chairman, it looked as if Shamrock Rovers was going to be doomed to extinction. Rovers were eventually rescued by John McNamara, who agreed to purchase the club.

GERRY MACKEY

'I had the unpleasant experience of dealing with the people involved – be it the Kilcoynes, the Jesuits, who had initially sold the site to the Kilcoyne's, or the FAI – to the point where it looked like Rovers were going to go out of business. There was a fateful meeting in Merion Square, in the FAI offices, that was the first time I met John McNamara. He turned out to be the saviour because if he hadn't come along then Rovers were gone. I almost became resigned to the fact that Rovers were going.

JIMMY CONROY

'The club almost went out of business, but in the end a settlement was reached and the champagne came out. As part of that meeting, the FAI agreed to assist us in every way to get our ground back. Subsequent events [Louis becoming President] show that a couple of cheap bottles of plonk and a few photos in the paper was their entire effort.'

'WE STOOD ALONE'

In the summer of 1990, houses were finally built on the land where Rovers had played for sixty-one years. The turf where Paddy Coad had revolutionised Irish football was turned into a housing estate; the terraces where generations of Dubs had grown up were sold to the highest bidder. Never again would the green and white of Rovers take to the field at Glenmalure Park.

PAT BYRNE

'You have to look at the Jesuits. They were more involved in that than anybody. They owned a 99-year lease but they just wanted rid of it. They did it for greed as much as anything else. The Jesuits are as much to blame as anyone else. The government have to be questioned too. Shamrock Rovers were an institution in Ireland and for the government to allow an Irish institution to be sold for a million quid is beyond me. I cannot understand that. It affected so many people's lives and had given pleasure to so many people.'

FRANK ALLEN

'There was very seldom an Irish international side without a few Shamrock Rovers players on it. That's why I feel that the FAI should have had a greater loyalty to the club. Rovers have produced more Irish internationals than any other club and the FAI should have stepped in to help us. What made me so bitter afterwards was the FAI making Louis Kilcoyne President and his later involvement with the Olympic Council. History has shown that he has all but destroyed one of the great institutions of Irish sport.'

JIMMY CONROY

'We tried to get the government to put a compulsory purchase order on the site, which was a good idea but it never materialised. They didn't care.'

SONNY O'REILLY

'I always felt that the FAI and the government should have done more to save Milltown. They should have stepped in and said that the land had to be kept for football.'

ROBBIE FOY

'The Jesuits said to the Kilcoynes, "We'll sell you this land and you can do whatever you like with it". So the Kilcoynes bought it and sold it almost straight away to property developers. They pulled a fast one. The problem with this country is that you if pull something like that people admire you for it.'

FRANK ALLEN

'The councillors rejected the planning proposal and said that Milltown had to be kept for sport, but then An Bord Pleanala, an unelected body, overturned the councillors decision. It made me lose faith in local democracy. Nobody who is involved in sport wanted the ground sold but An Bord Pleanala were able to do it. If the votes of democratically elected local politicians don't mean anything, what is the point in electing them?'

JIMMY CONROY

'You go out and elect 18 people for local government, someone goes to them for planning permission and they all turn it down, surely that has to mean something. 18-0, you can't get more of a consensus than that. Rovers biggest victory we used to call it. Then it goes to Bord Pleanala, three people who we never knew who they were and they over-turn it. Can anyone tell me that's right? What's the point in local elections when that happens? I feel very strongly about that and it left me very bitter.'

ROBERT GOGGINS

'On the day An Bord Pleanala announced that they were giving planning permission, the Evening Herald carried the story on the front page - "Milltown: It's Houses". Once we heard that, we knew it was over. No one seemed to give a damn about Shamrock Rovers, not even the FAI. I have to say that Eamon Dunphy didn't help matters. He was very close to the Kilcoynes and he belittled people who were involved in KRAM and the supporters club. Rovers' supporters really stood alone during that whole affair.'

MARTIN MOORE

'The trouble was, all these people said, "Ah Milltown, sorry to see it go", but nobody lifted a finger to help us. I mean, Louis became President of the FAI afterwards! There was a rumour that he would have presented the cup in '91 if we'd have won, and that Rovers would have refused to take it. Just stood on the pitch. I would have loved to have seen that. That would have been the business.'

Monument in Milltown.

PAT BRADY
'The cynical view was that the Kilcoynes wanted out for some time and found a variety of excuses to do so. If you look at the years '83 – '86, there just had to be money made. There were decent gates, big friendlies, lots of trophies, some big transfers – it's hard to see how money wasn't made.'

MARTIN KEATING
'Kilcoyne made money available for transfers but got big money in from selling people like Jim Beglin, Liam Buckley, Liam O'Brien and Alan Campbell, all of whom went to big clubs. The first season we won the league – '84 – the bar in Milltown was shut at six o'clock. It was incredible, he shut the bar at six and threw everyone out!'

ROBBIE FOY
'Louis was one of the only people in the FAI who could even tie his own shoelaces. He's a clever bloke and he could do things. Now they've made him Honorary Life President. Is it personal between Louis and Rovers fans? Jesus, yes.'

'IT WAS THE WORST DAY OF MY LIFE'

To many people, closing the gates on Milltown represented the death-knell of the entire league. The sale of Milltown has left a legacy of bitterness which is still evident to this day.

155

GERRY MACKEY

'It was an end of an era. There is an extent to which things will never be the same again for me. I'm still a Rovers man but the buzz has gone out of it.'

FRANK ALLEN

'I had a friend who moved into one of the houses [in Milltown]. I had to call up to her on one occasion and I felt physically sick when I was in the house. It felt so wrong, I knew that where I was standing was somewhere on the pitch. I had to get out. All the problems Rovers have had since, I'd put that all down to what Kilcoyne did to the club.'

NED ARMSTRONG

'I went to Milltown for over 50 years, from 1936 to 1987. I had my own spot, standing on the unreserved stand – the cheap side – about level with the penalty area at the Gonzaga end. You used to get groups from different areas of the city standing in their own spots in the ground. I felt disgusted when they sold it. You loved going to Milltown, everything was geared towards going to Milltown on a Sunday. After that, a lot of the supporters didn't bother going anymore. They went to Milltown and that was it, they didn't want to go anywhere else. They thought that was it. It was a sickener. I was almost fed up with all football after it.'

PAT BRADY

'If someone who wasn't encumbered by the greed factor wanted to sell Milltown in order to relocate the club to an area with better demographics then it might have worked. But that wasn't the case and so the battleground became Milltown and the club has never gotten over that. It was a complete disaster and, ultimately, it led to people such as myself ceasing to be fans of Shamrock Rovers. It says something too about the League of Ireland – the lack of vision, the lack of any strategic sense of where the domestic game is going.'

MARTIN MOORE

'I think that if we had stayed in Milltown we would have ended up selling it and moving elsewhere eventually. If the club had said, "Alright, we are going to leave Milltown because we can't afford it, but we are going to built a beautiful ground elsewhere" we could have lived with it. But not the way it happened.'

MARIE CRADDOCK

'The last time I was involved in Rovers was 1959 because I got married and left for England. I always went to games when I came back to Ireland, but I haven't gone to any since Milltown was sold. I still look out for the scores but the interest is gone to a large degree.'

JAMES COOKE

'Three generations of my family went to Milltown. I will always treasure my memories of Milltown. I had my own little spot, it was about two crush barriers down from the shop in the Shed. Our own little group assembled there but most of the group stopped going to games after we lost Milltown. Not only did the closure of that great ground almost kill our club, it also deprived me of some good friends that I had made.'

ROBBIE FOY

'The ground was all separated. The Shed went to a GAA ground in Kinnagad, the nets went to Tolka, the floodlights went to Tree Rock Rovers hockey club. The only consolation is that they [the Kilcoynes] got so little money out of Milltown. They only got £900,000 or so from Milltown, which is a pittance. Had they waited ten years you could have stuck a couple of zeros on the end of that.'

MACDARA FERRIS
'For me Milltown will always be Shamrock Rovers. I'm very lucky in the sense that there are a lot of Rovers fans my age who were never in the ground. It's a strange feeling going past the site now. I've never gone into it since the houses went up. It was the first football ground I was ever in so it will always be special.'

PAULINE FOY
'When my son was around ten himself and his friends started getting interested in Rovers, as all the boys from around this area did. Now that Milltown is gone, Rovers have lost a whole generation of children from around here [Milltown area].'

FERGUS McCORMACK
'Losing the ground was obviously a terrible thing, but to me the biggest crime was losing the identity in south Dublin. From Dun Laoghaire, through Ringsend, Rathfarnham, Terenure and beyond, it was all Rovers. Supporting Rovers was a badge of honour in south Dublin.'

ROBBIE FOY
'A lot of residents in Milltown were always dead against the ground anyway, so they had it replaced with a nice middle-class housing estate. My dream has always been to buy a house in Milltown, hand it over to a biker club, run everyone out of the estate and knock it all down.'

MARTIN MOORE
'I had a cousin who used to go to Rovers but emigrated to Australia a couple of years before we left Milltown. My brother went over there a few years ago, around 1996, and he said to him, "Does Martin still go to Milltown?" "No, Milltown's gone, they lost it about 10 years ago". He actually rang me. It was afternoon there but it was 3 in the morning here. "Martin, its Joe. Is Milltown really gone?" "Yeah" "When did it go?" "Let me see, today is Wednesday…Monday…Tuesday…1987". He just couldn't believe it.'

FERGUS McCORMACK
'You hear of taxi drivers who refuse to go into Glenmalure. I don't even go down the Milltown Road, I just don't want to see it.'

KITTY MELON
'I started going to Milltown in the 1930s, I couldn't believe it when they sold it. I often think of people like Billy Lord, who went to Milltown every day of his life before he died in 1985. What would poor Billy Lord have said if he knew they were going to sell Milltown?'

JACK WILSON
'I've only been on the Milltown Road once since they sold the ground, that was when Paddy Coad's daughter asked me to bring her up to the monument [commemorating Rovers]. Even when I'm in taxis, I divert them up through Clonskeagh, I just don't want to see what Milltown is like now. Walking out of Milltown for the last time, after the game against Sligo, was the worst day of my life. Without a doubt, the worst day. It nearly killed me.'

'Glenmalure Park, Milltown. 1926 – 1987'.

CHAPTER 10

MEETING LOUIS

IF EVERY STORY HAS A villain, Louis Kilcoyne fits the bill for Rovers. Seventeen years after selling Glenmalure Park, the clubs' former chairman is every bit the Great Satan he was on the fateful day in 1987 when Milltown closed its gates for the last time. Stories still abound of supporters bumping into their former chairman: 'I bumped into Louis, I chased him down the road'. Bravado for the most part, although certain incidents have been confirmed. To this day, one of the most popular terrace songs is an ode to Louis' recent health scare:

'Who's that lying on the carpet,
Who's that lying on the floor,
It's Louis on his back and he's had a heart attack,
And he won't be screwing Rovers anymore'.

His years at Rovers saw the club reach its lowest ever point — finishing bottom of the table for the only time in its history in 1976 — and its highest point — winning four league titles in a row in the mid-1980s. In between these extremes saw the Giles era, an era personally manufactured by Louis, which was without doubt the most ambitious in Irish football history.

The Four-in-a-Row triumph in the mid-80s is the most celebrated feat in the clubs' history, yet Louis' role in this achievement has been completely airbrushed out. Interestingly, he has almost no interest in discussing it.

So why did he get involved with Shamrock Rovers? Louis declared as a sports promoter in 1970 and says that his interest in domestic Irish football grew from that. The Kilcoyne brothers – Louis, Paddy and Barton – had initially sought to take over Drumcondra FC but that deal fell through. After that, it was as much a matter of chance as anything else. The Kilcoynes were looking to get into football, the Cunninghams – who had run Rovers as a family business for forty years – were looking to get out. It took the two families less than

Louis Kilcoyne (right) on the pitch that he would soon sell to property developers. Rovers manager Jim McLaughlin is on the left.

a month to strike a deal. By the start of the 1972/73 season, the Cunningham dynasty was over and the Kilcoynes were running the ship.

'They [the Cunninghams] were very frustrated because the game had diminished so much. By the time we came in there was little or no interest [in the game]', he explains. 'We had the view that this was a sleeping giant and that we could resurrect it. We were very naive, to say the least'.

Louis' 'naivety' lasted 17 years before he decided to throw in the towel. He makes no bones about the fact that taking over Rovers was a business move. His language does not disguise the fact that he was always more interested in the bank balance than the match results: 'You can win a cup or win a league but big deal'

Ever since the media revealed Milltown's fate, Louis has cited poor attendances as a mantra to defend selling the ground. The intriguing paradox of the great Rovers side of the 1980s was that, although they played fast, entertaining football and were extremely successful, they never attracted large crowds. Some argue that Irish football was in too steady a decline to attract crowds, others argue that Rovers were simply too strong; the lack of competition made the league 'boring'. Louis argues both.

'The visiting teams wouldn't travel to Milltown with any degree of hope, they'd only bring a bus or two of supporters with them', he says. 'We were too strong. The game was a dead duck from the '60s onwards, by the '80s the public had other things to do. It just petered out. After 17 years, we gave up'.

Louis is a smooth operator. He smokes cigars and talks in a cool and assured manner. Before he ever got involved with Rovers, he brought Pele's Santos to Dublin to play Drumcondra. A few years later he went one better by bringing the entire Brazilian side over to play an Irish side under the name 'Shamrock Rovers'. In the mid-70s, Louis brought the Rovers squad to Japan, where they defeated the Japanese national side in front of 60,000 people. He brought Johnny Giles – his brother-in-law – home to Milltown, along with seasoned pros such as Ray Tracey, Paddy Mulligan and Eamon Dunphy. He has contacts. Good contacts.

In 1985 Louis purchased Glenmalure Park from the Jesuits, who had leased it to the club since 1926. It is at this point where Louis' story gets cloudy. 'We were paying them [the Jesuits] relatively reasonable rent but we offered to buy them out in a way that was beneficial to them so they accepted', he recalls. 'While sponsors and government aid hadn't arrived, because we were in Europe all the time we had visions of becoming a European side so we had to develop Glenmalure Park'.

It seems strange that the Kilcoynes would want to develop the ground in 1985 but want to sell it two years later. It is generally believed that the sole reason the ground was purchased was in order to sell it. Furthermore, it is often argued that the Jesuits were under no illusions as to what the fate of the famous ground would be.

'There were a lot of painful aspects to running Shamrock Rovers', he says. 'There are a few so-called good memories but they never paid any bills'.

Louis wanted out of the club and wanted to recoup as much of his money as he could. When news filtered down to Rovers supporters, there was outrage. Demonstrations were held and the supporters went on a round of political lobbying. However, everywhere they went, the supporters ran into a dead end. Abandoned by everyone in a position of power, the supporters were fighting a losing battle to hold onto their ground. Did Louis understand the emotional reasons behind the fans desire to hang onto Milltown?

'The quick answer is yes', he retorts, 'but it is one thing to desire something so long as someone is paying the piper. I could understand their angst and desire or whatever. But, so what?'

The plans to sell Glenmalure received a serious blow when the local councillors unanimously voted down the proposal. Louis describes this decision as 'bullshit', saying that An Bord Pleanala had no problems in granting planning permission.

'Politicians my arse', he says defiantly. 'A few fellas came knocking on the door about it but they were only responding to constituents. There was no serious effort made, certainly not on the government's part. Despite all the heated arguments about principles and Glenmalure being a Mecca, no one ever produced anything serious [in terms of financial offers]'.

When Rovers vacated Glenmalure Park, the club was moved to Tolka Park. Here, Louis' story gets mixed up even further. The financial reality of the club, he says, made him want to get out: 'We were fed-up propping Rovers up year-in-year-out. There was nothing to encourage us to continue'. Yet, when the move to Tolka Park was announced Louis attempted to sell it to supporters as a relocation to a suburb with a greater encatchment area. While on one hand saying that he wanted out of Rovers, Louis still talks of building the 'stadium of the future' in Drumcondra, claiming that he had a 'blueprint for the future'.

However, with a final decision on Glenmalure still pending, the supporters launched a boycott of the northside venue. The boycott was an attempt to starve the Kilcoyne's out of the club before the sale had gone through. With the Kilcoyne's gone, the club could move back into its home.

'It was bloody awful', recalls Louis. 'I was spat on and abused, it wasn't pleasant but I had to take it. I felt for them [the supporters] because they were emotionally involved. Many of their fathers would have been Rovers supporters and you could understand their hurt. I just had to get on with it'.

Get on with it he did. In the summer of 1990, houses were built on the square of land where hundreds of thousands of Dubliners had flocked to witness some of the greatest footballers this country has every produced. As the Republic of Ireland competed in their first ever World Cup finals, the club which had produced more Irish internationals than any other was being destroyed. Never has Irish sport witnessed such a cruel irony.

In a further insult to Shamrock Rovers, Louis Kilcoyne was later elected President of the FAI, having been offered a way back into the game by Cork City. It seems a remarkable decision for the national football association to appoint as President the man who nearly killed off the country's most famous club. It would be akin to appointing Oliver Cromwell President of Gaelic Studies. What makes Louis' appointment even more amazing is the fact that he openly states his belief that Irish domestic football is fighting a losing battle.

'In the '40s and '50s people were happy to go out and watch a game because they had no other options', he says. 'Today, they have options. We are a better off society now. There is the cliché of televised football, but people have options now and all that conspires to do domestic football in'.

It says a lot about the FAI that their most senior members believe domestic football to be little more than a waste of time. No other national football association in the world would elect as President a man who, not only almost killed the country's most successful club, but sees no future for domestic football. Louis resigned from his position in. In July 2002, the FAI awarded Louis Kilcoyne the title of Life Vice President.

Much time has passed since Milltown's gates were closed and this has made Louis blasé about what happened. I ask Louis how he expects to be remembered in the clubs' history: 'Like shit', he replies, but this doesn't bother him. 'You have to put it in perspective, you're talking about a relative handful of people who would begrudge me or be upset. In the greater context, there are other things in life. In football records, it will be written that I sold Glenmalure Park, but beyond that there won't be too much negativity about me'.

Seventeen years after he sold Glenmalure Park, Ireland's most famous football club is still on the move and is now perilously close to extinction. How does that make him feel?

'I feel awful', he says.. 'I feel awful that I was a part of the demise of the club, without a doubt. It's not a good feeling but a decision had to be made, a business decision had to be made, and that overruled everything else'.

Louis says he still attends League of Ireland games and claims that the Rovers result is the first he looks for - 'that's second nature', he says. Despite this, he has not seen Rovers play since he left the club in 1988: 'There's no point. They've enough problems without bumping into me'.

Louis Kilcoyne ran Shamrock Rovers from 1972 until 1988. For the past seventeen years, he has been a figure of hate like never before seen in domestic Irish football. The club which he once ran has spent seventeen years homeless and on the verge of extinction because of a decision he made. The once great Shamrock Rovers have won just one trophy during this time, all because of a decision he made. Does he regret it?

'I regret putting seventeen years into the club', he says. 'I wouldn't touch it again. I enjoyed attempting to revamp football, whatever about Rovers, but I wouldn't' do it again'.

Finally, after seventeen years, Louis and Rovers fans can agree on something.

CHAPTER 11

THE HOMELESS YEARS
1988–PRESENT

Having sold Glenmalure Park to property developers, the Kilcoynes then offloaded Shamrock Rovers Football Club to Dublin businessman John McNamara. Although supporters had hoped that the McNamara buy-out could lead to a possible return to Milltown, they soon had to face up to the reality that the club's spiritual home was gone.

Rovers had just completed the boycott season in Tolka Park and so, with the club under new management, the supporters met to vote on their next move. The new owners of Rovers had a controversial proposal: the club would move away from the detested Tolka Park, but only as far as Dalymount Park, home to local rivals Bohemians. KRAM, who had for eighteen months boycotted their club in a bid to drive out the owners, congregated to take the historic vote. When the proposal to lift the boycott of the club was put to the crowd, all three hundred members present voted in favour. However, when the supporters were asked to move to Dalymount Park, sixteen supporters voted against.

JIMMY CONROY

'I was one of the sixteen to vote against the move. I didn't go to Dalymount. We didn't picket it or anything, a democratic decision had been made to bring the club to Dalymount, but I didn't go myself. I went to all the away games in those two seasons, but none of the home ones. There was no animosity or anything, it was a personal decision. I felt we should have gone for bust with Milltown, I was a bit more hot-headed in those days. We used to meet with the FAI on a weekly basis; sometimes Rovers were playing on a Friday night and I'd be up with the FAI, I wasn't just sitting on my arse!'

MARTIN KEATING

'I didn't go to Dalymount. The boycott had to finish if McNamara was to take the club over, which is fair enough because you can't expect a guy to take over a club if a boycott is still on. But I just felt that going up the road to Dalymount was a sell-out. But the lads were meeting McNamara and the FAI at 11am and the meeting were going on till four in the morning, they were worn out. It was like when prisoners are beaten into submission. Dalymount Park? With Bohs? Christ Almighty! Bohs were laughing at us. Here was me standing outside Tolka for eighteen months and all of a sudden we're up in Dalymount. I thought it was a sell-out. The FAI put a gun to our heads and said "unless you agree to the Dalymount move, there isn't going to be a Shamrock Rovers".'

'I can't even remember most of the team'

For the supporters who did journey to Phibsboro to see Rovers in action, it was a sorry time in the club's history. Just two years previously, the club had won it's fourth league title in a row and were seemingly unstoppable. Now, they were playing in front of scant crowds and paying rent to their greatest rivals.

Not only did many supporters stay away, an entirely new playing staff was hired, with only Jody Byrne and Harry Kenny remaining. Although the Kilcoyne's sold McNamara an entity entitled 'Shamrock Rovers Football Club', the reality was that the new owners were merely buying the name and a set of jerseys. Some supporters stayed away on principle, to others the club was dead in all but name. To this day, thousands of Dubs will still say that they stopped following Rovers the day the club left Milltown. To them, it just wasn't the same club anymore.

David Byrne

'One of our lowest moments was the first home game in Dalymount when Athlone Town beat us 1-0. I remember it well because Austin Brady, the Athlone right back, was our postman. But we counted a total of 88 people in the ground that day. That's when I really took to Rovers. I drifted in and out during the four in a row but it was only when things

Dave Connell bloodied during game v Bohs.

got really crap that I decided that I wanted to do this week in week out. When we went to Dalymount the club only had two bags of footballs and a set of jerseys. They got the team out of nowhere, I can't even remember most of the team because they came and went so quickly. We had five Hungarians and a few Americans and a couple of journeymen we found.'

JOHN DORNEY
'The first time I saw Rovers play was "at home" in Dalymount in late 1989 against Bohs. At that time Rovers were still waiting on the An Bord Planala decision on whether houses could be built on Milltown, and the match programme had a hopeful article about moving back there. By the time I went to my second match – also against Bohs – in the early part of the following year, Milltown had already been demolished and the club was forced to look at the realities of long term homelessness. The club was on its knees.'

KIERAN MAHER
'John MacNamara rang me and asked me to re-sign for Rovers. It was so different though – we were playing in Dalymount with our arch rivals and it was like starting out all over again. You were running out onto the pitch wearing the Shamrock Rovers jersey but you knew it wasn't the same. It just felt wrong.'

'WE COULDN'T BELIEVE THE SIZE OF THE CROWD'

Everyone involved in the club knew that Dalymount could only be a short-term solution. As the 1989/90 season drew to a close, the club made a dramatic announcement: Rovers were moving to the RDS. The Royal Dublin Society is Ireland's premier horse-jumping arena. Situated in Ballsbridge, the RDS is located halfway between Milltown and Ringsend, the two areas of the city most identified with Rovers.

Ricky McEvoy at the RDS.

On 16 September 1990, the RDS played host to Shamrock Rovers against St. Patrick's Athletic in the first ever League of Ireland game at the venue. The game was heavily plugged in the press as the rebirth of Rovers and 22,000 people flocked to see the game, the largest crowd at a Rovers home game in over two decades.

Sadly, the sides failed to deliver. Rovers were under the management of Noel King, whilst St. Pat's were managed by future Ireland boss Brian Kerr, neither of whom were renowned for their attacking play. Negative tactics, coupled with a sense of occasion alien to both sets of players, conspired to serve up a drab encounter in which neither side managed to score. For the fans, it was a missed opportunity.

ROBBIE FOY
'Going into the ground they were giving out free sticks of Rovers rock candy – it was superb! The teams came out and they played the theme tune to 2001 Space Odyssey and this girl carried a flag saying "Welcome home Rovers". I burst into tears. Of course, it didn't help that I'd been drinking since 9 o'clock that morning.'

JIMMY CONROY
'We got an open top bus from the White Horse Inn to the RDS for the first game. It was great, everyone on the street was cheering us.'

JUSTIN MASON
'It was a terrible game. We played Pats a few months later and they beat us 4-2 in a cracking game, it's just a pity that they couldn't have done that in the opening match. I think we lost a lot of potential League of Ireland fans that day.'

'Mick Byrne jumps for the ball during the first game in the RDS' (pic: Sportsfile).

DAVID BYRNE

'For the first game there I was saying to my dad that we better go earlier, and he says "The place holds over 20,000, I think we'll be alright". We couldn't believe the size of the crowd. If we had even kept half the crowd interested it would have been a massive boost. But of course the game was so terrible. Typical Pats.'

ROBBIE GAFFNEY

'I played for Pats against Rovers on the first day of the RDS. It was a very strange game to play in because we couldn't get over the size of the crowd. The game had to be delayed because people just kept coming in. Unfortunately, the game was completely crap. The surface at the RDS was desperate. It wasn't a football pitch, your feet would be sinking into the ground. You'd finish a game and you'd be completely drained.'

RICHIE PHILPOTT

'Initially I was sceptical of the move to the RDS but gradually you began to hear of the amount of interest from the public in the move. There were 22,000 at the opening match against St. Pat's, but the two teams contrived to serve up the most tedious 0-0 draw of all time, which was one of the worst crimes ever committed against League of Ireland football. If they had gone all out attack and served up a 3-3 draw the spin-off benefits would have been gigantic. I remember leaving the ground practically in tears because I knew that most of the crowd wouldn't be back. And they weren't.'

RONAN O'DONOGHUE

'The first day in the RDS should have been perfect. Noel King should have gone for broke and lost 7-4, but it was a dull game and it finished 0-0. The move to the RDS was one of the last great hurrahs for League of Ireland football and it was a terrible shame when it failed.'

Team shot 1991.

FRANK ALLEN
'For a while it looked like the RDS might start a new era at the club, but it wasn't to be. At the end of the day, it was a show-jumping arena. It just couldn't compensate for Milltown.'

'THERE'S A LEAGUE IN THIS TEAM'

Twenty-two thousand people attended the first Rovers game in the RDS. Two weeks later, however, when the Hoops took on Derry City at the same venue, the crowd had halved to 11,000. As the weeks wore on, the numbers continued to dwindle. Despite not being able to hold regular crowds of over 6,000, Rovers crowds during the early RDS years constantly hovered around 4-5,000, which was more than other Dublin clubs were attracting and more than had been attending Milltown on a regular basis.

With good crowds pouring through the turn-stiles, the club soon found that money was available to bolster the side. Noel King had departed as manager, with Ray Treacy taking over the reigns. The style of football employed by King had never endeared him to the supporters, yet Treacy soon had the team playing the passing game which the club traditionally prides itself on. The side was playing good football but struggling with results and had to make do with mid-table finishes. However, the spine of the side was strong and as the 1993/94 season kicked off there was quite confidence in the Rovers camp.

JIMMY CONROY
'We didn't do well in '92/'93 but we played nice football. I remember Bohs beating us 1-0 that season and I went for a pint after the game and met up with Peter Eccles [Rovers captain]. It was just the two of us at the bar and we were yapping away and he says to me, "Jimmy, this is a good Rovers team, there is a league in this team". The thing was that we were losing games that we were playing very well in. The belief was there.'

Terry Eviston.

Peter Eccles with league trophy.

TERRY EVISTON
'I was up front with Stephen Geoghegan – I was the older head and he was the younger guy who really blossomed. We had Alan Byrne in the middle of the park, he was absolutely outstanding. In fact, there was talk of Leeds United coming in for him at one stage. John Toal and Paul Osam, Gino Brazil at the back with Peter Eccles, both of whom were outstanding professionals. Eoin Mullen was fantastic that season, as was Derek Treacy.'

ALAN O'NEILL
'I signed for Rovers at the end of the 1992/93 season. The way I saw it, I had unfinished business with Rovers – I had won the cup with them [in 1978] but never the league. We got beaten in our first league game, hadn't a particularly good league cup and we drew our second game. We only managed one point from two games and we were going down to Galway and there was now huge pressure on Ray because he had spent money but we had only one point. We went down to the Greyhound Stadium in Galway for what was a crunch game and we ended up winning the game 6-1. That launched the season for us.'

Under the system in use at the time, the league broke into two groups – top half and bottom half – after twenty-two games. By the time the league broke up, Rovers were on 48 points, nine ahead of closest rivals Cork. With ten games remaining, it appeared that league success was a formality.

169

However, Rovers being Rovers, nothing went to plan and the Hoops lost their next four games, allowing the Cork side back into the race. It appeared as though Rovers had blown it.

DAVID BYRNE
'We all thought we'd blown it. We went to Galway and Cork went up to the Brandywell in Derry. We go 2-0 down and Cork go 2-0 up and all the Rovers fans thought the league was gone. Most of the lads went to the bar in the ground after around twenty minutes. I decided to stay out and there were only two of us behind the goal when we got one back. I ran into the bar shouting "Its 2-1" but everyone thought the game was over. Just on the stroke of half time we equalised and I ran back in "Lads, it's 2-2". People came out then and the news came in that Derry had equalised. One of the lads brought an inflatable sheep and they hoisted it up the flagpole. We heard that Cork had gone 3-2 down and then Rovers got the late winner. It was madness, total pandemonium.'

Rovers won their next three games meaning that, with two games remaining, a victory at home to Shelbourne would bring the league title to Rovers for the first time since 1987. Defeat to Shels would mean the title being decided on the last day of the season when Rovers took on Cork City in the RDS.

RICHIE PHILPOTT
'It was absolutely pissing rain on the day of the Shels game and I was stuck in a conference that I couldn't get out of. The conference didn't finish until 5:30 which was the same time as the game was kicking off. I literally ran from town to Ballsbridge. I was practically giving myself a heart attack. I arrived at the ground half an hour late and completely soaked, I ran up the stairs and just as I reached the top Rovers scored to make it 2-1. I'll always remember this guy who I'd never seen before just ran up to me and jumped on me. We knew we'd won the league and we just went bananas. I had a hangover for around a week.'

ALAN O'NEILL
'We played Shels on what was really an unplayable pitch. I remember being at fault for the Shels goal and we ended up going 1-0 down. I remember at the time, Sean Creedon was on the radio and he was an avid Cork supporter and for two weeks before the match he was preaching that he wouldn't mind Rovers doing well but he would prefer to see it go to the last match of the season. But we weren't having any of that and we came back and beat Shels 3-1. The last match of the season turned into a carnival. We ran out 3-0.'

MARTIN MOORE
'It was the best league win because of what we'd been through. You don't appreciate victory until you've been in the depths.'

PAT BRADY
'We picked up the title against Cork in the RDS and Peter Eccles scored. That was a great moment because he had been the Player of the Year that year and it was a wonderful moment for him as a player. A great servant to the club.'

JIMMY CONROY
'That was the greatest title for me, even better than '84. We'd been through so much. We were winning things in the '60s and '80s but, not that we were arrogant about it, it just

'Champions again: Rovers celebrate the 1994 league title'.

seemed like the right thing to do – we were the biggest club. But we'd been through so much by '94 that it was special.'

TERRY EVISTON
'That league title was fantastic. We had a great mixture of youth and experience and it all gelled together. It was a very special season. It was a great side, although success was quite unexpected. They had only just kept out of trouble the season before.'

JOHN DORNEY
'At the risk of sounding like a glory hunter, I'd have to admit that what turned me into real Rovers fan was their league win of 1994. Not only was this triumph achieved by playing good football, it also temporarily gave the club back some its sheen as the Irish football club.'

RICHIE PHILPOTT
'The '94 season is probably my favourite ever season. Alan Byrne was outstanding that year, Stephen Geoghegan was superb and I also think that Eoin Mullen didn't get the credit he deserved.'

PETER MURPHY
'John Toal would be the most underrated player I've seen play for Rovers. He signed for Rovers in 92 and he was a kind of engine room type of player. I have one of the infamous purple jerseys from the league winning season with Toal and the number 6 on the back of it.'

Just six years after the club had descended into a state of civil war, Rovers had returned to the top. For the supporters, the league title of 1994 was vindication for sticking with the club through an horrendous few years. Milltown would never be forgotten, but with the league trophy residing in the RDS, it appeared as if the club was ready to move on. However, the euphoria was short-lived. The title win of '94 papered over the cracks, but the legacy of Milltown's sale was to go from bad to worse.

It all began in the close season of 1994. John McNamara had assembled Ireland's premier side relatively inexpensively. Following the league success, players had attracted interest from other clubs and suddenly there was pressure to improve contracts. McNamara and Ray Treacy decided against offering more money to players and instead decided to rebuild the team. It was the beginning of the end for the two men who had helped reshape the club. One of the players to leave the club was centre-back Peter Eccles, who had become a folk hero to supporters:

PETER ECCLES
'If we'd signed more players we would have won the league again but Ray [Treacy] slipped up there. Alan Byrne was the best midfielder around, Stephen Geoghegan was the best forward around and I would have been considered one of the better centre halves, and Ray let the three of us go. Some people say that Geoghegan and Byrne walked out, but I didn't think enough was done to try and keep them. It was a strange decision to let the three of us go. Paul Osam was fantastic too and it was a joke to let him go. It was a huge blunder. Ray thought he could do it but unfortunately he was proven wrong.'

Alan Byrne.

TERRY EVISTON

'Ray had got a lot of stick because there were a lot of young lads in the team [the season after winning the league]. In fairness to Ray, he was managing just before the wages started to spiral. We weren't on big money back then, he kept a lid on it. It was part-time and it was nice to get a few extra bob but it wasn't huge. Ray didn't believe the finances were there to sustain high wages and he stuck to his guns. The two lads – Alan Byrne and Stephen Geoghegan – left and went to Shels and that was the start of the wage spiral.'

JUSTIN MASON

'If you made a "Best XI" since 1990, at least eight of the '93/'94 side would be on it, along with people like Terry Palmer and Tony Cousins. They were a great side, it's such a shame they were broken up. If you look at the teams who won the league after that – Dundalk in '95, Pats in '96 and Derry in '97 – none of them were great sides.'

ROBERT GOGGINS

'When Stephen Geoghegan, Alan Byrne and Peter Eccles left the club there was a lot of bad feeling. The club didn't want Eccles to have a testimonial because he had left and when Eccles did have a testimonial dinner there was no representative of the club there.'

ROBBIE FOY

'I loved Alan Byrne. I got a taxi out to a pub I heard he was in just to beg him to stay at Rovers. I was doing promotion work at the time and I was saying, "Here's some CD's Alan, stay at Rovers".'

'IT GOT VERY NASTY'

Rovers began the 1994/95 season with a 7-0 drubbing at the hands of Polish side Gornik Zabrze. By the time the league campaign had begun, there was serious unrest on the terraces. The supporters were disillusioned with the running of the club and it was not long before they were calling for the heads of Treacy and McNamara. The chairman and manager responded by being highly critical of certain Rovers fans through the match programme. In one famous outburst, Treacy urged "the boo boys" to leave Rovers and follow Dynamo Tiblisi, presumingly the first foreign-sounding club that came into his head.

JIMMY CONROY

'By the time we went to Poland, the whole team had been ripped apart, it's no wonder we lost 7-0. That's when the fans turned. When a club gets success, it wants to be the best at everything. The fans wanted to have the best team, the best programme, the best supporters club, the best bloody corner flags, and we didn't think the set-up at the club was right.'

JOHN DORNEY

'My formative years as a Rovers fan were ones of virtual civil war within the club as John MacNamara's RDS dream crumbled around him. He and Ray Treacy wrote regular verbal attacks on the fans, who in turn abused them and the failing fortunes of the club and the team.'

MACDARA FERRIS

'I couldn't understand the hounding of Treacy. I differentiated between the board and the manager and I blamed the board for the players walking. To me, Treacy was the man who delivered a league title to the club and I would have had a lot of time for him. But it got very

'In happier times: club chairman John McNamara, who saved Rovers from extinction, celebrates the league title'.

nasty. I was sitting up in the stand away from the singing fans but you could hear the shouts of "Treacy must go".'

JUSTIN MASON
'Treacy had the club playing brilliant football. But in the end he had to go because he lost the fans and the dressing room. If players aren't winning matches they start questioning their own ability but then they start questioning other peoples ability. There was one particularly nasty incident outside Tolka Park when the fans turned on him. It got ugly but that's football, it happens.'

FERGUS McCORMACK
'If Rovers won the Champions league I would still complain about the way the club is run. McNamara came in and saved the club but then it all went a bit wrong. He settled for the RDS. If you look at the pitch out there, it was an absolute quagmire by the time we left. There was never a plan B. No-one was thinking "Where are Rovers going to be in 20 years". If you love something you want it to be run as best as it can. The club that you hate the most is probably your own club.'

ROWAN McFEELY
'John McNamara's relationship with fans had deteriorated somewhat. In a classic message to the fans, he asked us to refrain from singing "Sheep Shagging Bastards" towards clubs from outside Dublin. In a rather v-signed reply, we sang it for the entire 90 minutes of the next match, which I think was against Shels – not exactly a rural club!'

TERRY EVISTON

'The season after we won the league was dreadful. Ray brought in some younger players but the crowd turned on him. That's the nature of supporters, if things aren't going right then it doesn't matter how well you've done in the past. It got very personal though, we were having to sneak out the back door of the RDS after games. That affects the players, it gets at your confidence. You sense the atmosphere, especially in League of Ireland where you can hear every comment. It got very nasty. John McNamara did fantastic things for Rovers. He tried to do everything right. He did as much as he could and then he started getting abuse and he didn't need that.'

PAT BRADY

'I think McNamara was unlucky the way the supporters turned on him. He had put a lot of money into the club, but football supporters are a funny bunch and they get ideas in their heads. But – and it's unfair to say this retrospectively – the RDS was the time to sit down and have a look at the long term future of the club and that wasn't done.'

MARTIN MOORE

'Treacy wrote loads in the programme about "the boo boys", saying that "the boo boys" were out to destroy the club. These were the same people who had travelled half way across Europe to watch Rovers lose 7-0 in Poland, so to say that they wanted to see the club go down was a bit much.'

RONAN O'DONOGHUE

'Treacy produced a fantastic team out of nothing. He was extremely realistic about finances but fans want a winning team. Himself and McNamara were driven out of Rovers, but the people who ousted them made a spectacular bags of it. They drove them out but things just went from bad to worse.'

'IT WAS TOTALLY OUT OF THE BLUE'

Rovers struggled through the '94/'95 season, finishing mid-table, and began poorly the following season. Supporter discontent about the running of the club increased to the extent that supporters took to surrounding the players dressing room after matches demanding resignations. On more than one occasion, players pleaded with supporters to remain calm, reminding them that children were present in the players' area. Following a 2-0 home defeat to Sligo Rovers late in the '95/'96 season, the 'boo boys' finally won out and Treacy fell on his sword. McNamara followed him a matter of weeks later. During the Sligo game, Terry Eviston was sent off and Alan O'Neill made a vital error which cost the Hoops a second goal. Ironically, it was to O'Neill and Eviston that Rovers turned.

ALAN O'NEILL

'Ray resigned and the next day I got a phone call from John McNamara. I presumed he was going to tell me who was taking over but he asked me whether I'd take the job. The silence was deafening. I didn't say anything for around two minutes. It was totally out of the blue for me and I told him I'd have to think about it. I told John that I would want Terry [Eviston] to take the job with me and he agreed. I immediately got on the phone to Terry and went down to his house. We had a good squad of players, so between the two of us we decided to go for it. Before we took the job we met Ray Treacy because Ray had been a major influence on my career and I certainly wasn't going to go behind his back, especially

'Loyalty in a game gone mad: Having joined the club as a teenager, Derek Treacy played out his entire career with Shamrock Rovers'.

since I had made a stupid error against Sligo that had probably been the final nail in his coffin. Ray being Ray and being the big man that he is gave us his blessing and wished us well. That just goes to show what Ray is like.'

ROWAN MCFEELY

'The funniest moment of the week was RTE news announcing that Alan O'Neill and Terry Eviston were to take charge of team matters. Against Sligo, Terry had been sent-off and Alan had kicked a clearance against Ian Gilzean which rebounded into the net. RTE decided to show our new management performing – one walking to the dressing room and the other majestically setting up our opponent's second goal.'

The new managerial team took over a side towards the bottom of the league who had not scored a goal in several hundred minutes of football. O'Neill and Eviston's first game in charge was in the RDS on a Wednesday afternoon when Dundalk took on Rovers. Derek Treacy scored the only goal of the game to give Rovers a 1-0 victory. It was the beginning of a seven game unbeaten run that would endear the new managerial team to the Rovers faithful. 'Alan and Terry's Barmy Army' was born.

TERRY EVISTON

'We hadn't scored in a good few games and then in our first game in charge we beat Dundalk 1-0 with Derek Tracey getting the goal. He scored and ran over and jumped up on me. It was just such a release. Everything had been so tense for a long time, it was a great feeling. We ended up nearly chasing a European spot.'

ALAN O'NEILL

'The first game we had was against Dundalk and it was a make or break day. I remember Mick Byrne had two great chances and I made a couple of good saves that day but we scraped it and won 1-0. We put a run of about twelve games together where we went unbeaten and suddenly we were within a chance of getting into Europe.'

JUSTIN MASON

'There were only around 250 people at the Dundalk game but it was like we'd won the European cup when that goal went in. We ended up going on a bit of a run and finished fifth.'

'YOU'VE ALWAYS GOT TO LOOK OVER YOUR SHOULDER'

Alan and Terry had transformed the club's fortunes on the pitch and were offered a contract extension by John McNamara. However, as the season drew to a close, McNamara stood aside and sold the club to Premier Computers, headed by Alan McGrath.

When Premier Computers arrived on the scene, a new buzz word began to circulate amongst Rovers supporters: Tallaght. McGrath unveiled an ambitious plan to end Rovers' nomadic existence by building a state-of-the-art stadium in the Dublin south-west suburb. The logic behind the move was impeccable: high rent and an increasingly poor playing surface were taking their toll at the RDS, which, since the demolition of the Grandstand in 1995, was a one-sided ground. Whilst crowds at the RDS had been relatively good, in Tallaght Rovers would have a potential support base of almost 100,000 people.

The Tallaght stadium was originally earmarked for St. James' Gate, a club managed by former Rovers legend Pat Byrne. The former international midfielder joined up with the new owners of Rovers and accepted the job of trying to get Rovers to Tallaght. However, within weeks, Byrne was installed as manager and O'Neill and Eviston were left crying foul.

ALAN O'NEILL

'We weren't sure what his [Pat Byrne] role would be, but we knew about the politics in football so the alarm bells rang. We made some good signings in pre-season – [Pat] "Nutsy" Fenlon and Tony Cousins, for example. We played Shelbourne in our first League game of the season and got beaten – not a great start but, hey, there's thirty or so games to go. The next night I met the chairman and he told me he was relieving me of my position as manager. I was really shocked. Despite being relieved of my position as manager, I agreed to remain as a player. I had Rovers in my blood. Then during an infamous radio interview the next morning Pat was very derogatory to the contributions myself and Terry had made over the previous eight or nine months, he said how things were going to be done much more professionally. I couldn't see how after those statements that I could play for Pat Byrne. But that's football, you just move on.'

TERRY EVISTON

'It was the politics that cost us. We lost the first game of the season to Shels and the next day Alan was called in and sacked. It left a very sour taste. I was with the lads on the training ground and I get a phone call from Alan and he says, "We're sacked". We weren't even given a chance, but that's football. You've always got to look over your shoulder. Pat [Byrne] later said that he couldn't understand why I'd walked out on the club because they'd only sacked Alan, but was I wasn't going to stay around.'

'THE CLUB IS SHAMROCK ROVERS IN NAME ONLY'

In truth, the remaining seasons of the 1990s all gel into one. The hope which Premier Computers brought to Rovers soon turned into a nightmare (See the following chapter). Without a home, the club wandered from Tolka Park, to Santry's Morton Stadium, to Richmond Park in Inchicore. A succession of managers – Pat Byrne, Mick Byrne, Damien Richardson, Liam Buckley – all attempted to restore the club's on-field stature but the reality of life on the road ensured that Rovers were generally closer to the bottom than the top.

Richardson and Buckley managed to briefly restore the club's pride, although both fell just short of ever bringing silverware to Rovers. Ultimately, Richardson will be remembered for his articles in the match programmes as much as his managerial prowess. Whereas most managers use the programme as a vehicle to communicate team news to supporters, Richardson saw it as a serialisation of his life story. The man who once described League of Ireland football as "a cosmic ballet of wondrous beauty", had this to say the week after defeat to Cork:

'It is a feeling of utter desolation. In a sporting sense there can be nothing as emotionally devastating as the concession of a ninety second minute winning goal. Whether one possesses the stoical stature of an empirical philosopher or a more mundane propensity for self-gratification, the cataclysmic effect of ones removal from pole position is the most injurious. However, by virtue of the fact that the operative word in the above encapsulation is could, I would suggest for your deliberation, that it is the propensity of champions to have the ability to suffer the ignominy of irretrievable capability for proper perception.'

"There's only one Tony Cousins, he scores the goals by the dozens".

Under Richardson's reign, supporters would often miss the game because they would spend a full ninety minutes merely trying to pronounce the manager's programme notes.

HUGH O'CONNOR
'Rico was a good man for using the thesaurus on his computer. I remember one of his programme notes and he started going on about the despondency of the dark winter enveloping the players. His tongue must have been firmly in his check. I only ever flick through programmes and I usually wouldn't even read the managers notes but I used to read Rico's column religiously. You'd go to a game thinking "What the hell is he going to be going on about this week". I worked with a Pat's fan who came in to work the day after a Rovers – Pat's game clutching the programme, pointing at Rico's notes and saying "What the hell is this bloke on about".

ROBBIE FOY
I was standing at a bus stop after a game and I was reading the programme. I got to Rico's notes and I had to just hold my hands up and say, 'I'm sorry lads, what does this mean?' I was standing with a well educated bunch of lads and not one of them could figure out what he was talking about.'

While the 1996/97 season had started with the optimism of the Tallaght move, by the middle of the season supporters were restless at the lack of movement on the stadium issue. Stumbling block after stumbling block delayed the planning process and Rovers were soon starring at the prospect of long-term homelessness.

MACDARA FERRIS
'A lot of people didn't make the move to Tolka because they thought we'd only be there for a season. But then one season turned into two and three and so on and people just got out of the habit. They'd found other things to fill their Friday and Sunday's.'

MICK BYRNE
'I came back as manager but there was just no money at the club. Everything was running at a loss and we were struggling to get planning permission for the new ground, which hurt people. Since Rovers left Milltown there have been eight managers. That's crazy, every second year someone is getting sacked. It's all got to do with money.'

PAT BYRNE
'I came back to the club to try and get the stadium finished but I was asked to take over as manager. There was nothing coming in through the gates and the money was so tight. At the moment, the club is Shamrock Rovers in name only.'

JUSTIN MASON
'We went back to Tolka, although we were told that it was only for a season, possibly two, while Tallaght was being built. It was tough going back there so soon after what had happened in '87 but people were happy enough for the short-term. Around five months into that season I started getting very edgy because it was still only talk of Tallaght. No one realised that eight years later we'd still be waiting.'

ROWAN MCFEELY
'The first day of the 1997/98 league season was a weird one. We beat UCD at Belfield 3-0. It

179

was on that day that Princess Diana died. It was one of those odd feelings that you have when something big in the world has just happened. I obviously had never met her, never held much out for the Royals in general, but this was akin to something our parents had talked about when other famous people had died. It was just an odd day. We were top of the league.'

PETER MURPHY

'In the '90s we always seemed to do well against Bohs. Even in '96, we were nearly relegated and they nearly won the league and we still beat them twice. On one occasion we beat them twice in a week because we beat them in the league and the Leinster Senior Cup. After that a few lads printed up "Twice in a Week" t-shirts and sold them at games.'

JOHN DORNEY

'For me personally, the high point of the last decade was a match against Dundalk that saved us from relegation in 1997. The Hooped travelling support took over Oriel Park for the night, making it like a home game for Rovers and two goals from Tony Cousins and one from Derek Tracey banished the bad times, at least for a while. The final goal was a breakaway, ending in Tracey diving to head Rover's third and clinching goal. I was squashed under a tide of delirious bodies in Dundalk's old stand. In the final minutes we just stood and sang "We shall not be moved" – meaning the team was staying up, but also that we the fans kept alive the spirit and history of the club, and we weren't going anywhere. Its this passion of the fans that keeps Shamrock Rovers in existence in times like these. Its just as well, because its all we have.'

TERRY PALMER

'I signed for Rovers from UCD. It took me a while to find my feet at Rovers, it was a big change. It was strange to make the move from standing on the terrace to playing for the club. It was a very big deal, but even more so for my dad. He's followed Rovers his whole life, as has his whole family. It was great for me but you could really see how much it meant for him to have his son playing for Rovers and then actually captaining Rovers. It takes time to develop a relationship with the fans but they are no fools. They can spot a player who wants to play for the club and that is all I've ever wanted to do. I only want to play for Rovers.'

FERGUS MCCORMACK

'Tony Cousins shortened his career by playing through injury to keep us from relegation. I want to go to Tallaght and win stuff and basically have a Tony Cousins Day. We need to honour the people who broke their balls for this club and got nothing in return.'

MACDARA FERRIS

'My favourite player was Tony Cousins because he saved us from relegation in 1997. On countless occasions we were losing games and he just popped up and score in the last minute. He played for us with a banjaxed knee when we needed him. You'd also have to mention Derek Tracey. He's played his entire career at Rovers – over 450 league appearances – which is phenomenal, especially in the modern era when players move around all the time. Tracey and Cousins played for the National League team against Ireland B. One of the coldest nights I've ever been at a football match by the way. And they did quite well.'

ROWAN MCFEELY

'1996/97 was the year of Tony Cousins. I can't remember any other player ever saving us more than he did.'

HUGH O'CONNOR
'Derek Tracey was probably the most consistent male figure in my teenage years. Every bloody week he'd be there, be it at right back, right wing, left wing, in the middle, up front, he'd always be there. In terms of consistency and loyalty he was second to none. You get the feeling he'd play for Rovers for free. In fact, he probably is!'

'YOU CAN ALMOST FEEL THE MAGIC SLIPPING AWAY'

As well as disappointing league campaigns, the 1990s has the dubious honour of being the only decade where Rovers have not won the FAI Cup. The club reached the final in 1991, only to be defeated by a Galway side whom Rovers had brushed aside in the league just weeks earlier. In the 1990s and early 2000s, Rovers didn't just get knocked out of the FAI Cup, they were often spectacularly dumped out – defeats to first divisions sides Waterford ('97), Athlone ('98) and Dundalk (2002), together with a semi-final defeat to Bohs (2001) and a final defeat to Derry (2002), sticking prominently in the minds of all Rovers fans.

JOHN BYRNE
'After the Athlone game there were loads of people hanging around outside the changing room basically wanting to beat up the players. There was a lot of soul searching done on the way home that night; it was one of those moments that you start thinking that Rovers are becoming the same as everyone else, just another club. You can almost feel the magic slipping away.'

JIMMY CONROY
'Even after the decline in crowd numbers had set in during the 1970's, we still got really big crowds for cup games back then. The cup is ours and we want it back. We haven't won it since we left Milltown and I don't think we'll win it again until we find a proper home. In the meantime, that "cup specialist" tag will drive us mad.

Trevor Molloy.

THOMAS FREYNE

'The teams went in at half time and it was 2-0 to Dundalk. The fans got together and decided to give it loads for the second half, but around five minutes into the second half a Rovers player got fouled and the ref didn't give it. Dundalk went down the other end and scored their third. That was it, it was over. We were stunned.'

JOHN BYRNE

'We played Dundalk in the cup semi-final and they went two nil up. At half time I remember telling people that we had to get behind the team, I must have made an awful idiot of myself. We went behind the goal and started singing away but straight from kick off, bang, three nil. That was it over.'

HUGH O'CONNOR

'At half time of the Dundalk game the fans made a decision to make as much noise as they could in the second half. By the end of that game there was just pure anger amongst the supporters. I remember one fan climbing on top of the tunnel trying to rip it apart, it looked like he was going to have an aneurysm. I thought he was going to massacre the entire squad.'

Ultimately, a decade which promised so little ended up delivering on its word. The 1990s began with the very existence of the club under threat and it ended in a similar fashion. Whether Rovers are too far in the rut to dig themselves out remains to be seen.

CHAPTER 12

TALLAGHT
THE STADIUM, THE
SPECULATORS AND THE
STRUGGLE FOR SURVIVAL

On 12 April 2005, a small band of Rovers supporters gathered in Court 16, the unlikely arena in which the club's fate was to be decided. Before them, Justice Peter Kelly deliberated on what action to take to rescue a company with debts of almost €3m.

Amongst the supporters lined up in the public gallery were Thomas Freyne, Jonathan Roche and James Nolan, three of the Trustees of the 400 Club, a supporters trust which was rapidly gaining ambitions to take over Rovers. The 400 Club had been in an open state of conflict with club chairman Tony Maguire for several months, even taking the unprecedented step of with-holding their financial contributions to the club in protest at Maguire's regime.

As relations between supporters and directors worsened, the idea of the club entering examinership, a limited form of liquidation, was mooted. In early April, Branvard – the company which traded as Shamrock Rovers – entered examinership in a bid to restructure its considerable debts.

As Justice Kelly poured over the application, he had two options: he could agree to the club's wish and appoint an accountant to oversee the running of the club for a specified time period, or he could refuse the request and order the club to be placed into liquidation, effectively putting an end to a 104-year-old Dublin institution. As he examined the club's debts, Kelly made no secret of his unease at Rovers' failure to repay over €500,000 in back-taxes owed to the Revenue Commissioners. The Revenue debt accounted for almost one-fifth of the total debt owed by the club, with everyone from the Department of Justice (€15,550) to the AUL Sports Complex (€3,960) on the list of creditors. Briefly, it appeared as though the decision was to go against the club. For a few anxious moments it seemed as though the glorious history of Shamrock Rovers was to come to an end in the High Court.

However, Justice Kelly finally placed the club into examinership, giving Rovers a lifeline on which to cling in their increasingly desperate struggle to stay afloat. The decision also marked the end of the road for Tony Maguire, the beleaguered chairman who had endured a remarkably stormy relationship with the supporters. Fans had been calling for Maguire's head for over a year and he eventually fell on his sword three weeks later on 5 May 2005.

Protest v Derry.

Maguire's resignation brought to an end three of the most turbulent years the club had ever seen. The chairman had gambled on a policy of maintaining high spending in the hope that the Tallaght stadium – first promised in 1996 but as of yet still not constructed – would provide sufficient funding to repay the debts. Ultimately, it was a failed policy and one that almost brought an end to Shamrock Rovers FC.

In the summer of 1996, Premier Computers – a group fronted by Alan McGrath, Brian Kearney and Mark Howell – bought Shamrock Rovers off John MacNamara. The club moved out of the RDS and into Tolka Park on Dublin's northside. However, unlike when Louis Kilcoyne declared his ambition to bring the club to the Drumcondra venue almost a decade earlier, McGrath insisted that the move would just be for one season. After one season in Tolka, Rovers would be ready to move into what McGrath promised would re-launch the club: the Tallaght Stadium.

In the mid-1950s Tallaght was a village of just 700 residents. Since the 1960s, however, the southwest suburb has mushroomed into one the most populated towns in Ireland. With over 70,000 people living in its confines, Tallaght boasts a larger population than the likes of Galway city. However, the area had also fallen victim to the laissez-faire planning which dogged Dublin's new suburbs.

Massive housing estates had been constructed to contain the city's rocketing population, yet a dearth of amenities had led to huge social problems. Once just a small village, within the space of twenty years Tallaght had exploded. With no investment or commitment to provide amenities or jobs for the area's new residents, Tallaght soon became a by-word for neglect. Premier Computers had initially envisaged bringing St. James' Gate F.C. to Tallaght, but that club soon folded, prompting the group to turn their attentions to Rovers. On the face of it, Rovers and Tallaght appeared to be a dream marriage: the

184

club would provide a focus and a social outlet for a community who could provide Rovers with thousands of new supporters. Top architects were flown in and supporters braced themselves for a re-birth of Rovers.

However, from the outset the stadium was besieged with planning problems and it wasn't long before McGrath, together with former player Pat Byrne, who had taken over first as commercial manager and soon after as club manager, were expressing doubts over whether the stadium would be completed. In May of 1997, exactly one year after purchasing Rovers, McGrath resigned as chairman and was replaced by Brian Kearney.

Kearney finally succeeded in getting planning permission for the new stadium on 14 January 1998, but that permission was delayed by objections from Frank McCarthy, headmaster of the nearby Old Bawn Community School. The stadium was to be built on council-owned land which the school had been using for football pitches and McCarthy objected to the land being taken away from local children. Despite assurances from Rovers that the ground would always be made available to the school, and despite a general consensus amongst local politicians that the move would be a fantastic amenity for locals, legal wranglings with the school occupied most of 1998, ensuring the project was already well behind schedule.

McCarthy eventually withdrew his opposition to the stadium in November 1998, but at this stage Joe Colwell had replaced Brian Kearney as club chairman. Although objections to the stadium had been dropped, it was not long before another problem was thrown at the Hoops. When applying for planning permission, Rovers had downsized the scale of the project to a 6,000 all-seater stadium at the request of An Bord Pleanala. However, in order to fulfil the planning guidelines, Rovers had to have room for a car park with a capacity of at least eight hundred cars. Although everyone had presumed the Council would give Rovers an extra piece of land in order to fulfil the planning criteria, several councillors expressed concern and a crucial meeting to address the topic was postponed. Joe Colwell stated publicly that a refusal by the Council to grant the extra land would effectively condemn Shamrock Rovers to extinction. With the fate of the club hanging in the balance, the councillors voted by 22 – 4 in favour of giving over the extra land.

It appeared as if the final hurdle to Tallaght had been overcome, even if another full year had been lost. On 3 March 2000, so confident were the club of completing the stadium that An Taoiseach Bertie Ahern appeared on site to conduct the official turning of the sod ceremony. However, with the men behind Premier Computers no longer on the scene, Rovers found themselves with one very basic problem: a shortage of money.

Colwell had inherited a wildly ambitious, multi-million euro project but lacked the finances to pull it off. The men who had designed the proposed stadium, and who had the financial clout to construct it, had left the club. Colwell now had planning permission for a state-of-the-art facility but lacked the ability to actually construct it.

On 24 March 2000, Colwell instructed the County Council to hand the lease for 12.18 acres of the 13 acre site over to a company called Mulden International Limited. Fronted by two of the wealthiest men in Ireland – Bernard McNamara and Jeremiah O'Reilly – Mulden was to complete the stadium on Rovers' behalf. Colwell assumed he had secured the club's future, the Council were satisfied that they were to finally get a stadium in Tallaght, and the supporters were convinced they would finally have a ground to call home.

The following October, just seven months after taking control of the lease, Mulden International leased eight acres of the land to a company called Sloanpark Company Limited, placing the responsibility of stadium construction on the new company. Mulden had, in effect, transferred ownership of the stadium to Sloanpark. However, they held onto four acres, and it was these four acres that were to cause so many headaches for all involved over the following four years.

Work on the stadium began immediately, with builders moving onto the site in October 2000 and, over the course of twelve months, they constructed the bones of the west stand. However, it became apparent that McNamara and O'Reilly were looking to construct alternative developments on their four acres. Planning permission for a hotel was refused and the pair quickly lost interest in Tallaght.

In October 2001, exactly one year after construction of the stadium began, building work ceased and has not resumed since. For four years a shell of a stadium has acted as an eye-sore for the people of Tallaght. Meanwhile, Rovers have edged closer and closer to extinction.

Joe Colwell handed the club over to Tony Maguire, who had previously been chairman of Tallaght Town F.C, a club operating in the Leinister Senior League. Tallaght Town had ambitions to one day enter into the League of Ireland and had initially opposed the move of Rovers to the area on the basis that it would affect their plans. Maguire himself had strongly opposed Rovers' plans, but soon after Tallaght Town and Rovers merged into one and Maguire found himself at the helm.

With no money to finance the completion of the stadium, Maguire began the search for potential investors. Aided by Michael Kearns, who took on the mantel of Stadium Director, Maguire first attempted to strike a deal with a local publican, who initially agreed to finance the stadium but soon pulled out. Ben Dunne became the next name linked with the site, with the former Dunnes Stores boss apparently eager to construct a gym on the site in return for finishing the stadium. The Ben Dunne deal was so far advanced that Rovers informed the media. However, Dunne soon pulled out, leaving Rovers with much egg on their face.

With Dunne out of the picture, Rovers finances were going from bad to worse. Players' wages began to go unpaid and in a humiliating case a dry cleaning company took Rovers to court over an unpaid laundry bill. It was around this time that Rovers took the interest of a mystery investor. The investor became the talk of the club, with Maguire and Kearns hailing him as the saviour of Rovers. Negotiations were complicated, however, by the presence of Mulden International's four acres. The investor – later named as Conor Clarkson, property developer and race horse owner – would finish the stadium on the basis that he could construct retail units below the stands. However, he needed Mulden's land and Mulden appeared reluctant to sell. Although it appeared as if the two sets of property speculators were at loggerheads, Clarkson and MacNamara/O'Reilly were far from enemies. In fact, Clarkson's race horse, Kicking King, was sponsored by none other than Bernard MacNamara. Despite their closeness, the groups appeared unable to strike a deal which would see all parties benefit.

All the time, Rovers finances worsened. Cheques were bouncing and players weren't happy. Maguire had maintained a policy of attempting to field a side capable of challenging for honours, while at the same time attempting to guide the club into the new stadium. The reality was that the club could afford neither of these lofty ambitions. As cheques continued to bounce, Maguire was rapidly losing control of the situation. As the 2003 season drew to a close, Rovers' supporters held an impromptu collection for the players at half-time, raising a token 500, which the players' – somewhat ironically – donated to an anti-depression charity. At the end of that season, nine players left the club to find pastures new. Yet, as the 2004 season began, the same problems arose, with some players owed four-figured sums by the club.

On numerous occasions, news filtered through to the fans that Mulden had agreed to sell up to Clarkson, thus paving the way for the completion of the stadium. But it was one false dawn after the next. The club applied for a one-year planning extension in October 2003, which the Council granted, but no work was carried out over the following twelve-months. When Rovers applied for a further extension towards the end of 2004, the Council dramatically refused. By pulling planning permission away from Rovers, the Council appeared to be ending the Tallaght dream once and for all.

Supporters immediately called for Maguire's head. Anti-board feeling had been rising over the previous two years, with a game against Derry City in late 2004 delayed for ten minutes after supporters staged an on-pitch protest calling for the board to resign. Failure to secure the long-term future of the club, whilst also jeopardising the short-term existence of Rovers, was turning the supporters against the board of directors. The week after the planning decision, however, the Council clarified their position. It soon became clear that planning was refused, not because they no longer wanted Rovers in Tallaght, but because they wanted to clear up the issue of ownership between Mulden and Clarkson. The Council made clear their intention to build the stadium in partnership with Rovers, once they could remove Mulden from the equation.

Animosity between directors and supporters at Rovers had been rising for months. The situation at the club now resembled the end scene of Quentin Tarantino's Reservoir Dogs, with the directors, supporters, potential investors and the County Council all pointing guns at each other. By refusing planning permission for Rovers, the Council had effectively pulled their trigger. Just as in Tarantino's famous scene, the bloodbath that would follow would claim more than one scalp.

The 400 Club was established by Jack Wilson, a member of the board of directors of Rovers, when the club's finances first took a serious nosedive. The initiative was a simple one: four hundred supporters would pledge 10 a week to the club, thus offering a potential €16,000 a month to the club. The 400 Club was administered by the board of directors and was essentially just a supporters' trust to help finance the administration of the club. However, as relations between the board and supporters diminished, supporters voted to take control of the 400 Club themselves. They would still help finance the running of the club but would ultimately control their own bank account. Money would only be released to the club whilst supporters were prepared to bankroll the current board

400 Club card.

of directors. 400 Club member Mark Lynch was elected to the board of directors but soon resigned from that position.

The development of the 400 Club mirrored the development of any democratic movement around the world. If people without a voice are given a limited opportunity to voice dissent, it is only a matter of time before they will call for a revolt. After the County Council refused the club an extension on their planning permission, that is precisely what the 400 Club did. The Trustees of the 400 Club informed the board of directors that they were no longer willing to bankroll their ownership of Shamrock Rovers and received a mandate from their members to withhold all money from the club. The supporters and directors were now in an open state of war.

Conor Clarkson had at this stage given over 60,000 to Rovers and was still committed to securing a deal with the club that would see him finance the completion of the stadium under terms that would see him operate commercial units within the stadium. However, the Council's decision had dealt a fatal blow to Clarkson's plans. Faced with the decision between sticking with Clarkson or hammering out a deal with the Council, Tony Maguire chose the former and initiated a High Court judicial review of the Council's ruling. At a general meeting between Maguire and the supporters, the chairman was forced to admit that Mulden International was financing the judicial review. For supporters, it was the final straw. The club's chairman was now the public face of a High Court challenge by property speculators against a local authority who were prepared to completely finance the new stadium using government grants.

However, any judicial review was destined for failure seeing as though the Council were operating within their rights not to extend planning permission for a project that had been stalled for four years. With no planning permission and with supporters threatening a mass boycott of home matches, the weight had shifted dramatically against Tony Maguire. The 400 Club were now in the driving seat and entered negotiations with the board of directors. In November 2004, the debts facing Branvard – the company trading as Shamrock Rovers – stood at 1.8m. Five months later they had grown to €2.3m. The company was insolvent and was haemorrhaging money at an alarming rate. It was clear to everyone that the situation could not continue and so the 400 Club and the board of directors began to discuss the possibility to entering examinership.

Examinership is a limited form of administration, whereby a High Court-appointed accountant examines the company's operation, courts potential investors, restructures its debts and then recommends to the High Court whether the company has any chance of survival. Having secured a new investor, the accountant then strikes a deal with creditors, usually offering somewhere in between five and ten cents for every euro owed. In other words, a €2.3m debt could be 'restructured' into a €200,000 debt.

The appointment of an examiner effectively signalled the end of the road for the board of directors. Along with 400 Club representative Mark Lynch, directors Jack Wilson and Michael Kearns had already resigned, as had Alan Duncan. Tony Maguire, Paul Boyle, Tony Ennis and John Breen were now all that remained of what was once an eight-man board. Under the terms of the examinership, the club was to be run by a board of management until a new investor could be found. That board of management was made up of the examiner (Neil Hughes), two 400 Club representatives (Dave Carpenter and James Nolan) and two Branvard directors (Tony Maguire and John Breen). During the period of the examinership, the 400 Club agreed to completely bankroll the running of the football club. The supporters were calling the shots.

However, there was to be an unexpected twist to the tale when the FAI discovered irregularities in Rovers' application for a football licence for the 2005 season. It was discovered that the club had submitted their 2003 accounts instead of their more up to date 2004 accounts. Although Maguire insisted it was a simple mistake, allegations began to surface that the club had essentially conned the FAI into granting them a licence. For the national association, it was a step to far. At a meeting on 4 May 2005, the FAI made clear to Tony Maguire that they would be seeking his resignation. The following morning, Maguire officially ended his term in charge of Shamrock Rovers.

Rovers formally entered examinership on 11 April 2005. Over the following three months, the 400 Club paid the day-to-day costs of the club, together with clearing debts owed to players and making monthly instalments in a bid to reduce the substantial debt owed to the Revenue Commissioners. Although this debt was initially thought to be €500,000, an examination of accounts revealed that Rovers had not paid tax in several years and the real bill to Revenue stood at over three times that figure.

Neil Hughes, the court-appointed examiner, sought new investors in order to take the club forward as a viable business. Six official bids for the club were received by the deadline of 4 May 2005, although three of these bids subsequently dropped out.

The three remaining bids came from Brian Quigley, Brian Phelan and the 400 Club. The supporters had put together a bid in the eventuality that no suitable outside investment would be found. Through members pledging long-term membership, the 400 Club had raised in the region of €250,000. However, both Quigley and Phelan were thought to have offered bids in the region of €1.5m. Of the two, Quigley's offer became the forerunner.

Brian Quigley was born in Sunderland and, along with business partner Brookes Mileson, had created a multi-million euro business empire. Mileson had generated headlines in Scotland for taking Gretna F.C., a village club based in the regional leagues, all the way to the Scottish First Division. Mileson pumped £1m a year into Gretna and also funded a variety of community-based sports programmes in north England and Scotland. With Rovers, Quigley saw his chance to do the same.

Negotiations between Quigley and Neil Hughes centred on the new stadium in Tallaght. South Dublin County Council reaffirmed their commitment to construct the stadium, with Rovers as primary tenants. Although the club would not own the new stadium, they would enjoy a similar arrangement as many top European clubs have with local councils.

However, negotiations stalled on several issues, most notably the Council's refusal to allow the English millionaire manage the stadium on a daily basis. When the 400 Club met on the evening of 22 June 2005 in Trinity College, members were informed that Quigley had until 12pm the following afternoon to agree a deal with the Council. As the clock ticked the following morning, it became clear that Quigley was withdrawing from the bidding process.

Hughes immediately entered negotiations with Brian Phelan. However, Phelan too withdrew from the process amid claims that he was not satisfied with the nature of the proposed tenancy in the Tallaght Stadium. With Plan A and Plan B now gone, Hughes and the 400 Club fell back onto Plan C: a supporter takeover. Writing in the summer of 2005, the issues of ownership of both the Tallaght Stadium and Rovers has not yet been resolved. In late June, the Council secured the release of the leases to the stadium site off both Sloanpark and Mulden International, removing the last obstacles to completing the stadium. The Council have stated their commitment to completing the stadium using grants obtained by the Department of Sport, a commitment the government, conscious of the local frustration in Tallaght at the constant delays to constructing the stadium, has agreed to. The Council has stated their belief that the new stadium will open in June 2006. However, the exact terms of tenancy are yet to be finalised.

Rovers, in the meantime, will resort to fan-ownership. Aided by a six-figured loan from long-time supporter Ray Wilson, the 400 Club officially bid for Rovers and that bid was accepted by Neil Hughes. Senior members of the 400 Club – James Nolan, Jonathan Roche, Thomas Freyne, John Byrne, Eamon Keenan, Noel Byrne and Dave Carpenter – have sought to bring the club back onto a more sound financial footing. The problems faced at Rovers are mirrored across the league. Players' wages have rocketed over the past decade, with gate receipts not responding in similar fashion. Indeed, as Ireland's obsession with the English Premiership continues, attendances at many clubs have fallen, placing domestic football in a huge crisis. However, whilst these problems are faced across the board, they have been exasperated at Rovers by the lack of a home ground, which has deprived the club of much-needed advertising revenue and also led to expensive ground rental contracts.

Many football clubs around the world are owned by the supporters – Barcelona is perhaps the most famous example – and it is a situation that can lead to prosperity. With a new stadium planned, Rovers supporters can be optimistic that the future of the club can be secured. However, a long and troublesome road lies ahead before this future will be secure. As Rovers supporters have proven time and time again, their loyalty to the club knows no bounds. If anyone can secure this future, surely it is the fans.

---

[1] In Ireland the term 'football' can be used to describe both Gaelic football and Association football (soccer). In the interests of clarity, I will refer to Gaelic football as 'Gaelic' and Association football as 'football' throughout the book. This might not please the GAA fraternity too much, but I figure they're not going to read this book anyway.

[1] Jim McLaughlin was manager of Rovers from 1983 – 1986, with Dermot Keely taking over the reigns for the final year of the Four in a Row.

Above and below: Tallaght stadium.

Forthcoming Titles Autumn/Winter 2005

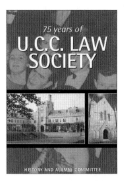

A History of the U.C.C. Law Society
HISTORY AND ALUMNI PROJECT COMMITTEE

The Law Society has had a varied and interesting history. From its humble origins as a society created for the educated elite to its current manifestation as a college society active in organizing charity, educational and departmental social events, not to mention its successful track record in debating and hosting many speakers of repute, the Law Society has changed as much as the society that surrounds it. Including many archive photographs and pieces by guest writers, this book outlines the changes, controversies and history of the Law Society since the 1920s.

1-84588-513-9   €17.99

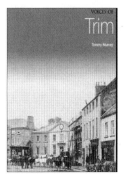

Voices of Trim
THOMAS MURRAY

Compiled by locally renowned author and historian Thomas Murray this book focuses on the life and times of Trim in the past centuries. With interviews ad stories from and about the town and its hinterland's unforgettable characters and events it is a charm for any native and a beautiful introduction for the visitor or new arrival. Featuring snapshots of the changing lives and lifestyles of a provincial town and with an unrivalled collection of old photographs to accompany the text it is bound to have a wide appeal.

1-84588-514-7   €17.99

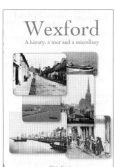

Wexford: History Guide & Miscellany
NICHOLAS ROSSITER

Nicholas Rossiter is a money advisor working in Wexford. In his spare time he writes, produces and broadcasts a series of radio programs that combine Local History with Folk Music, a combination he finds very effective and attracts contributions from across the world. He has been heavily involved in researching Wexford's History and has a considerable corpus of material at his disposal. Through this large body of material he takes the reader on a journey through Wexford's history and culture from early times to the present.

1-84588-528-7   €17.99

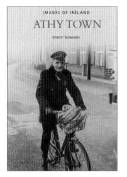

Images of Ireland: Athy Town
ROBERT REDMOND

Athy is a sizeable and fast developing town in County Kildare. It is a designated heritage town and has a rich history dating back to the 12th century. Robert Redmond is well established as a photographer in his town and has taken photos all over County Kildare and Athy in particular. There are wonderful and varied pictures featured in this book. Social, religious and sporting events are illustrated, not to mention, the people and picturesque landscape of Robert's much loved town.

1-84588-502-3   €16.99

If you are interested in publishing with Nonsuch Publishing please contact us at
Nonsuch Publishing, 73 Lower Leeson Street, Dublin 2

www.nonsuch-publishing.com